ROUTER PROJECTS and JIGS

By

Robert Rosendahl

B. Sc. Ed. , MA. Ind. Ed., Certified Carpenter

Rick Rosendahl

B. Ed., Cabinet maker

Oak Park Enterprises Ltd.

Printed in 1994
Second printing in 1995
Third printing in 1997

Canadian Cataloguing in Publication Data

Rosendahl, Robert R. and Rosendahl, Rick L.
Router Projects and Jigs

ISBN 0-919823-04-1

1. Router (tools). 2. Jigs and fixtures.
3. Woodworking. I. Title.
TT203.5.R68 1994 621.9'12   C88-098155-5

© 1994 by Robert R. and Rick L. Rosendahl
Printed and Bound in Canada by Kromar Printing
Oak Park Enterprises Ltd.
Box 280, Elie, Manitoba
Canada, R0H 0H0
1-800-665-0252

Preface

The authors have over 60 years accumulated experience in the use of the routers and woodworking techniques. Their creative and unique applications of the router are evident in the **Router Projects and Jigs.**

The projects in this book are presented to give woodworkers practical applications to start on, build up confidence, and harder projects to challenge them. Step by step instructions are clearly enhanced by extensive use of photos and drawings. From the many photos taken in the authors shops one gets the feeling of actually being there with them during the project planning, processing, and assembly.

Condition of the machinery and the quality of the materials directly affect the project results and user safety. The authors and publisher cannot be responsible for the readers interpretation of the projects in this publication. Every precaution has been taken to ensure accurate instruction.

Acknowledgements

No book is ever the product of the author or authors alone. Bob and Rick wish to acknowledge the assistance provided by the following individuals. The first thanks must go to the wives, Reta and Wendy Rosendahl, without whose patience, understanding and superb proofreading ability this book would have never seen the light of day.

Thanks also go to John Hayes, whose skills with a computer helped make the book easy to look at and read, and to Fred Cleverley, who is the editor of the Router News-Bits! and who helped with some of the editing in this book. Thanks to Keith Freeman who took all of the photographs.

There are also many people behind the scenes who helped produce Router Projects and Jigs, including Oak Park's vice president, Dean Rosendahl, production coordinator Brian Sprott and office staffer Sandy Nichol. Dean is largely responsible for the many line drawings that help with the understanding of the projects. Brian was the sounding board on the suitability of many of the projects, and provided many of the practical checks on the techniques suggested. Sandy contributed many hours to the typing and preparation of the material.

Then there are the dozens of people with a keen interest in using the router who have helped with their ideas and their techniques, many of which have been incorporated in this book. They all deserve credit for making Router Projects and Jigs as interesting as we hope you will find it.

Contents

Appendix

Introduction

Introduction by Fred Cleverley, editor of Router News Bits!, longtime friend of Bob and Rick Rosendahl and an amateur woodworker.

It is more than a dozen years since Bob Rosendahl published The Router, a book which has become the definitive text for woodworkers throughout Canada and the United States who have caught Bob's enthusiasm for this unusual piece of power equipment. This book is now in its ninth printing and is still in demand as more and more home and professional craft workers seek to duplicate, in their own workshops, the unique, attractive and interesting projects Bob builds during the dozens of shows, seminars and demonstrations he attends each year.

One of the questions Bob and his son Rick have heard often at these events is when will there be another book. Router Projects and Jigs is the answer to those questions. Coauthored by Bob and Rick, it contains dozens of projects which make use of the basic router skills so well presented in The Router. It contains literally hundreds of tips on technique accumulated through years of experience in using routers and talking to thousands of enthusiastic individuals whose many suggestions have been invaluable.

As well, it is a stand-alone text. While reading the original book and practicing what it teaches is recommended for anyone who wants to make more use of their router, Router Projects and Jigs can be used as a first text by the beginning enthusiast. Each project is graded according to the skill required to build it, and the extensive collection of appendix material provides, in itself, a basic course that includes everything from selecting and sizing wood to gluing and clamping the finished project. Whenever a particular procedure is used in two or more projects, the appropriate appendix gives step-by-step instructions on what to do.

This book has taken more than three years of research to produce. Each project has been built not once, but dozens, sometimes hundreds of times and all the short-cuts learned have been included. Some of the less complicated projects are so economical on material that two or more items can be produced from a single piece of wood. In some of the more elaborate items, such as the featured walnut chest, can be found a miniature degree course in the production of fine furniture.

As in their demonstrations, their seminars, their videos and at the increasingly popular hands-on router weeks held by Bob and Rick each summer in Winnipeg, the emphasis in this book is safety. The reader cannot help but be impressed by the idea that woodworking, particularly when using a router, is really safe fun.

From a personal viewpoint, I have found, in Bob's first book, his videos and through an opportunity to attend one of his hands-on courses, an entirely new fascination with my router. Once relegated to an obscure shelf in my workshop, my router now finds a prominent place as part of a system that includes Oak Park's router table, a set of spacer fences, a pattern jig and patterns, a more varied assortment of bits than I once dreamed possible and a reference shelf on which sits both an earlier and later edition of The Router and, well protected from dust, a set of Bob's videos.

I have been fortunate to become associated with the Rosendahl family through editing the newsletter, Router News-Bits! and by helping out, in a limited way, during the summer hands-on courses.

Router Projects and Jigs will take a prominent place in my workshop, although I must confess that I am a bit reluctant to allow members of my family to browse through it. I'm afraid they will ask for far more of the projects than I expect to have time to build. Just as an example, I built two of the basic boxes in the hands-on course I attended two years ago. This year I built 15, and that was still not enough to distribute to family members who wanted them.

I have no hesitation whatsoever in recommending Router Projects and Jigs to anyone who has shown the slightest interest in woodworking. Just flipping through it is enough to create a desire to switch on a router, or to go out and buy a router if you don't have one.

Unit 1
BOXES

Practically every building project is a box in some shape, size, or form. Houses, cupboards, desks, and television sets are all forms of the box. In this unit we will concentrate on small boxes that can be used around the home or office to hold pins, coins, ear rings, paper clips, paper, or what ever you decide to store. They are easy to build, decorative to display, and provide useful storage.

WHAT YOU WILL LEARN BY BUILDING BOXES

First, small boxes provide excellent practice in cutting your materials to the right size. If you are wrong, the boxes will not fit together the way you want them to.

Then, you will discover how joints work. How different joints work differently. How different joints require different gluing. Once you understand joints, and their different characteristics, you will be able to decide on which joint will work best when you are making other projects.

You will better understand how a material list is made up, and how you can figure easily the sizes you will need to change the size of a project as listed.

Then, small boxes provide an excellent way to learn how to use the router itself. You will learn the direction of feed, the use of fences, and how using a table-mounted router differs from using the tool as a hand-held unit.

Finally, working with small boxes provides a basic course in router safety. Although it is hard to believe, most router injuries happen after the machine is switched off. Some woodworkers are so anxious to clean off the table and get to the next cut that they attempt to brush away the cuttings with their hands before the router has actually stopped. Don't do this. If you have to clean before the machine stops, use a brush.

Some of the boxes you can make by following the instructions you will find in this unit.

1 A. Basic Box

Figure 1-A-1 Dress up a basic box with molds, inlays, or bases.

Boxes are fun to make, economical on material, and fun to receive as a gift. You can decorate boxes with decals, paint, router molds, or allow an exotic wood to make the statement. Put an inlay in the lid, if you wish to improve the appearance. Whatever you decide to do with this basic box, it is the simplest and easiest one to make. See figure 1-A-1.

Project Requirements

Recommended: Cedar

Also suitable: Oak, Walnut

Material list

    2 - 4" x 5" x 3/8" top / bottom
    2 - 3 5/8" x 5" x 3/8" sides
    2 - 3 5/8" x 3 5/8" x 3/8" ends
    1 - 5" x 6" x 3/4" base

Router tools

    Table mounted router
    Table fence

Router bits:

    3/8" rabbet bit
    3/8" solid carbide spiral bit
    5/32" roman ogee bit
    3/4" V groove bit

Skill Level

X	Basic			Basic Plus
	Moderate			Advanced

Construction details in:

The skills necessary to complete the projects in this book are presented in appendixes at the back. The following skills are used in this project. You may wish to review the following appendixes before you start.

Appendix I - Choosing / Sizing Material

Appendix II - Gluing and Clamping

**Appendix III- B. Table fence
                D. Measuring made simple**

Appendix V - B. For inlay option

How to build this project

Always take care in selecting the wood for any project. Decide which pieces will look best for the top and bottom, which for the two sides and which for the two ends.

Make sure all pieces are cut square and to the exact size listed, so they will fit properly. Joint, plane and cut according to the materials list.

Base

Since we have added a base to this box, let's start with it first. Chuck up the 5/32" roman ogee bit in the table-mounted router. Set the depth of the cut to use the full profile of the bit. See figure 1-A-2. Isolate the bearing by adjusting the table fence. See Appendix III-B.

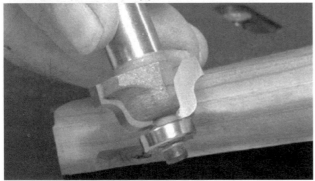

Figure 1-A-2 Use the roman ogee bit to mold the top of the base.

Rout the top of the base. This means that the top will be face down on the router table. Cut an end-grain side first. Next rotate the base counter-clockwise to cut a straight grain side. Then cut the other end grain side and finally the last straight grain side. Doing it this way avoids leaving exposed tear-out on the edge grain sides.

The illusion of feet on the base can be created by using the upper part of the same roman ogee bit (which cuts a small cove) and using stop cuts on the back face edges and ends. See Appendix III-B. By starting 3/4" in from each corner and stopping 3/4" from the next corner on all sides of the bottom, it looks as if the base is supported by corner feet. See figure 1-A-3.

Figure 1-A-3 Make corner feet with the cove part of the roman ogee bit.

Making the Box

Now for the box itself. What makes this project interesting is how the joints work to make the box. See figure 1-A-4. The router is

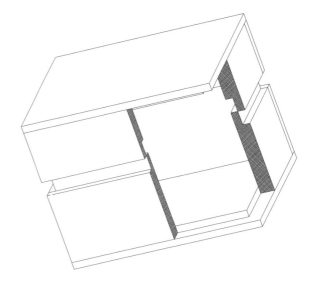

Figure 1-A-4 Dados become rabbets when cut apart.

the most efficient tool available to produce perfect joints.

However, to use it easily and effectively it is best to separate your thinking time from your cutting time. This box uses identical rabbet joints all around. It is just a matter of marking in advance where the cuts will be made (thinking time) and then making the cuts (cutting time).

First chuck up the rabbet bit in the table mounted router. Set the depth of cut to half the thickness of the material. Check this set up with a piece of 3/8" scrap material. How to do this is in the Appendix III-D-a. When making the rabbet joints be sure to use a router bit that has the diameter that is large enough to use only the cutting side of the bit.

First mark an "X" with a pencil (so you can sand it off later) on the face of each piece. You will make the cuts on the other side, so if you can see the "X" you know you are cutting the right side.

Then sort the pieces. The top and bottom will be cut on all four sides, the side pieces only on each end. No cuts are made on the end pieces, so set them aside before you start cutting.

It is a good idea to cut the sides first, since only two cuts are required. If you cut the pieces in a random fashion, it is easy to forget whether you want to cut just the ends or all four sides. Do the two-cut pieces first, then the four-cut pieces. See figure 1-A-5.

Figure 1-A-5 Rabbet the ends of the sides and all around the top and bottom.

You should not have to adjust the depth you have set, for the entire project.

Next, rabbet all four sides of the top and bottom pieces. See figure 1-A-6. Remember, you do not have to touch the end pieces. This is the time to test fit the box together. It is not absolutely necessary to test fit, but it will give you a lot of satisfaction. Besides, it is a good time to lay out the pieces so that you can make the initial dado cut by which the lid fits over the lip on the box itself.

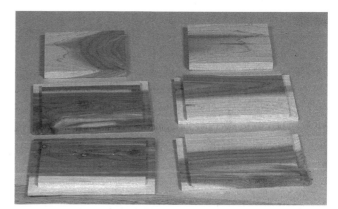

Figure 1-A-6 Layout of pieces with rabbets complete.

Inside dado for the lid

Again, it's thinking time, time to mark where this inside dado will be cut on the side and end pieces. Put the top and bottom aside so you will not cut them by mistake.

Use a 3/8" spiral bit, set at one-half the thickness of the stock, for these dado cuts. Use one of the rabbet cuts as a guide to setting the depth, then check it on a piece of scrap stock the same way you did when you set the rabbet bit depth. Then position the fence so that the cut will be approximately one inch away. This is not an absolute measurement, since it just controls which part of the box is the lid and which part is the bottom.

To make the inside cut for the lid, we will run a dado near the top of the box on the inside of each end and side piece. See figure 1-A-7.

Once you have made the cuts on the sides and ends, mark where they are on the outside lip of the rabbet on the side pieces. See figure 1-A-8. Remember to do this, because once the box is glued it is your only indication of where the inside dado cut is located.

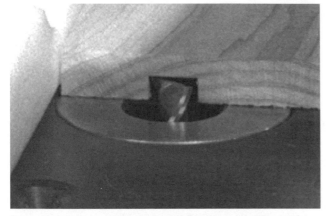

Figure 1-A-7 Dado about one inch from top on sides and ends.

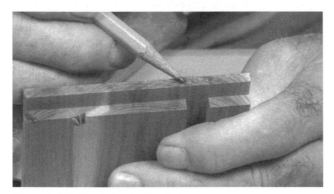

Figure 1-A-8 Mark the inside dado.

Safety

To save your fingers always complete your thinking and marking of pieces as separate operations. Once you have all of the pieces marked for face side, to cut you just have to look for the X and think about keeping your fingers away from the router bit. SAFETY ALWAYS FIRST!

Do you have the inside dado marked? Check before gluing.

Clean, glue, and clamp the box together. Be sure it is square. For gluing and clamping instructions see Appendix II.

When the glue has set, position the table fence so that the bit is at the mark where the dado is on the inside of the box. Overlap just a little bit. Use the 3/8" carbide spiral for the outside dado. If you have sanded the box, you may have to check the bit depth to be sure it is half the thickness of the material. The height of the bit will determine the fit of the lid to the bottom. The higher the bit the looser the fit. Remember about the finish on the box, do not make the lid too tight. Cut the outside dados in the box sides first. This will remove the end grain from the sides and make it easier to cut the ends. See figure 1-A-9.

Figure 1-A-9 Cut the outside dado in the straight grain sides first.

Insert wooden pieces (3/8" x 1" x 3/16") into the outside dados just cut. Put a piece of masking tape across each shim to ensure that they stay in place. See figure 1-A-10. These blocks hold the box from collapsing inward when the final end dados are cut.

Figure 1-A-10 Tape a small block in the dado on both sides before cutting the end dados.

Cut the dados in the ends. You should be able to see right through the box. Remove the wooden pieces and the masking tape. The lid should separate from the bottom. See figure 1-A-11.

Figure 1-A-11 Lid and bottom separate.

The inside and outside dados now become rabbets allowing the inside rabbet to lap over the outside rabbet. This allows the lid to fit perfectly.

Dressing it up

Chuck up a round over bit in the table mounted router. Position the table fence to iso-

late the bearing. See Appendix III-B-c. Set the depth of cut to give the full profile plus 1/16th for the profile line. Round over all edges of the face side of the box top.

Chuck up the 3/4" V groove bit. Set the depth of cut to just allow the V groove to protrude 1/16". Put the lid on the box bottom. You may want to tape the box together if the lid fits loose. Set the fence to the right of the cutter so the cut line in the box is directly over the bit. Cut a small V on the lid/bottom cut line all around the box. This gives a pleasing appearance to the box. See figure 1-A-12.

Figure 1-A-12 Cut a V on the top/bottom cut line.

Box and base assembly

Center the box bottom on the base piece. DO NOT MEASURE! Line one side and end of the box with the profile line on the base. Make a small pencil mark on the base where the other sides of the box extend. This will leave the space that needs to be divided equally between the base and the box. Mark it at half the distance from the mark to the closest profile line on the side and the end of the base. Set the box bottom at these new marks and you will have centered the bottom on the base. Glue it in place being sure it is square. See figure I-A-13.

Figure I-A-13 Glue the base to the box.

Finishing touches

Sand and finish the project. Dress this basic box up with molding on top and a base below as we have here. Make the square cornered box and stack one box on another or make boxes to fit inside boxes. Using 3/8" material change the size of the material by I" all around to make a box to fit inside this one. It cannot have a base piece on it. If you wish to make inlays in your box see Appendix V - B.

How to make a different sized box

If the box described is not the size you want to build, here's an easy way to size the material for a larger or smaller one. First, pick the overall size of the box you want. The top, bottom and length dimensions of the two sides will be exactly this size. The ends are smaller by one thickness on the width and length and the two sides are smaller on the width by one thickness of the material you are using.

If this sounds too simple, try it out on some scrap to convince yourself that it works. If you really insist on a technical explanation, this is a characteristic of the rabbet joint.

Notes:

Figure I-B-I Box with box joints and hinged lid.

I B. Another Small Box

Box joints decorate and join this box to hold jewelry, receipts, or other small items that require containment. See figure I-B-I.

Project Requirements

Recommended: Oak

Also suitable: Cedar, Mahogany

Material list
    I - 4 I/2" x 6 I/2" x I/2" - box lid
    2 - 3" x 6" x 3/8" - box sides
    2 - 3" x 4" x 3/8" - box ends
    I - 3 5/8" x 5 5/8" x I/8" - ply bottom

Router tools
    Table mounted router
    Table fence
    I/4" spacer fence

Router bits
    I/4" carbide spiral router bit
    I/8" carbide spiral router bit
    5/32" roman ogee router bit

Hardware
    I pair of 3/4" brass butt hinges and screws.

Skill Level

Basic		X	Basic Plus
Moderate			Advanced

Construction details in:

The skills necessary to complete the projects in this book are presented in appendixes at the back. The following skills are used in this project. You may wish to review the following appendixes before you start.

Appendix I - Choosing / Sizing Material

Appendix II - Gluing and Clamping

Appendix III- A. Direction of feed
           B-d. Table fence stopped cuts

Appendix IV- A. Box joints uniform thickness

How to build this project

Select the materials. Joint, plane and cut all materials to size according to the material list. Be sure to cut to exact size and ensure that all stock is cut square. Appendix I contains a discussion on Choosing and Sizing Materials.

The lid

Set up the router table by chucking up the 5/32 roman ogee router bit. Adjust the depth of the bit and the fence so that only the round over portion of the cutter comes in contact with the stock. See figure 1-B-2. Run a test piece of stock to be sure that you are cutting the full quarter round on the stock. Be sure to use the proper direction of feed. *With the lid face down* mold a round edge all the way around the face side of the lid stock. Mold end grain, straight, end and straight.

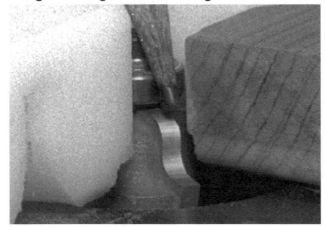

Figure 1-B-2 Round over top of lid.

Reset the height of the bit and fence to only expose the cove cut of the ogee bit. Check this cut with a test block. Run a cove cut around the bottom side of the lid stock (face up on the table) to create a cove on the underside of the box lid. Follow the same direction of feed as shown for the quarter round cut. See figure 1-B-3.

Figure 1-B-3 Cove cut on underside of lid.

Making the box joints

We now want to set up the router table to do the box joints on the ends and sides. **First the ends.** Chuck a 1/4" spiral router bit into the router and install a 1/4" spacer fence over the table mounted router. Be sure to set the height of the 1/4" bit a little above the thickness of the material being used. This will insure that the box joint fingers will protrude through the sides. Check your fence set up with two sample pieces of stock. See Appendix IV-A. If the joints are too loose, tap the fence away from the bit. If the joint is too tight, tap the fence toward the bit. Use scrap until you get the fit you want.

Mark a fence side on the pieces of material. Clamp the box ends together and run box joints on both ends of the material making sure the marked sides are against the fence. Be sure the pieces are square and tight to the fence. See figure 1-B-4.

Figure 1-B-4 Box joints on the ends.

Now we want to cut the box joints on the **box sides**. The procedure is the same as the box ends except we must offset the cuts by 1/4". See figure 1-B-5. Be sure to cut both ends of the stock with the 1/4" offset. See Appendix IV for box joints on a spacer fence.

Figure 1-B-5 Offset box joints in the sides.

The box bottom

Before we can assemble our box we have to cut a slot into the box sides and ends to hold the bottom. Chuck a 1/8" spiral bit into the router. Adjust the height of the bit to 3/16" or half the thickness of the side and end material. The location of this next cut is very crucial. See figure 1-B-6.

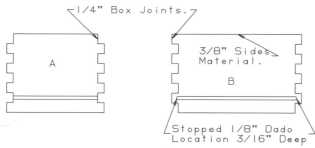

Figure 1-B-6 Dado to receive the bottom.

Adjust the fence on the router table as shown in this diagram. Run a 1/8" dado for the 1/8" ply bottom in the sides and ends as shown. Use a stop block on the router table fence so you can start and stop the dado in the proper place on the sides. See Appendix III-B-d. If you cut through the dados on the sides you will end up with a hole in the box joint. The dados run right through on the end pieces. When the cuts are complete, dry fit the pieces to check that all the bottom dados match. See figure 1-B-7.

Figure 1-B-7 Bottom dados must match in the sides and ends to receive the 1/8" bottom.

Gluing it up

We are now ready to glue the box together. Box joints can be hard to glue. We recommend that you use a small brush to spread the glue. Place masking tape on the inside of the box. Then glue and clamp the box together. Do not forget to install the box bottom while you are gluing the box together, it cannot be done later. Any excess glue will spill on the tape and can be removed by pulling the tape off the inside corner before the glue dries. See Appendix II for gluing and clamping.

Sand the box and the lid. Install the brass butt hinges and do the final sanding and finishing.

Different Sizes

It is a characteristic of box joints that the length of the sides and ends are the same as the outside dimensions of the project. Just decide what size you want your box to be, and that will be the length of sides and ends that you need.

Last determine your width and material thickness. Easy, right!

Notes:

1 C. Jewelry Box

Figure 1-C-1 Combine box joints with a fancy mold for this jewelry box.

We have titled this project jewelry box because it makes a decorative holder for earrings, necklaces, and rings. Box joints are used for joinery in this project. A liner makes a lid lip and the decorative mold gives the box a unique appearance. See figure 1-C-1. The style of this box makes it necessary to use a solid wood material.

Project Requirements

Recommended: Walnut, Cedar

Also suitable: Oak, Cherry

Material list:
 2 - 2 5/8" x 9 1/8" x 3/8" sides A
 2 - 2 5/8" x 6 1/8" x 3/8" ends B
 2 - 6 1/8" x 9 1/8" x 3/8" top/bottom C
 1 - 30"x 1 3/4" x 1/4" lining material D

Router tools:
 Table mounted router
 Table fence
 Spacer fence 3/8"

Router bits:
 3/8" Spiral
 Drawline bit

Skill Level			
Basic		**X**	Basic Plus
Moderate			Advanced

Construction details in:

The skills necessary to complete the projects in this book are presented in appendixes at the back. The following skills are used in this project. You may wish to review the following appendixes before you start.

Appendix I - Choosing and Sizing Material

Appendix II - Gluing and Clamping

Appendix IV- A. Box joints rectangular

How to build this project

Select the materials by choosing the wood you will use. Joint, plane, and cut all materials to size following the material list.

There is an extra 1/8" on sides A and B (not shown on Drawing) which is needed for box joints. Appendix I gives step by step instructions for choosing and sizing project material.

Cutting the box joints

Identify and mark one edge and face side of each piece. Chuck up a 3/8" solid carbide Spiral bit. Set up the router table with a 3/8" spacer fence to cut box joints in the sides (A) and ends (B) with the proper offset. Check your fence set up with two sample pieces of stock. For assistance with Spacer Joinery see Appendix IV-A.

Complete a dry fit with the four pieces to ensure that all the box joints fit together properly. Lay the top and bottom on the fitted pieces to make sure all parts are square and lined up. See figure 1-C-2.

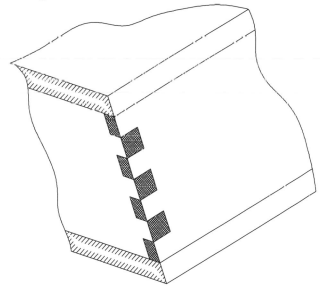

Figure 1-C-2 Stack top, box jointed sides/ends, and bottom.

If the box joint is satisfactory glue and clamp the four (A)and (B) pieces together. (Use masking tape on the inside of the joint to prevent the glue from spreading on the inside corner. Excess glue and the tape can be removed at the end of the gluing process before the glue dries).

Check to make sure that the box is square before letting the glue set. Use a small square to check each corner. Check all joints to be sure they have a tight fit.

Let the glue set and remove the clamps. Clean up and sand the outside of the box joints.

Assembly

Position the top and bottom (C) on the completed sides. Check the side assembly to be sure the parts are even on the top and bottom. The top and bottom are cut over-sized and should be positioned so there is an even border over hanging the sides all around the box. Glue and clamp the top and bottom to the sides. When the glue is set remove the clamps and clean up excess glue. See Appendix II for gluing and clamping.

Using the decorative router bit, rout the top and bottom. Adjust the bit height so that the top and bottom glue lines are inconspicuous. See figure 1-C-3. Make the mold cuts trim the top and bottom.

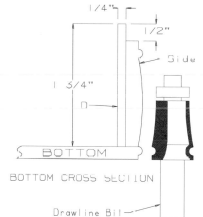

Figure 1-C-3 Mold the top and bottom with the drawline bit.

Cutting apart

Cut the box into two equal halves (to make a lid/bottom parts of the box). Use a thin kerfed blade in the table saw to make this cut. See figure 1-C-4.

Using the same decorative drawline router bit, rout both the lid and the bottom on the newly cut edges.

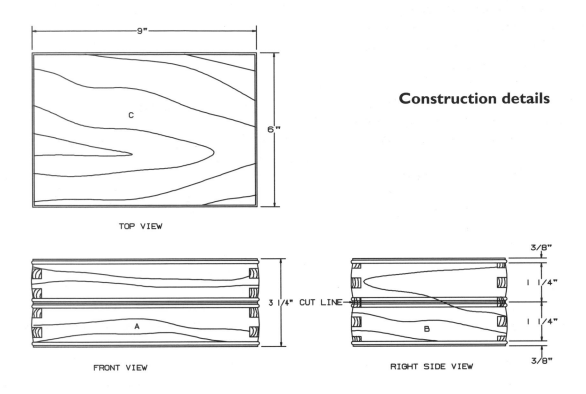

Construction details

Figure 1-C-4 Cut line to separate the lid from the bottom.

Cut the 30" lip material to fit into the box bottom like a liner. You can use butt or mitre joints. Glue the liner in place and let the glue set. This is the final operation and it creates a lip to hold the lid to the bottom. See figure 1-C-5.

Remove the clamps. Clean up and finish sand the project. Apply a finish of your choice.

Different sizes

As with the previous project, the sides and ends can be cut to the size of the box desired. The top and the bottom should be cut 1/8" over-size to allow for a decorative molding to be routed.

Notes:

Figure 1-C-5 The box liner makes a lip inside the box.

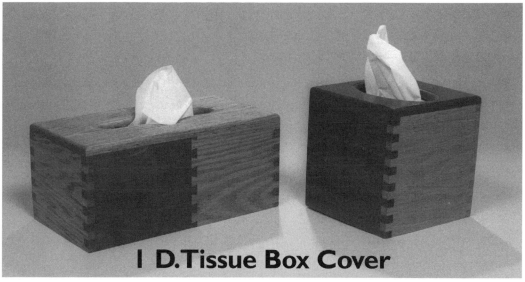

I D. Tissue Box Cover

Figure I-D-I Create a tissue cover.

Make wooden covers to use over facial tissue cardboard cartons for decoration. Wooden tissue box covers can be made with a variety of joints and decorative processes such as inlays, dovetail splices, and pattern hole cutouts. See figure I-D-I. Here are the instructions for the rectangular tissue box.

Project Requirements

Recommended: Oak, Walnut

Also suitable: Ash, Cherry

Material list (Rectangular)
- 2 - 4 1/4" X 10 1/2" X 3/8" sides.
- 2 - 4 1/4" X 5 1/2" X 3/8" oak ends.
- 1 - 5 1/2" X 10 1/2" X 3/8" oak top.

(Optional for dovetail spliced sides)
- 2 - 4 3/4" x 6" x 1/2" walnut sides
- 2 - 4 3/4" x 6" x 1/2" oak sides

To make dovetail splices in the tissue box sides use the material list above. The extra is to allow for trimming.

Material list (Square)
- 5 - 5 5/8" x 5 5/8" x 3/8" top, sides, ends

Router tools:
- Table mounted router
- 3/8" Spacer fence
- Pattern jig
- Tissue slot pattern
- 7" base plate
- 1" brass guide and ring nut

Skill Level

	Basic		Basic Plus
X	Moderate		Advanced

Router bits:
- 3/8" solid carbide spiral bit
- 3/4" Plunge round over bit
- OPTION: 1/2" 14 degree dovetail bit

Construction details in:

The skills necessary to complete the projects in this book are presented in appendixes at the back. The following skills are used in this project. You may wish to review the following appendixes before you start.

Appendix I - Choosing /Sizing Material

Appendix II - Gluing and Clamping

Appendix IV- A. Box joints rectangular

Option: IV- E. dovetail splice

Appendix V - D. Pattern cutting

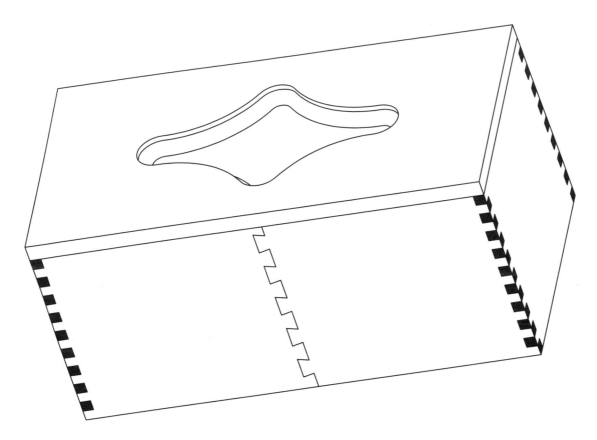

Figure 1-D-2 Rectangular tissue cover, with optional dovetail sides.

How to build this project

Choose the wood for this project. Joint, plane and cut all materials to size according to the material list. Be sure all stock is cut square to the exact size listed. Appendix 1 contains instructions on choosing and sizing materials.

Sides and ends

Chuck up a 3/8" spiral bit. Set up the 3/8" spacer fence to make box joints. See Appendix IV-A for cutting box joints. Make a sample cut first in off cut project material to check for box joint fit. See figure 1-D-2 and 1-D-3. When your are satisfied with the fit, cut box joints in the sides and ends.

The top

Remove the router and 11" plate from the table and install the pattern jig in the table top.

Insert the tissue top stock in the pattern jig and center it with furniture blocks and pattern bolts. See figure 1-D-4. Slide the tissue box pattern over the stock and lock the pattern with the pin. See Appendix V-D for pattern cutting.

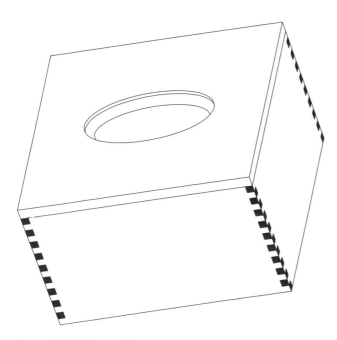

Figure 1-D-3 Square tissue cover.

Figure 1-D-4 Secure the top stock in the pattern jig.

Install a 1" guide and 7" base plate on the router. Mount the 3/4" plunge round over bit in the router. Set the depth of cut at 7/16", using set-up bars, to cut through the 3/8" top material.

Plunge through the material keeping the guide flange tight to the pattern and rout the tissue slot. Be sure to move in a clockwise direction for this internal cut. This cuts and molds the opening in one operation. See figure 1-D-5. Be sure to clean the cavity periodically to make sure debri does not get between the guide and the pattern.

Dry fit all the parts. Glue and clamp the pieces together. Sand and trim as needed. Finish sand, stain, and decorate as desired.

You may want to round off the top corners of the tissue cover. Use the same roundover bit in a table mounted router with a table fence.

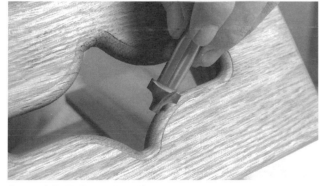

Figure 1-D-5 Cut and mold in one operation.

Using dovetail splices

If you have decided to try the decorative dovetail splices in your tissue box as shown in the photo, you will have to prepare the side stock first. Use 1/2" material in two contrasting woods and you will require slightly longer and wider pieces for the dovetail overlap and for trimming.

Chuck up a 1/2" 14 degree dovetail router bit in the table mounted router and position the 3/8" spacer fence over the table. Clamp the contrasting wood pieces together with an off set and run dovetails across the width. See Appendix IV-E. Dovetail splices. Glue the splice and plane both surfaces of the pieces to get rid of any tear out and bring the size down to 3/8" thickness. Cut the width and length of the spliced sides to the size indicated in the material list (Rectangular). Go back to "How to build this project" and follow the instructions.

Square Cover

Tissue boxes can be made in a variety of sizes using different shaped openings. See figure 1-D-6. This cover fits over the smaller cardboard tissue box and has an oval opening in the top. Use the 3 x 5 size oval pattern for the tissue hole and a 1 3/8" guide instead of the 1" guide. Follow the same procedure as above but cut your material to fit over the smaller tissue box.

Figure 1-D-6 Oval opening

Offset the pieces and run the box joints in the tissue box ends and sides. See Appendix IV-A.

Position the top with the oval opening on the square box. Round the edges of the top if desired.

Dry fit, glue, sand and finish.

1 E. Roll Up Box

Figure 1-E-1 Roll up box

This is not your ordinary box. When it is completely opened up, the contents are laid out before you on the flat. There is no digging to the bottom to see what has sifted down. However, depending what you store in this box you may want to devise hangers or holders for the items you put in the box. It is ideal for small tools or items that could get lost easily in a drawer. The authors intend to use their box for storing brass guides. Small computer repair tools, sewing fixtures, and sized screw drivers are other possible items for this kind of storage. See figure 1-E-1.

Project Requirements

Recommended: Box-Oak,
           Spline-Walnut

Material list:
    4 - 4" x 8" x 3/8" oak sides
    4 - 4" x 5" x 3/8" oak ends
    these are rough cut. See figure 1-E-3
    16 - 5/8" x 4 1/2" x 3/16" walnut splines

Router tools:
    Table mounted router
    Table fence
    Brass insert and ring nut
    1/4" spacer fence

Router bits:
    1/4" carbide spiral bit
    3/16" slot cutter
    3/4" V groove bit
    3/8" carbide spiral bit

Hardware:
    3 - pair 3/4" narrow butt hinges
    1 - latch (novelty box type)

Skill Level

Basic			Basic Plus
Moderate		**X**	Advanced

Construction details in:
The skills necessary to complete the projects in this book are presented in appendixes at the back. The following skills are used in this project. You may wish to review the following appendixes before you start.

Appendix I-Choosing / Sizing Material

Appendix II - Gluing and Clamping

Appendix III- B. Table fence set up
                    D. Measuring made simple

Appendix IV- Box joints

Appendix VII- J. Angle fixture

Important sketches for the Roll up box

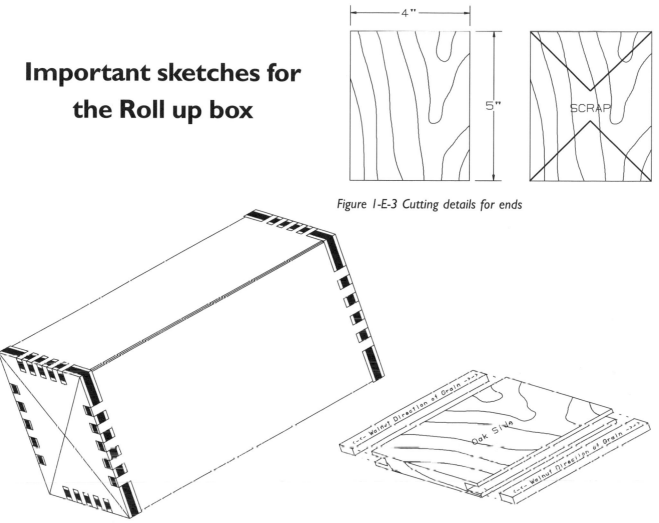

Figure 1-E-3 Cutting details for ends

Figure 1-E-2 Drawing of closed box

Figure 1-E-4 Spline and slot cutting details

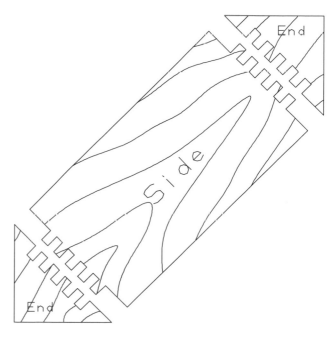

Figure 1-E-5 Centering the box joints on the sides and ends

How to build this project

Choose the wood for this project. Joint, plane and cut all materials to size according to the material list. Be sure all stock is cut square to the exact size listed. Appendix 1 contains instructions on choosing and sizing materials.

See figures 1-E-2, 1-E-3, 1-E-4, and 1-E-5 for material details.

Getting started

Set up the router table using a 3/16" slot cutter and a table fence. Set the depth of cut to center the 3/16" slot in the 3/8" material. Set the fence to allow the cutter to make a 5/8" deep slot in each end of the sides and in each end of the four ends to receive the walnut spline. See figure 1-E-6.

Figure 1-E-6 Slots cut to receive the walnut splines.

Cut and glue the splines in place. Be sure the grain of the wood is according to the plans. When the glue is set trim the splines flush with all edges of the sides and ends.

Chuck up a 1/4" spiral bit in the table mounted router. Adjust the table fence at 2" from the center of the bit. This will be half the width of the ends and sides. Adjust the depth of cut to the material thickness. See Appendix III-D-b.

Cut a centre slot in the four end pieces first. Using a backer stick cut a 1/4" slot in the splined ends of each end piece. (see figure 1-E-7) This cut will be used later for box joints after the spacer fence is in place. REMEMBER — THIS CUT IS MADE IN ONLY THE SPLINED ENDS OF THE END PIECES, NOT THE SIDES.

Figure 1-E-7 Cut 1/4" slots in the splined ends.

A similar cut must be made in the sides. First, readjust the fence so that it is 1/4" closer to the bit. See figure 1-E-8. This will give the proper offset for the box joints which fasten the

ends to the sides. Put a mark on each side to indicate which edge will face the fence. Again using a push stick, cut a slot in the splined ends of each side.

Figure 1-E-8 Cut 1/4" slots in splined side, 1/4" closer to fence.

Then install a 1/4" spacer fence and adjust it so that properly fitting 1/4" box joints can be produced. Use scrap to get the proper fit. Adjust the bit so that the depth of cut will equal that already cut in the initial slots. See figure 1-E-9. Cut the joint slots in the end pieces first. Slip the 1/4" slot already cut over the spacer fence and, using a backer stick, cut TWO slots on each side of the slot already cut. Repeat for all four end pieces. See figure 1-E-10.

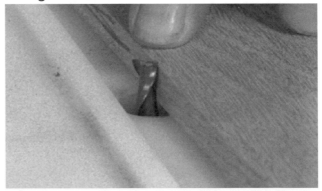

Figure 1-E-9 Set the height of the bit for box joints.

Figure 1-E-10 Cut the rest of the slots on the spacer fence.

Next, cut the box joints in the ends of the sides. DO NOT CHANGE THE SPACER FENCE. You will be able to cut two slots on one side of the previously cut centre slot, and three on the other. You will be left with tabs on both sides, but don't worry about it, as these will cut off later. See figure 1-E-11. Be sure that the two slots on one side are on the same side each time.

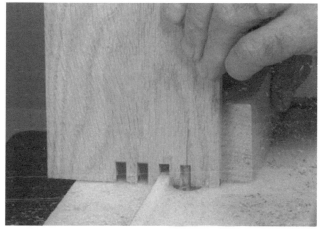

Figure 1-E-11 Tab on each edge of the sides.

Removing the end tabs

Chuck up a 3/8" spiral bit in the table-mounted router, and adjust the depth of cut to the same as the box joint slots. Clamp the table fence to the table at one end, start the router, and swing the fence into the rotating cutter for about 1/16", leaving 1/4" of the bit exposed. Stand the side pieces up using a support stick on the outside, held with the left hand to keep the sides vertical. Cut the tabs off both ends of each piece. See figure 1-E-12.

Figure 1-E-12 Cutting the tabs off the sides.

Angling the side edges

Chuck up the V groove bit and adjust the table fence and bit to cut a 45 degree bevel on the inside of each edge of each side piece. See figure 1-E-13. Do Not bring this cut to a sharp edge. See figure 1-E-14.

Figure 1-E-13 Bevel on the inside box side edge.

1/16" =

45°

Figure 1-F-14 Drawing of the lip left above the bevel.

The end pieces are now ready to cut according to the drawing Figure 1-E-3 using the table saw and the angle fixture. See Appendix VII - J. Cut the ends on a 45 degree angle as shown. See figure 1-E-15 and 1-E-16.

Figure 1-E-15 Cutting angles with the angle fixture.

Note: The box joint slot fits around a poly finger during this angle cut.

Figure I-E-16 Angle fixture acts as a shute board on the table saw.

Dry fit the box together. Because there are many loose pieces, this is not an easy box to glue together.

Glue and clamp the box pieces together. Appendix II contains information on gluing and clamping.

Sand where necessary. Install the hardware. Stain or finish as you wish. You have a unique roll up box.

Notes:

1 F. Chest of Box Drawers

Figure 1-F-1 Chest of box drawers

I F. Chest of Box Drawers

Why make just one box when you can make eight, and create a puzzle for yourself at the same time. By the time you finish you will agree that this chest of drawers can be a puzzle to put together, but an interesting puzzle. This decorative storage unit is ideal for small items. See figure I-F-I. Any seamstress will love it. It could be useful in a workshop as well, to hold those tiny items that always make their way to the bottoms of existing drawers, and in the process become needles in the proverbial haystack with people looking high and low for them.

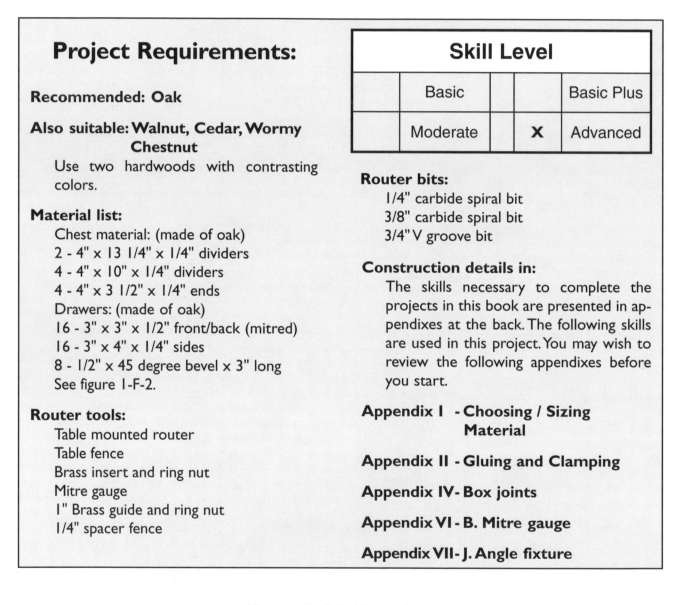

Project Requirements:

Recommended: Oak

Also suitable: Walnut, Cedar, Wormy Chestnut
Use two hardwoods with contrasting colors.

Material list:
Chest material: (made of oak)
2 - 4" x 13 1/4" x 1/4" dividers
4 - 4" x 10" x 1/4" dividers
4 - 4" x 3 1/2" x 1/4" ends
Drawers: (made of oak)
16 - 3" x 3" x 1/2" front/back (mitred)
16 - 3" x 4" x 1/4" sides
8 - 1/2" x 45 degree bevel x 3" long
See figure I-F-2.

Router tools:
Table mounted router
Table fence
Brass insert and ring nut
Mitre gauge
1" Brass guide and ring nut
1/4" spacer fence

Skill Level			
	Basic		Basic Plus
	Moderate	**X**	Advanced

Router bits:
1/4" carbide spiral bit
3/8" carbide spiral bit
3/4" V groove bit

Construction details in:
The skills necessary to complete the projects in this book are presented in appendixes at the back. The following skills are used in this project. You may wish to review the following appendixes before you start.

Appendix I - Choosing / Sizing Material

Appendix II - Gluing and Clamping

Appendix IV- Box joints

Appendix VI- B. Mitre gauge

Appendix VII- J. Angle fixture

How to build this project

Choose the wood for this project. Joint, plane and cut all materials to size according to the material list. Be sure all stock is cut square to the exact size listed. Appendix I contains instructions on choosing and sizing materials.

Lay out all the slots in the dividers as shown in the plans. See figures I-F-2 to I-F-10 for the lay out drawings for the drawer and the chest.

Drawer details

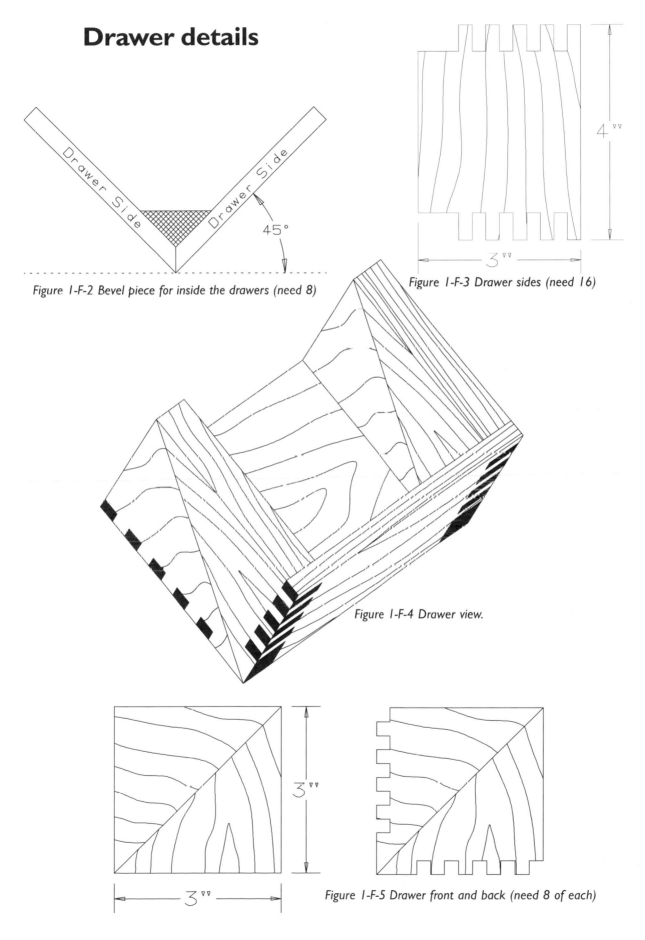

Figure 1-F-2 Bevel piece for inside the drawers (need 8)

45°

Drawer Side   Drawer Side

Figure 1-F-3 Drawer sides (need 16)

4″

3″

Figure 1-F-4 Drawer view.

3″

3″

Figure 1-F-5 Drawer front and back (need 8 of each)

Case details

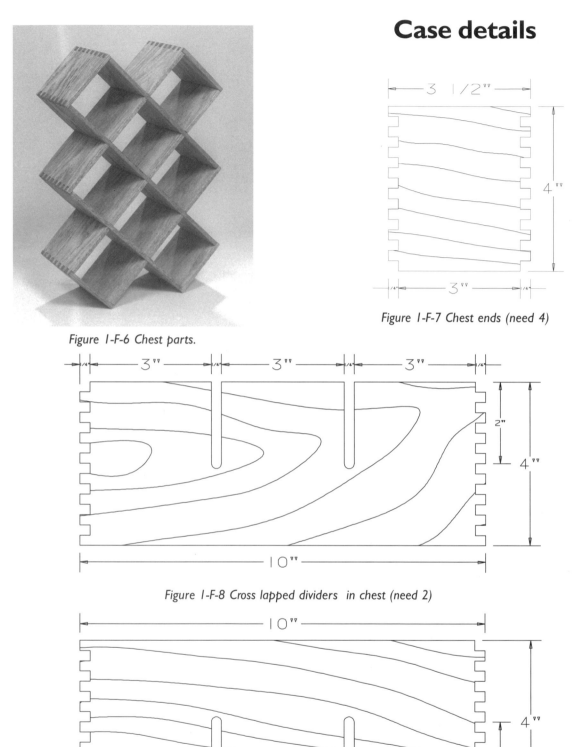

Figure 1-F-6 Chest parts.

Figure 1-F-7 Chest ends (need 4)

Figure 1-F-8 Cross lapped dividers in chest (need 2)

Figure 1-F-9 Cross lapped dividers in chest (need 2)

Note: Pay close attention to how these parts are Box jointed.

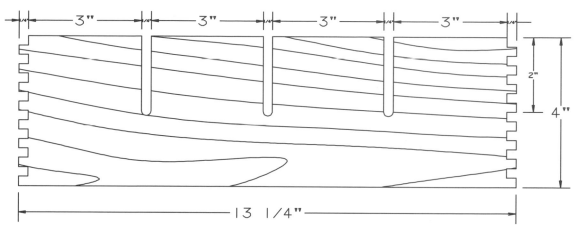

Figure 1-F-10 Chest parts crosslapped (need 2)

Chuck up the 1/4" spiral bit in the table-mounted router. Install the 1" guide in the base plate using the ring nut. Clamp the dividers into the mitre gauge. All cross laps will be half the width of the chest dividers. Set up a stop block or clamp to insure the mitre gauge cuts no further than the half-way mark. See Appendix VI-B.

Cut the slots for the dividers following the details in the above plans. See figure 1-F-11.

Figure 1-F-11 Cross laps on the mitre gauge.

Install the 1/4" spacer fence over the table and with the 1/4" spiral bit chucked up make a test box joint to ensure proper fit. Adjust the depth of cut to slightly more than the thickness of the material. Cut all the 1/4" box joints in the dividers and ends. Be sure you follow the detail plans for each divider and end. Remember all face edges will go to the fence. See figure 1-F-12. See Appendix IV for Spacer joinery.

Figure 1-F-12 Layout of finished dividers and ends.

Checking the fit

Once all the parts have been box jointed, dry fit into the chest assembly. Follow the photograph assembly shown here. See figure 1-F-13 and 1-F-14.

Figure 1-F-13 Partial assembly of chest pieces.

Figure 1-F-14 Assembled chest - no drawers.

Making the drawers

Box joints only work well on end grain of the wood. Chipping will occur even on an angle so it is necessary to make sure the drawer front and back are mitred to provide end grain for the box joint cuts. Rip the front material from 1/2" stock to a full 3" width. Use the angle fixture with the table saw to cut the following mitres. See Appendix VII - J. Angle Fixture.

Cut a 45 degree angle on one end of the stock. See figure 1-F-15.

Figure 1-F-15 45 Degree angle cut.

Cut this angle piece off using the square cut on the fixture. See figure 1-F-16.

Figure 1-F-16 Square cut on the angle fixture.

Cut thirty two of the above pieces. Reverse this block and glue the 45 degree angle together. Watch the direction of the grain. Check the details for drawer fronts in the plans. See figure 1-F-17.

Figure 1-F-17 Glue drawer fronts together.

When the glue dries clean the excess away and sand both sides of the drawer fronts.

In the table mounted router chuck up a 1/4" spiral bit. Install the insert and ring nut to narrow the bit hole. Secure the table fence leaving 3/4" between the bit and the fence. Set the depth of cut at slightly more than 1/4". Run a 1/4" slot in each edge of end grain in the drawer fronts and backs as shown in the plan details. See figure 1-F-18.

Figure 1-F-18 Slot in the edge grain.

When all the fronts and backs are completed with these slot cuts, install the spacer fence over the table and run a test piece to check the box joint fit. Adjust the depth of cut to exactly the same as the previous slot cut. Using the previous 1/4" slot over the spacer fence cut box joints on both end grain sides of all drawer fronts and backs. See Appendix IV-B.

Adjust the bit height to slightly more than 1/2" and box joint the sides of the drawers. You should have a face edge marked and remember to keep this mark to the fence as you cut box joints in the drawer sides.

There should be five consecutive box joints in each side. You will note that there is a larger section left over. These ends will be removed once all the box joints have been completed. Remove the spacer fence.

Chuck up the 3/8" spiral bit and set the depth of cut to the same as the box joint in the sides. Secure the table fence on one end, start the router, and swing the fence into the rotating bit to about 1/16". The bit will be rounded slightly into the fence.

Using a stop block on the out feed side of the fence and a support block in your left hand, stand the drawer side on end and cut the tab off by running the cut to the stop block. Do this for all the sides. See figure 1-F-19.

Reset the router table with a V groove bit and table fence. Adjust the fence and bit to cut a sharp 45 degree angle on the drawer sides. See figure 1-F-20.

Figure 1-F-20 45 degree cut on drawer sides.

Glue, clean, and sand the drawers. Insert the cant strip in the bottom of each drawer. See detail drawing for exact size needed. See 1-F-21.

Figure 1-F-21 Cant strip in bottom of drawers.

Assemble and glue the chest. Insert the drawers in the chest. You now have an eight drawer storage chest that is decorative and functional.

Notes:

Figure 1-F-19 Cut tabs off the sides.

FRAMES and DISHES

We can never have too many frames for the pictures that most people collect of family and friends. Wood is an ideal material for frames because it comes in a variety of colours and textures to set off our important family pictures or for that statement mirror in the front entrance. The mirror/picture frames in this unit have been chosen for beauty and simplicity.

Throughout history, dishes have been fashioned of an almost unlimited variety of materials. From a large leaf dish to manufactured fine bone china, people have eaten from and served food in wooden dishes. Because the surface of the wooden dish will be in contact with food, be sure to use a non toxic finish. Do not make dishes from exotic woods that may have poisonous properties.

WHAT YOU WILL LEARN IN THIS SECTION

In this unit you will become familiar with the use of the plunge router. This is the recommended style of router to buy, since it allows the owner to start the machine with the bit clear of the wood, and then to plunge the bit into the wood at the desired point, rather than having to tip the bit in as was necessary with the older, barrel-screw type routers.

The plunge router and the solid brass guides are particularly useful when following patterns. The techniques make following patterns easy and the projects in this section provide good practice in this work.

This section also teaches how to produce a series of spaced patterns, which in turn is useful in making multiple picture frames.

Finally, this section allows the woodworker to practice using the router to produce exact circles, and how to cut a series of circles from a single piece of wood.

The router not only produces the best joints, it is a machine that can be used to produce finished cuts on irregular edges, cuts that require little or no sanding before being finished.

Frames and dishes.

2 A. Candy Dishes

Figure 2-A-1

The bridge or whist club will be impressed with your wooden snack dishes shaped like the card suits See figure 2-A-1. They are easily routed in a very short time.

Project Requirements

Recommended: Oak, Walnut

Also suitable: Cherry, Ash, Maple

Material list:
    4 - 8" x 11" x 3/4" oak dish stock

Router tools:
    Table mounted router
    Table fence
    Pattern jig
    Club pattern
    Spade pattern
    Diamond pattern
    Large heart pattern
    7" base plate
    1" brass guide and ring nut

Router bits:
    5/8" flat bottom core box bit
    1 1/4" plunge round over bit
    5/32" roman ogee bit with bearing
    1/4" round over bit with bearing

Skill Level

X	Basic		Basic Plus
	Moderate		Advanced

Construction details:
    You may wish to review the following appendixes before you start.

Appendix I - Choosing and Sizing Material

**Appendix III- A-d. Safety pin use
            B-c,e. Table fence set up**

Appendix V - D. Pattern cutting internal

How to build this project

Choose the wood for this project. Joint, plane and cut all materials to size according to the material list. Be sure all stock is cut square to the exact size listed. Appendix I contains instructions on choosing and sizing materials.

Position the pattern jig in the table hole and install the first dish stock piece in the pattern jig. Center and secure it by using furniture blocks. See figure 2-A-2.

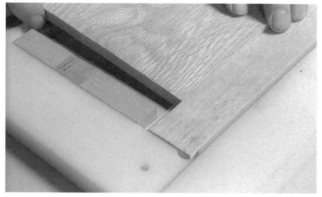

Figure 2A2 Position stock in the pattern jig.

Slide the club pattern in place over the stock. Lock the pattern in place with the pin provided. It should already be centered because the stock being used almost fills the stock cavity. Chuck up the flat bottom core box bit in the plunge portable router. The 7" base plate, the 1" brass guide and ring nut should be in place. Be sure the guide and ring nut are tightened. Set the depth of cut to 5/8". Use brass set up bars.

With the guide flange against the pattern edge, plunge the bit into the stock. Move slowly clockwise in the pattern shape about half way around. Stop to remove debris that tends to get between the guide and pattern. Keep routing the cavity until you have a smooth bottom 5/8" deep cavity in the club shape. This will leave about a 1/8" bottom in the dish. See figure 2-A-3.

Figure 2-A-3 Pattern jig and guide.

When you are satisfied with the cavity, remove the pattern and dish stock. Secure the next piece of dish stock in the pattern jig and slide the spade pattern over the dish stock. Lock the pattern in with the pin. Repeat the above procedure with this pattern.

In the same manner rout out the dishes for the diamond and heart shapes.

Put the pattern jig aside and set up the table mounted router with a 1 1/4" plunge round over bit. Set the depth to the full round over of the bit. Adjust and secure the table fence to round the corners of the dishes. See Appendix III-B-e.

Figure 2-A-4 Round the stock corners.

Holding the stock pieces on edge and using a backer piece to prevent chipping, round off all the corners of the dishes.

Tip

This rounding operation goes smoother if you remember to rout with the straight grain of the stock against the table. See figure 2-A-4.

The outside edges

To make the dish easier to lift, a larger, ogee-style cut is made with the bottom on the table. Chuck up the roman ogee bit in the table-mounted router and set the depth of the cut to the full profile of the bit. Use the safety pin as a fulcrum and ease the stock into the cutter to route around the outside. See Appendix III A-d. Again, cut a cross-grain edge first and then a straight-grain edge. See figure 2-A-5.

Figure 2-A-5 Mold the outside edge of the dish.

To finish the top of the dish, chuck up the 1/4" round over bit in the table mounted router. With the safety pin in place, round the outside face side of all the dishes. When cutting the top of the dish cut a cross grain end first, then a side, then the other end and finally the other side. Remove the safety pin and put the dish cavity over the bit. Allow the bearing to follow the dish shape to round off the inside top edge of the dish cavity. You will be moving the stock in a clockwise direction. See figure 2-A-6.

Figure 2-A-6 Top edge rounded. Use table mount.

Round the outside and inside face edges of all the dishes.

Sand and finish the set of snack dishes with a food finish such as mineral oil.

Notes:

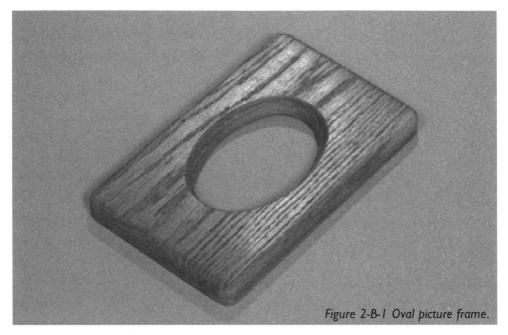

Figure 2-B-1 Oval picture frame.

2 B. Oval Picture Frame

We can never have too many picture frames. Cameras are more used than ever before and pictures of family and friends abound. Children and grandchildren bring pictures home from school. It is nice to display some of our special pictures or give frames as gifts. Here is an especially easy to make picture frame that will please your friends and family. See figure 2-B-1.

Project Requirements

Recommended: Oak or Walnut

Also suitable: Mahogany, Cedar

Material List:
    1 - 6" x 8" x 3/4" oak or walnut

Router Tools:
    Table mounted router
    Table fence
    Pattern jig
    Oval pattern (5 x 7)
    1" brass guide and ring nut
    7" base plate
    Square pattern (optional)
    5/8" brass guide (optional)

Router bits:
    Plunging Ogee bit 3/4"
    Flat Bottom Plunge bit 3/4"
    1/4" Round over bit with or without pilot
    Keyhole bit (optional)

Skill Level

X	Basic		Basic Plus
	Moderate		Advanced

Construction details:
    The skills necessary to complete the projects in this book are presented in appendixes at the back. The following skills are used in this project. You may wish to review the following appendixes before you start.

Appendix I - Choosing and Sizing Material

Appendix III- B. Table fence set up

Appendix V - D. Pattern cutting

How to build this project

Choose the wood for this project. Joint, plane and cut all materials to size according to the material list. Be sure all stock is cut square to the exact size listed. Appendix I contains instructions on choosing and sizing materials.

Center the stock in the pattern jig. Use furniture blocks along one side and the top. Snug the stock in place with pattern bolts on the other side and the bottom. See figure 2-B-2.

Figure 2-B-2 Pattern jig and oval pattern.

Centering the oval

Slide the oval pattern over the stock in the pattern jig. Slide the pattern up so that the top of the oval is flush with the top of the stock. Make a pencil mark at the bottom of the oval. Remove the pattern and make another mark half-way between the first mark and the bottom of the stock. Re-insert the pattern and position it so that the bottom of the oval is lined up with your second pencil mark.

If you then turn the jig upside down you will be able to drill a hole for the positioning pin through the existing jig hole. If you then turn the jig over, you will be able to put a pin in this hole, to make sure the pattern does not move while you are routing.

Mount a plunging ogee bit in the router. Install a one-inch guide in the 7" base plate, making sure the bit is in the centre of the guide. Use set-up bars, or a piece of material to set the depth of cut to 5/8".

Position the guide along the long edge of the oval shape and plunge the bit into the stock. *Move from left to right.* This will mold and shape the piece in one operation. The plunging ogee bit will not cut all the way through the stock. To ensure a smooth cut be sure to get rid of wood chips. Debris between the pattern and the guide will cause an irregular cut. Use a vacuum or stop periodically to dump the chips from the cut See Appendix V D. Pattern cutting. See figure 2-B-3.

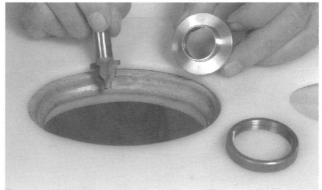

Figure 2-B-3 The oval cut.

Rabbeting the back

When the oval shape has been completely molded, remove the stock piece and reinstall it upside down.

CAUTION: Do not flip the piece end for end.

To make a rabbet in the back of the picture frame, slide the oval pattern back into place and lock it shut with the pin. Change to the 3/4" flat bottom plunge bit and, still using the 1" guide, set the depth of cut to 1/8" or until it meets the ogee cut from the face side. Position the guide along a side of the oval. Plunge the router into the cut and move from left to right. This will leave a groove in the back of the frame for the picture and free the center plug. Be sure there is a place for the plug to drop away from the bit.

Option: The only drawback to the frame as described above is that the recess for the picture and/or glass is also oval. Most pictures come in a square or retangular format. Here's an option to the rabbet cut that will make it easler to frame the picture without too much trimming.

To make a square recess for the picture and glass rather than an oval one, substitute a square pattern instead of the oval one for the rabbet.

With the flat bottom bit and 1/8" depth of cut rout the back of the frame in a 1/8" depth to the square shape. This will leave a recess for the picture and a glass. It will allow the oval plug to drop away. See figure 2-B-4.

Figure 2-B-4 Square cut back.

The square pattern has a key hole above the square that can be used for a hanger hole if desired. To make a hanger hole change to a key hole bit and a 5/8" guide. Set the depth of cut to 3/8". Plunge the bit into the wide end of the key-hole pattern. Move up to the narrow end and back down to the wide end before removing the bit. This will make an undercut hanging hole just above the picture oval for hanging the picture on the wall. See figure 2-B-5

Figure 2-B-5 Use a key hole bit for the hanger hole.

To mold the outside of the picture frame mount the router in the table. Install a 1/4" round over bit in the router. Position the table fence exposing the mold desired. Make sure the bit bearing does not touch the stock. To isolate the bearing see Appendix III-B-c. Set the depth of cut to the desired round and mold the cross grain end first. Mold the straight grain side, the end and the other side. This completes the oval picture frame.

Sand and finish as desired

Notes:

2 C. Mirror Frame

We never seem to have a mirror when we need one. The pictured frame will suit any decor and may be constructed of a variety of wood species. See figure 2-C-1. It can also serve as a picture frame, as it can be simply made up in a variety of sizes.

Figure 2-C-1 Rectangular mirror frame.

Project Requirements

Recommended: Walnut

Also suitable: Oak, Cedar

Material list:
 2 - 2 3/8" x 20" x 3/4" walnut stiles
 2 - 2 3/8" x 10" x 3/4" walnut rails
 2 - 1 1/2" x 15 3/4" x 3/4" walnut molding

Router tools:
 Table mounted router
 Table fence
 Panel door fence system

Router bits:
 Stile and rail bit(s)
 3/8" rabbet bit
 1/4" round over bit
 5/32" roman ogee bit

Hardware:
 6 - #6 x 1/2" flat headed wood screws
 1 - 10" x 16" plated mirror

Skill Level

	Basic			Basic Plus
X	Moderate			Advanced

Construction details:
 The skills necessary to complete the projects in this book are presented in appendixes at the back. The following skills are used in this project. You may wish to review the following appendixes before you start.

Appendix I - Choosing and Sizing Material

Appendix II - Gluing and Clamping

Appendix III - B. Table fence set up

Appendix VI - A. Panel construction

How to build this project

Choose the wood for this project. Joint, plane, and cut all materials to size according to the material list. Be sure all stock is cut square to the exact size listed. Appendix I contains instructions on choosing and sizing materials.

Set up the router table with the panel door fence system. Install the stile and rail bit in the router. Run the cope cut on the ends of the rails. Appendix VI-A contains panel construction. Adjust the cutter to make the bead cuts. Run beads along one edge of each stile and rail piece. Dry fit the pieces. If satisfactory, glue the stile and rail together. Appendix II has information on gluing and clamping. Be sure the frame is square before the glue sets. See figure 2-C-2.

Figure 2-C-2 Stile and rail joint.

Top and Bottom pieces

Chuck up a roman ogee bit and set the depth of the cut to the full profile of the bit. Using a table fence, isolate the bit bearing. See Appendix III-B-c. Using a backer board clamped to each end in turn, mold all four ends of the top and bottom pieces. See figure 2-C-3. The backing board will produce a clean cut with no tearout. Once the ends are cut run the mold along the front edge of each piece.

Figure 2-C-3 Backer board clamped to mold ends.

Then chuck up a round-over bit and isolate the bearing with the table fence. Use backing boards when rounding over the ends and then round over the edges opposite the ogee molds.

Drill screw holes in the molding pieces as shown in figure 2-C-4.

Figure 2-C-4 Drill screw holes in molding.

Round over the face, outside edges of the stiles. See figure 2-C-5.

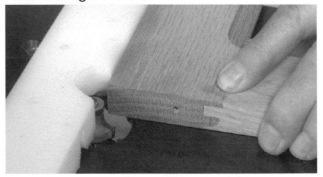

Figure 2-C-5 Round outside of stiles.

A rabbet cut must be made to hold the mirror in the opening. After the frame is clamped and glued, chuck up a 3/8" rabbeting bit in the tablemounted router and set the depth to 1/4". Using the pilot against the frame with the back face-down on the table, move in a clockwise direction so that you are always routing into the cutting edge of the bit. The rabbeting bit when used with the pilot leaves rounded corners. You can square these with a chisel, or round off the corners of the mirror to fit the opening. See figure 2-C-6.

Figure 2-C-6 Frame glued. Note rounded corners on rabbets.

Let the size of your mirror or picture determine the size of the frame you build.

Screw the moldings to the top and bottom of the mirror frame as shown.

Sand, stain or finish the project as desired.

Figure 2-D-1 Wheel dish.

2 D. Wheel Nut Dish

Wooden dishes, spoons, plates, and cutting blocks have been in use for centuries. Interestingly, for years wood had been used in bakeries to roll dough and for cutting boards. Wood was also used in restaurants to cut your steak on. Then the health department outlawed wood as a possible food contaminate. This resulted in all kinds of plastic replacements. Now after years of study, it has been shown that bacteria live in the plastic and quickly die in the wood. We are now back to wooden dishes for food.

Caution: Stay away from exotic wood for food service. Be very careful of the finish you use on wood meant for food. Make this wooden nut dish out of maple and walnut. See figure 2-D-1.

Project Requirements

Recommended: Maple, Walnut

Also suitable: Ash, Cherry, Oak

Material list:
    1 - 14" x 14" X 3/4" maple top
    1 - 14" x 14" x 3/4" walnut Base

Router tools:
    Table mounted router
    Table fence
    Wheel jig (Choose design and size) Featured 12" Standard.
    Sub top for table See Appendix VII-F.
    7" base plate
    1" brass guide
    Brass ring nut

Router bits:
    1/2" carbide spiral bit
    5/8" flat bottom core box bit
    3/4" round over bit
    301 molding profile bit (you can choose a profile)
    1/4" round over bit

Skill Level

	Basic			Basic Plus
X	Moderate			Advanced

Construction Details:
    The skills necessary to complete the projects in this book are presented in appendixes at the back. The following skills are used in this project. You may wish to review the following appendixes before you start.

Appendix I - Choosing and Sizing Material

Appendix II - Gluing and Clamping

Appendix III- A. Safety pin use

Appendix V - C. Wheel jig

Appendix VII -F. Sub top

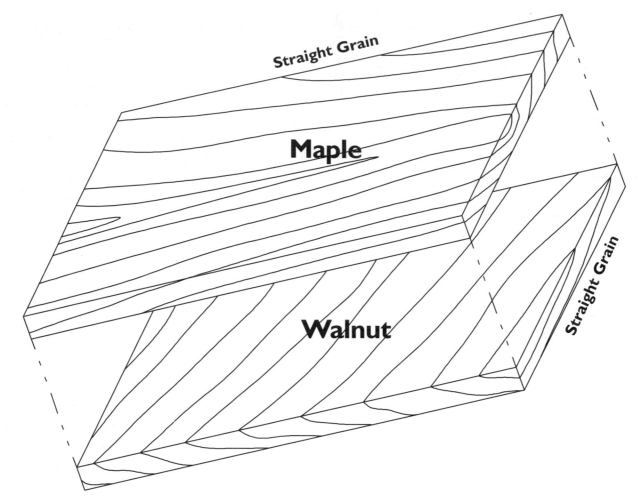

Figure 2-D-2 Cross layer the stock pieces.

How to build this project

Choose the wood for this project. Joint, plane and cut all materials to size according to the material list. Be sure all stock is cut square to the exact size listed. Appendix I contains instructions on choosing and sizing materials.

You may have to laminate pieces together to make up the 14" width. If so do this first. Clean, glue and surface both sides of the walnut and maple. Then laminate the two pieces together using a cross layered system. See figure 2-D-2.

Put the sub top over the router table top to give yourself a work surface to which you can fasten your dish stock. See Appendix VII-F. Fasten the dish stock to the sub top at the corners or with corner blocks attached to the sub top to tightly confine the stock.

On the maple side of the dish stock drill a 1/4" hole in the center. Install the 1/4" center pin and position the wheel jig. See figure 2-D-3.

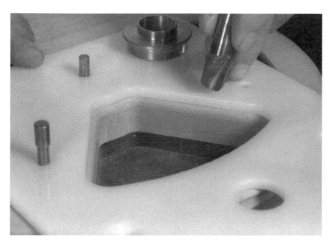

Figure 2-D-3 Wheel jig positioned on the stock.

The wheel effect

Chuck up the 1/2" spiral bit. Install the 7" base plate, 1" guide and ring nut on the router. A plunge router is almost a must for this operation. See Appendix V-C. Follow the instructions for making a wheel except that you will want to leave a bottom in each cavity rather than cutting right through. The dish cavities will be about 1 1/4" deep leaving about a 1/4" bottom. Because of the amount of wood to be removed, you may have to take it in three steps, two 1/2" passes and finish with a 1/4" pass. The turret adjustment on your router and brass set up bars will work well for this depth setting.

Rout the four cavities to the 1 1/4" depth. Chuck up the 5/8" flat bottom core box bit. Using the same guide set up clean all four cavities with the core box bit. Because this bit does not have a deep cutting ability it will take several passes for this operation. Check to make sure the bottom and sides of each cavity is smooth before you go on to the next cavity.

Cut circles in two passes

When the four cavities have been cut smooth, chuck up the 1/2" spiral bit and position the one inch guide in the 1" circle hole of the wheel jig. Because of the thickness of the material to be cut and the resulting chip load it is better to make this circle cut in two passes. Moving the router from left to right plunge the bit about 3/4" for the first pass. Clean the cut of debri and cut through the stock with the second cut.

Remove the wheel jig from the round stock. Remove the sub top and table mount the router. Chuck up the #2-301 molding bit or your mold choice. With the safety pin in place, mold the outside edge of the dish. See Appendix III-A for safety pin use. See figure 2-D-4.

Figure 2-D-4 Cavities and mold routed.

Rounding over

Install the 1/4" round-over bit in the table mounted router. Set the depth to the full 1/4" profile. Place the cavity over the bit and moving the dish against the bit pilot, round over the top edge. Round over each cavity in the dish in this manner.

Drill holes for the pick and nut cracker set in the blank spot of the dish. The center hole left from the wheel jig may be used for one of the picks.

Sand and finish the project. Because food touches the surface, you may want to use mineral oil for the finish

---

Notes:

Figure 2-E-1 Heart frame.

As with most frames you can decide what it will hold, pictures or mirrors. See figure 2-E-1.

Project Requirements

Skill Level

Basic	**X**	Basic Plus
Moderate		Advanced

Recommended: Oak

Also suitable: Walnut, Ash

Material List:

1 - 6 1/4" x 24" x 3/4" oak stock.

Router tools:

Table mounted router
Table fence
Heart pattern
1 " guide and ring nut
7" Base Plate
Shop jig (heart) See Appendix VII-C.
Pattern holder.

Router bits:

3/4" plunging ogee bit
5/32 roman ogee bit
3/4" flat bottom plunge bit

References:
The skills necessary to complete the projects in this book are presented in appendixes at the back. The following skills are used in this project. You may wish to review the following appendixes before you start.

Appendix I - Choosing and Sizing Material

Appendix III- B-c. Table fence

Appendix V - D. Pattern fixture

How to build this project

Choose the wood for this project. Joint, plane and cut all materials to size according to the material list. Be sure all stock is cut square to the exact size listed. Appendix I contains instructions on choosing and sizing materials.

Placing the hearts

First decide how much material you want left at the top and the bottom. For appearance purposes, we have made the bottom area larger, leaving 8" of clear wood at the bottom and 6" at the top.

Using a square and pencil, draw lines across the stock at these points. Using your pattern, position one heart just touching the top line and another just touching the bottom.

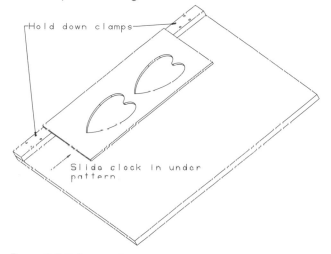

Figure 2-E-2 Pattern fixture.

The pattern jig is not used in this project. Rather, the heart pattern should be screwed to a side guide of the same thickness as the stock. See figure 2-E-2. See appendix VII-D. Clamp the stock into position under the pattern at the top heart. Using the 3/4" plunge ogee bit, with the 7" base plate and 1" guide, cut three quarters of the way into the stock, moving clockwise, periodically clearing the chips and keeping the guide tight against the pattern. See figure 2-E-3.

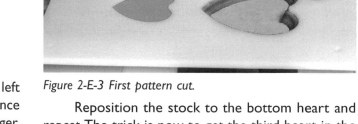

Figure 2-E-3 First pattern cut.

Reposition the stock to the bottom heart and repeat. The trick is now to get the third heart in the centre. Do this by sliding the stock so that the top of the pattern opening is over the bottom of the first cut. Mark the bottom opening of the pattern on the stock with a pencil. Slide the stock out of the way and put another pencil mark half way between the first mark and the top of the bottom heart. Reposition the stock so that the bottom of the pattern opening is over this second mark and you will be able to cut the third heart exactly half way between the top and bottom hearts. See figure 2-E-4.

Figure 2-E-4 Hearts evenly spaced.

Cutting the back recess

To cut a square recess behind each heart you will need a square pattern. You can either use the Oak Park pattern number PA056 or make one in your shop and mount it on a side guide in the same manner as you mounted the heart pattern. Locating where the cuts should be made is quite simple.

Marking the back

You already have lines on the front at the top of the top heart and at the bottom of the bottom heart. Add lines at the top of the middle and bottom hearts, and with a try square, transfer these lines to the back of the stock. The easiest way to do this is to first stand the stock on edge and continue the front lines along the edge, and then, with the stock upside down, continue the lines on the back.

The pattern square you have made should be one-half inch larger than the heart on each side. Since you will be using a guide, this will make the actual cut one-quarter of an inch larger than the heart on each side. Your back lines show you where the top of each heart is. Simply draw an extra line one-half of an inch above each of the existing lines. Using a set-up block makes this easy. Position your stock so that the top of the opening is over these new lines and, using a 3/4" plunge flat bottom bit rout out a cavity 1/4" deep. This should free the heart you have cut on the opposite side and leave you with a finished frame. See Figure 2-E-5.

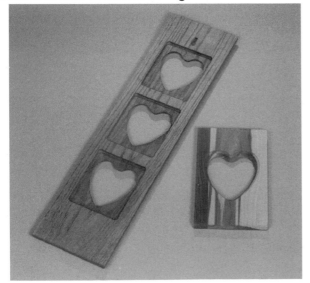

Figure 2-E-5 Square cuts in back.

Adding the hanger hole

If you decide to use a hanger hole, rather than a mechanical hanger, this can be routed into the back of the frame near the top by using a key-hole bit. You may want to add a slot for this cut in the square pattern you have made for the back recess.

Chuck up the 5/32" roman ogee bit in the table mounted router. See Appendix III-B-c. Position the table fence to isolate the bearing. Set the depth of cut to expose the bit profile. Mold the outside face edges of the picture frame by routing the end grain, straight, end, and straight grain sides.

Sand and finish the picture frame and install pictures of your choice.

Other Choices

The directions given are for a three-heart frame. The method can be used to produce any number of openings, depending on your requirements. Sand and finish your frame before putting the pictures in place. You will have produced a real eye catcher.

Notes:

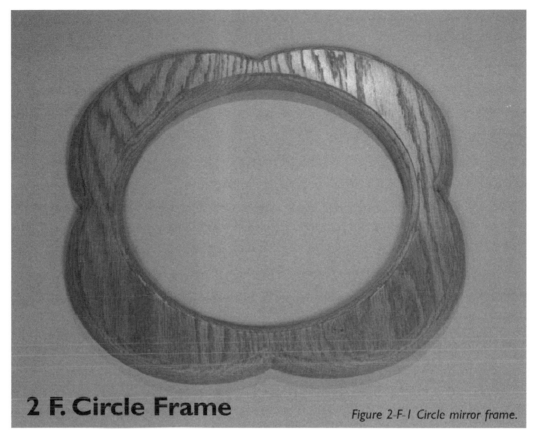

2 F. Circle Frame

Figure 2-F-1 Circle mirror frame.

One of the easiest shapes to make is a circle. Frames are a must in our society with pictures to display and mirrors a part of our furniture. A unique frame is always a focus point. Use the circle jig and your router to produce this different mirror frame. See figure 2-F-1.

Project Requirements	**Skill Level**			
		Basic			Basic Plus
Recommended: Oak	**X**	Moderate			Advanced

Project Requirements

Recommended: Oak

Also suitable: Walnut

Material list:
    1 - 17 1/2" x 17 1/2" x 3/4" oak

Router tools:
    Table mounted router
    Circle jig

Router bits:
    1 1/4" plunge round over bit
    3/8" rabbet bit

Hardware:
    1 metal picture hanger

Skill Level

	Basic			Basic Plus
X	Moderate			Advanced

References:
    The skills necessary to complete the projects in this book are presented in appendixes at the back. The following skills are used in this project. You may wish to review the following appendixes before you start.

Appendix I - Choosing and Sizing Material

Appendix III-A-d. Safety pin use

Appendix VII-F. Sub top

How to build this project

Choose the wood for this project. Joint, plane and cut all materials to size according to the material list. Be sure all stock is cut square to the exact size listed. Appendix I contains instructions on choosing and sizing materials.

This project uses five separate pivot points to develop the shape. Find the center of the stock piece by drawing two lines corner to corner. Where these lines intersect will be the center of the piece. See figure 2-F-2.

Figure 2-F-2 Finding centre of stock.

On each of these diagonal lines make a mark 3 1/2" from the center point. These points will be pivot points I to 4. See figure 2-F-3.

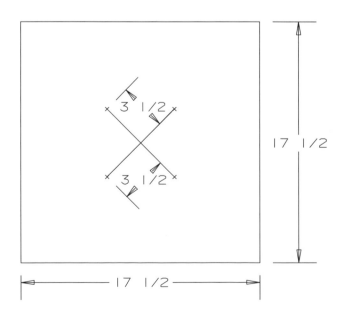

Figure 2-F-3 Four pivot points

After the outside cuts are completed, we will use the circle jig to cut the inside circle using pivot point 5, the center. Cover the router table top with the sub top. See Appendix VII-F. Secure the mirror stock to the sub top by using corner blocks nailed to the sub top. Make sure these blocks hold the stock without twisting. Put a center mark in pencil at the half way point on each side of the stock to guide you in cutting the scallops.

Drive a finishing nail into pivot point I to use as a center pin. Be sure the pin is perpendicular to the stock. Chuck up the I 1/4" plunge round over bit and install the circle jig on your plunge router. Drill a center pin hole in the circle jig 6" from the cutting edge of the bit. Chuck up a finishing nail in your drill like your stock center pin to drill the hole in the jig. Set the depth of cut to the full profile of the bit plus 1/16" to give a flash line. Place the jig hole over pivot point I and moving from left to right cut the first quarter cut in the outside of the frame. See figure 2-F-4 on page 2-20.

Move the circle jig to pivot point 2 and cut the second quarter. Cut the third and fourth quarter in the same manner. Discard the outside corners of stock. See Figure 2-F-5.

Figure 2-F-5 Circle frame.

Secure the stock by driving two finishing nails into the stock on either side of pivot point 5 and about an inch away. Make them flush with the surface and holding into the sub top. Position the circle jig over pivot hole 5 and moving in a clockwise direction, cut the inside circle for the mirror. Sand the molded edges.

Chuck up a 3/8" rabbet bit in the table mounted router. Set the depth of cut to 1/4". Put the center of the mirror frame over the bit face up. Moving the frame in a clockwise direction the pilot on the bit will bear against the stock to mold a rabbet in the back of the frame.

For safety's sake

Keep your hands on the outside of the frame away from the bit, while cutting this rabbet.

Dressing it up

If you wish to dress the outside edge of the back of the mirror, chuck up a 1/4" round over bit. Set the depth of cut to a small round and with the safety pin in place round the back outside edge of the mirror frame. See Appendix III-A-d. This is easier than sanding the edge.

Sand and finish the mirror frame. Cut and install the mirror.

Two for one

You can use the circular piece of stock in the middle for another circular frame if you wish by cutting another center circle out using point 5 as the center and a four inch radius. You would need to make another hole in the circle jig four inches from the edge of the cutter. This would give you a 2 inch circle frame with a seven inch diameter picture hole.

Complete this frame as you did the scallop mirror with a rabbet for the picture and round over mold on the back outside edge. This gives you two projects from one piece of stock.

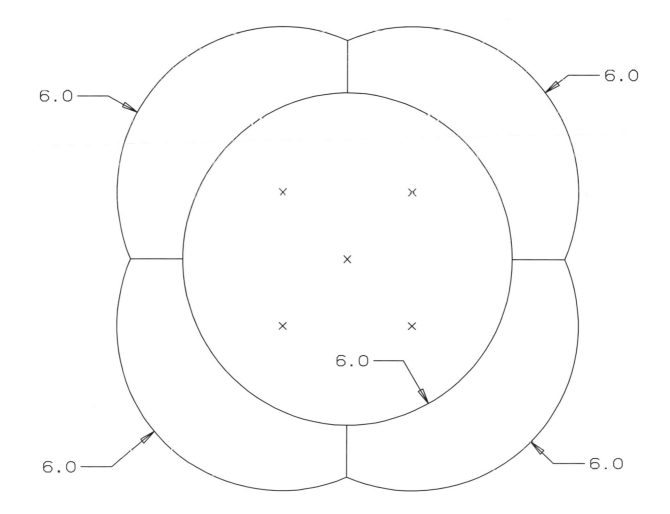

Figure 2-F-4 Drawing of pivot points and cuts.

Figure 2-G-1 Rosewood mirror

2 G. Full Length Mirror Frame

Everyone has a room that they would like to appear larger. This full length mirror will do just that and allow you to check your appearance before you leave home. See figure 2-G-1. This simple design will add a touch of class regardless of the species of wood you choose.

Project Requirements

Recommended: Rosewood

Also suitable: Oak, Walnut, Ash

Material list:
    2 - 2 3/4" X 13" X 3/4" rosewood rails
    2 - 2 3/4" x 56" x 3/4" rosewood stiles

Router tools:
    Table mounted router
    Table fence
    5/8" brass guide and ring nut
    7" base plate
    Shop made mortise jig. See Appendix VII-H.
    Shop made molding jig. See Appendix VII-I.

Router bits:
    3/8" rabbet bit
    3/8" carbide spiral bit

Hardware:
    8 - #6 x 1 1/4" flat headed wood screws
    2 - metal picture hangers

Skill Level

Basic		**X**	Basic Plus
Moderate			Advanced

References:
The skills necessary to complete the projects in this book are presented in appendixes at the back. The following skills are used in this project. You may wish to review the following appendixes before you start.

Appendix I - Choosing and Sizing Material

Appendix II - Gluing and Clamping

Appendix VII- H. Mortise
           I. Mirror fixture

Drawing details

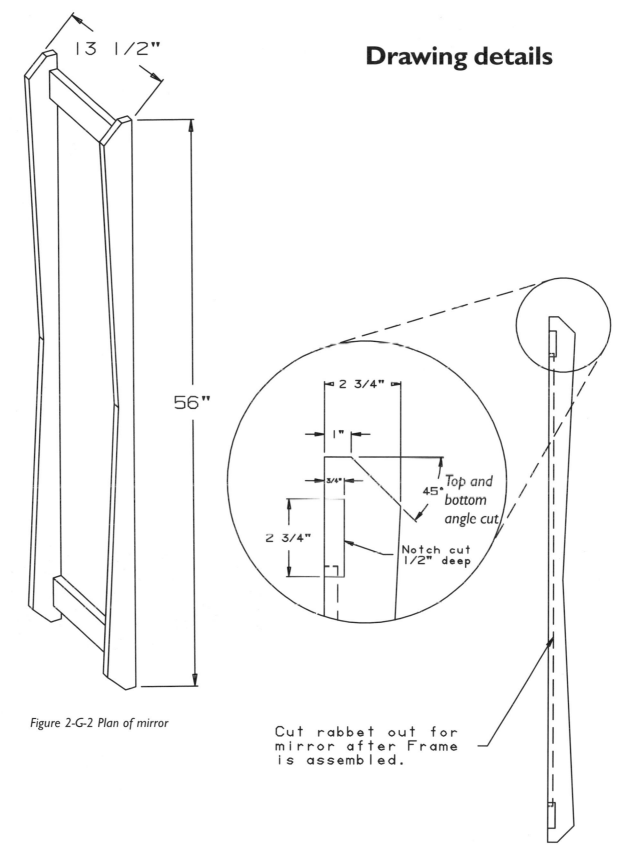

13 1/2"

56"

2 3/4"

1"

3/4"

45°

Top and bottom angle cut

2 3/4"

Notch cut 1/2" deep

Figure 2-G-2 Plan of mirror

Cut rabbet out for mirror after Frame is assembled.

Figure 2-G-3 Front and back details

How to build this project

Choose the wood for this project. Joint, plane and cut all materials to size according to the material list. See figure 2-G-2 and figure 2-G-3. Be sure all stock is cut square to the exact size listed. Appendix I contains instructions on choosing and sizing materials.

Construct the shop fixture to mold the sides of the mirror. See Appendix VII-1. See figure 2-G-4 and 2-G-5.

Figure 2-G-5 Mirror fixture

Lay out the stiles and shape them according to the plan by rough cutting them about 1/4" from the finish line with the band saw.

Install a 5/8" guide in the table mounted router and chuck up the 3/8" spiral bit. Clamp the mirror stile securely in the molding fixture. Depth of cut should be high enough to cut through the mirror stock. Cut one end of the mirror stile to the stop notch in the fixture. See figure 2-G-6. Keep your fingers away from the exposed router bit. See Appendix III-A for a method of guarding the router bit.

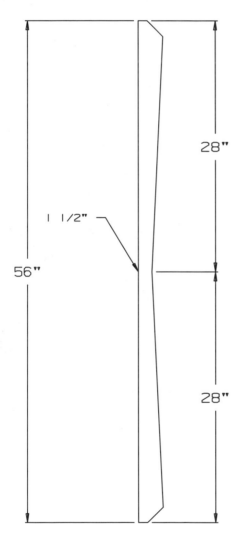

Figure 2-G-4 detail information on template for external routing jig.

28"

1 1/2"

56"

28"

Figure 2-G-6 Stop notch in fixture.

You are cutting down grain so you should not experience any tear out. Be sure to cut from left to right and begin with the pattern against the guide. **CAUTION**: Make sure that the moving router bit does not touch the wood until the pattern is securely against the guide. See figure 2-G-7. Unclamp and end for end the stile in the fixture. Repeat the pattern cut for the other end of the same stile. This is done to keep the router bit cutting down grain. Mold

Cut the top and bottom angle on the stiles using a table or mitre saw. See figure 2-G-3.

Lay out where the mortises will be cut to receive the rails. See figure 2-G-3. Be sure to make a left and right stile.

both edges of the second stile in the same manner.

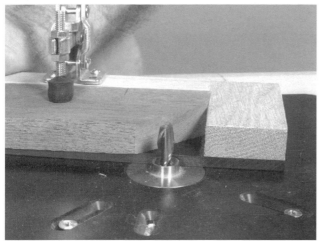

Figure 2-G-7 Mirror fixture, guide and bit to cut stile shape (external cut).

Mortise the stiles

From Appendix VII-H construct a mortise fixture. Fasten the mortise fixture over the stile in the marked location. Be sure to tighten the hold down clamps securely. See figure 2-G-8.

Figure 2-G-8 Mortise jig with bit and guide (internal cut).

Chuck up the 3/8" spiral bit into the portable router and install a 5/8" brass guide on the 7" base plate. Set the depth of cut to 1/2" and follow the mortise fixture with the guide to mortise the four slots for the rail positions. See figure 2-G-9.

Figure 2-G-9 Table saw angles and mortises cut in left and right stiles.

Mark and drill screws through back face of the rails 1/2" in from the edges. See figure 2-G-10.

Figure 2-G-10 Put frame together.

Glue and screw the frame together. Be sure the frame is square before you set the clamps. See Appendix II for information on gluing and clamping.

Figure 2-G-11 Support strips clamped to stiles.

While the frame is still in clamps, rabbet the back of the frame to accept the mirror and backing piece. Clamp or double stick tape a 3/4" full length strip of support material flush with each side to give the router support while the rabbet is being cut. See figure 2-G-11.

Chuck up a 3/8" rabbet bit in the portable router and using the pilot as a guide, rout from left to right around the inside back edge of the mirror frame to a depth of 3/8". Rout along a rail, stile, rail, and final stile. See figure 2-G-12.

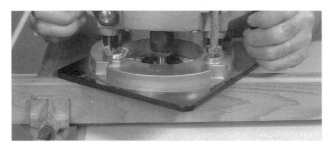

Figure 2-G-12 Rabbet to receive the mirror.

The rabbet bit leaves round corners that you can square with a chisel or you may want to round the corners of the mirror to fit.

Unclamp, sand, finish and stain the mirror to your desire. Be sure to stain and finish the rabbet that the mirror fits in because it will show on the face side in the mirror. Install the mirror and cardboard backing with a bead of silicon all around the back perimeter. See figure 2-G-13. Fasten the metal hangers on the top back of the stiles.

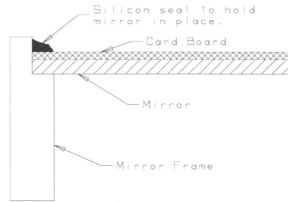

Figure 2-G-13 Use silicon to fasten the mirror and cardboard in place.

This mirror design can be made in a shorter version with the same fixtures.

Notes:

Unit 3
HOUSE GIFTS

We all like to receive gifts that we can use in the home. This unit offers house gifts both large and small. Build a cedar chest or a wall coat rack. Both are unique and decorative. The wonderful thing about our woodworking friends is that we often get gifts from them that we cannot buy.

What you will learn in this section

Beginning with a rabbet-dado joint, one of the strongest joints available, you will learn how to join woods of different thicknesses, how to produce multiple patterns and how to create joints that can be taken apart and put back together again after the project is completed. As well, you will enter the field of advanced router work, as this section contains the showpiece of Router Projects and Jigs, a handsome walnut chest that will be a credit to the builder wherever it is displayed.

HOUSE GIFTS

3 A. Small Chest

Figure 3-A-1 Small chest

Most furniture, drawers and other products are box variations. For this reason being able to make a square simple box structure with a variety of joinery is very important. This box in the size specified in this project can become a jewelery chest, a shop storage chest, or home storage receptacle for pictures, thread and a variety of other uses. See figure 3-A-1. The joinery in this box is adaptable to other box structures as shown in the Walnut Chest.

Project Requirements

Recommended: Walnut

Also suitable: Oak, Cherry

Skill Level

	Basic		X	Basic Plus
	Moderate			Advanced

Material list:
- 2 - 3" x 8" x 1/2"- sides
- 2 - 3" x 4 1/2" x 1/2" - ends
- 2 - 5 1/2" x 8 1/2" x 3/4" top and bottom

Router tools:
- Table mounted Router
- 1/4" Spacer fence
- Table fence

Router bits:
- 1/4" Carbide spiral Router bit
- 3/4" Plunge ogee router bit

Hardware:
- 4 - #6 x 1 1/4" flat head wood screws
- 1 - pair butt hinges 1" brass and screws

Construction details in:
The skills necessary to complete the projects in this book are presented in appendixes at the back. The following skills are used in this project. You may wish to review the following appendixes before you start.

Appendix I - Choosing and Sizing Material

Appendix II - Gluing and Clamping

Appendix III- B. Table fence set up

Appendix IV- D. Rabbet dado joint

How to build this project

Choose the wood for this project. Joint, plane and cut all materials to size according to the material list. Be sure all stock is cut square to the exact size listed. Appendix I contains instructions on choosing and sizing materials.

Box sides

Set up the router table with a 1/4" spacer fence and install a 1/4" carbide spiral router bit.

Cut rabbet dado combination joints in the sides and ends of the chest material. See Appendix IV-D. See figure 3-A-2.

Figure 3-A-2 Rabbet dado joint.

When cutting these joints, pay close attention to make sure the best face is out. With the dado cut, the best face is up. When cutting the rabbet joint, the best face is against the offset block.

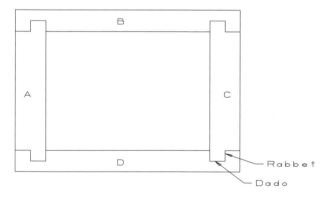

Figure 3-A-3 Rabbet dado layout.

Remember, fit problems may be caused by two things. The material is thicker than 1/2" or the rabbet cut was moved away from the offset block. Make sure the joints are cleaned up before you dry fit.

Top and bottom

Set up the router table with a 3/4" plunge ogee bit and a table fence. Set the depth of cut and the table fence to expose the desired BIT PROFILE. See Appendix III-B-c. Cut an ogee profile on all four sides of the top and bottom pieces of the box. Remember to cut the cross grain end first, then cut with the grain.

Testing the fit

Dry fit the sides and ends together and lay out the screw holes in the bottom. The screws are laid out to put one screw in the center of each side. See figure 3-A-4.

Figure 3-A-4 Bottom screw holes.

Glue and clamp the box sides and ends together, being sure to keep the pieces SQUARE. Sand the top and bottom. Unclamp, clean and sand the glued box. Attach the bottom to the box with screws as laid out above. Install hinges in the lid and attach to box. See figure 3-A-5.

Figure 3-A-5 Install the hinges.

Finishing the box

The simple joinery in this box makes it easy to construct but very strong. Complete this project by applying the finish of your choice.

3 B. Two Drawer Storage

Figure 3-B-1 Two Drawer Storage

Combine box joints, sliding dovetails, and contrasting wood to make this decorative storage for the top of your dresser or desk. The drawers in this storage are suitable for small items such as jewelery, buttons, and office supplies. See figure 3-B-1.

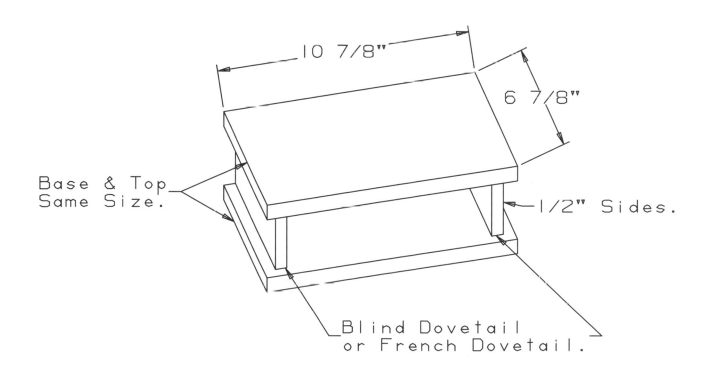

Figure 3-B-2 Case work

Project Requirements

Recommended: Oak, Walnut

Also suitable: Cherry, White Ash

Material List:

Case: See figure 3-B-2.
2 - 6 7/8" x 10 7/8" x 3/4" top/bottom.
2 - 3 7/8" x 6 1/4" x 1/2" for sides.
1 - 3 7/8" x 8 7/8" x 1/4" ply back.
Drawers: See figure 3-B-3.
4 - 3" x 4" x 3/4" for front and back.
4 - 3" x 6" x 3/8" for sides.
2 - 2 5/8" x 4 7/8" x 1/8" ply bottom.

Router tools:

Table mounted router
3/8" spacer fence
Table fence
Mitre gauge
1" guide and ring nut

Router bits:

3/8" solid carbide spiral bit
1/8" solid carbide spiral bit
1/2" 14 degree dovetail bit
5/32" roman ogee bit
3/8" rabbet bit

Skill Level				
	Basic			Basic Plus
X	Moderate			Advanced

Construction details in:

The skills necessary to complete the projects in this book are presented in appendixes at the back. The following skills are used in this project. You may wish to review the following appendixes before you start.

Appendix I - Choosing and Sizing Material

Appendix II - Gluing and Clamping

Appendix III- B. Table fence set up

Appendix IV- B. Box joints

Appendix VI - B.a Stopped dovetails

How to build this project

Choose your wood first. Cut, joint, plane each piece to the size in the material list. Be sure each piece is square. See Appendix I.

The drawers

The drawers are constructed with box joints. See figure 3-B-3. What you have to watch is that the fronts and backs are thicker than the sides. To get started chuck up a 3/8" straight or spiral bit, and install a 3/8" spacer fence over the table mounted router. Use scrap blocks until you get a snug fit. See Appendix IV-B.

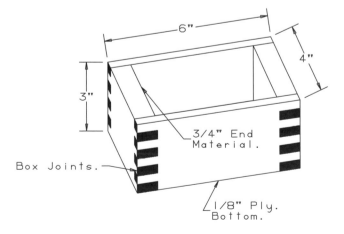

Figure 3-B-3 Drawers

The drawer sides

Adjust the depth of the cut to the thickness of the 3/4" front and back pieces. Then, on the side pieces, put a mark on the top edge of each. Clamp two side pieces together and run the box joint openings on these pieces. Use a backing block with a shaker peg to ensure that the pieces remain vertical while you are cutting the joint openings. Always start the top edge (the one you marked) against the spacer fence to the right of the router bit. Repeat until you have cut the box joint openings on both ends of all the drawer sides. See figure 3-B-4.

Figure 3-B-4 Box-joint the sides.

The ends

The box joint openings in the box ends are cut next. First, adjust the depth of the cut to match the thickness of the sides. Again, mark the top edge of each end piece. Using an offset jig (see Appendix IV) over the spacer fence cut the first 3/8" slot in each end piece. See figure 3-B-5.

Figure 3-B-5 Make the slot in the ends with an off set block.

As with the sides, you can clamp these end pieces two by two, so that the front and back of each drawer will be identical.

Whenever you are cutting box joints, it is important to remember which side will be the top. Never flip the pieces end over end to make the second cut.

After you have made the initial cut in each end piece, remove the offset jig and make the remaining cuts in the end pieces. If you follow this procedure, the sides and ends will fit flush at the top. If the pieces are the same width, the bottom will be flush.

Dry fit

Test the fit of the pieces which will make the drawers. Do this before you take down the spacer fence setup.

The Bottom

Remove the spacer fence and chuck up a 1/8" solid carbide, and adjust the depth of the cut to 3/16". Set the fence so that the cut will come in the centre of the bottom opening of the box joint in the front and back. See figure 3-B-6.

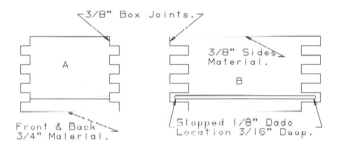

Figure 3-B-6 Dado to receive the bottom.

Cut the dado (groove) for the bottom in the front and back pieces, keeping the bottom of each piece against the fence and the face side up.

Cut the same dado in the sides, remembering that the cuts must not run right through to the end of the box-joint tab, or they will show in the finished drawer. Stopping a dado short of the end is called a stopped dado and the technique is covered in Appendix III-B-d.

Assembly

Before assembling, sand the inside surfaces of all sides and bottom. Glue and clamp the drawers, remembering to insert the bottom before putting the final side or end in place. Use masking tape on the inside of the box joints. This will help avoid having to remove unwanted glue which will squeeze from the joint. Be sure to remove the tape before the glue hardens. See figure 3-B-7.

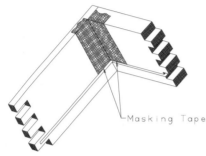

Figure 3-B-7 Masking tape on the inside collects the excess glue

The Case

The construction used in the case for the drawers provides a good example of the use of stopped dovetail work which is both strong and attractive. See figure 3-B-8.

Figure 3-B-8 Stopped dovetails with a mitre gauge

It is best to start with the dovetail cuts on the top and bottom. Set up the router table by installing a 1" guide in the base plate and a 1/2", 14-degree dovetail bit in the chuck. The depth should be about 3/8". It is important to remember not to the change this depth until both the slot and the side pins have been cut.

Use scrap material to obtain the fit you want. Appendix VI-B-a explains how to produce stopped dovetails with a mitre gauge. See figure 3-B-8. First cut the dovetail slots in the top and bottom of the case. See figure 3-B-9.

You have two drawers to fit between the stopped dovetails. The drawers are 8" (4"+4"). Determine where to cut the stopped dovetails to leave 8" room for the drawers plus about 1/4" for sliding. See Appendix III-D for centering measurement.

Figure 3-B-9 Stopped dovetails in top and bottom.

Then cut the dovetail pins on the sides. See figure 3-B-10. Remember to select and mark the face side of each piece before cutting. Test fit the pieces together.

Figure 3-B-10 Dovetail pins

Fit square pieces to round holes

The dovetail bit leaves round cavities at the ends of the stopped dovetail slot. When you cut the pins on the sides they are square on the ends. Using the mitre gauge, cut a notch in the fronts of the dovetail pins so the pin will slide over and cover the hole. See figure 3-B-11.

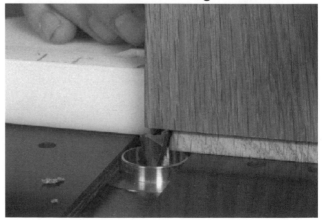

Figure 3-B-11 Cut a notch in the front side of dovetail pins.

Finishing the top and bottom

Chuck up a 5/32" roman ogee bit in the table mounted router. Set the depth of cut to expose the full profile of the bit. Set the fence to isolate the bearing. See Appendix III-B-c. Check the cut with a piece of scrap. Run an ogee mold around the ends and front edge of the top and bottom, but not the back edge.

To provide additional decoration you can also run a small cove on the under edge of the top. Just drop the ogee bit down to expose the cove portion and run this cove. See figure 3-B-12. A stop cove has been used to give the illusion of feet on the bottom. See Appendix III-B-d.

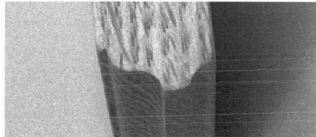

Figure 3-B-12 roman ogee mold with cove underneath

Glue, clamp and sand as necessary.

The back

To accommodate the back cut a 3/8" by 1/4" rabbet all around the inside of the back of the case, using the bit pilot as a guide. See figure 3-B-13.

Figure 3-B-13 Rout the rabbet in the case.

This rabbet will have round corners. Round the corners of the plywood back or square the corners in the rabbet cut with a chisel. Glue and clamp the plywood back into place. See figure 3-B-14.

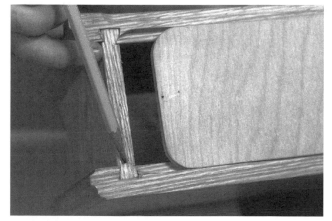

Figure 3-B-14 Round the corners on the back to fit the rabbet.

Finish the drawers

Finish the case and drawers with the finish of your choice. All that is left is to put the hardware pulls of your choice on the drawers.

Enjoy your two drawer storage.

Notes:

3 C. Coat Wall Rack

Figure 3-C-1

This item is handy at the back door or where we have family members going in and out. It is nice to have a place to hang a coat near an outside door. Any unused wall space can accommodate a coat rack. See figure 3-C-1. If your space is smaller make a smaller rack.

Project Requirements

Recommended: Oak

Also Suitable: Mahogany, Ash

Material List:

1 - 7 1/2" x 42" x 3/4" Oak
4 - Shaker pegs

Router tools:

Table mounted router
Table fence
Heart pattern
Shop made pattern jig Appendix VII-D.
1" brass guide and ring nut
7" base plate

Router bits:

5/32 Roman Ogee bit
3/4" Plunge round over bit

Skill Level			
Basic		**X**	Basic Plus
Moderate			Advanced

Construction details in:

The skills necessary to complete the projects in this book are presented in appendixes at the back. The following skills are used in this project. You may wish to review the following appendixes before you start.

Appendix I - Choosing and Sizing Material

Appendix III- B-c Table fence set up D-f. Measuring

Appendix V - D. Pattern cutting

Appendix VII- D. Pattern fixture

How to build this project:

Choose the wood for this project. Joint, plane and cut all materials to size according to the material list. Be sure all stock is cut square to the exact size listed. Appendix I contains instructions on choosing and sizing materials.

Position of pattern

Mark the stock equally to determine the position of the 4 heart designs. Use a square to mark the lines across the work piece as shown. See figure 3-C-2. We positioned the two end hearts 5" from the stock end to heart centre. The middle hearts are divided evenly from heart centre to centre. See Appendix III-D-f.

Construct your shop made pattern holder. See Appendix VII-D. Slide your stock into the first heart position. Secure the stock with two hold down clamps on either side of the pattern. See figure 3-C-3.

3-C-3 Stock in the pattern fixture.

Using the pattern

With the 1" guide mounted on the 7 " base plate and the 3/4" plunge round over bit mounted in the router, rout the first heart design into the stock. See figure 3-C-4. Because this is for design, do not rout right through the stock. Set the depth for 3/8". Keep the guide flange tight to the pattern to be sure not to spoil the design effect. Rout from left to right.

Figure 3-C-4 Cut the first pattern.

Hearts equally spaced

Unclamp and move the stock to the next heart design position as shown in figure 3-C-2. Clamp and rout the design in this position. Continue to rout the heart design in the four positions on the stock.

The outside edges

With a fence in position on the router table and the Roman ogee bit in the router, isolate the bearing and run an edge mold around the entire stock. See Appendix III-B-c. Drill a 1/2" hole in the centre of each heart design to receive the Shaker pegs. See figure 3-C-5.

Figure 3-C-5 Holes for pegs

The coat rack may be screwed to the wall through the shaker peg holes. Distance between the two outside holes is 32" on center as is most house framing. Then glue in the peg. The length of the coat rack can change according to space available. Any pattern design may be used instead of the heart. Sand and finish the wall coat rack.

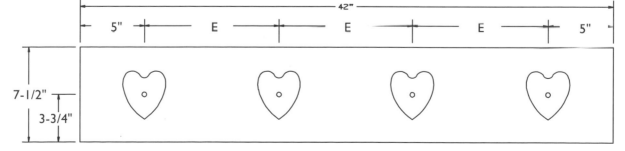

3-C-2 Mark the layout of the hearts.

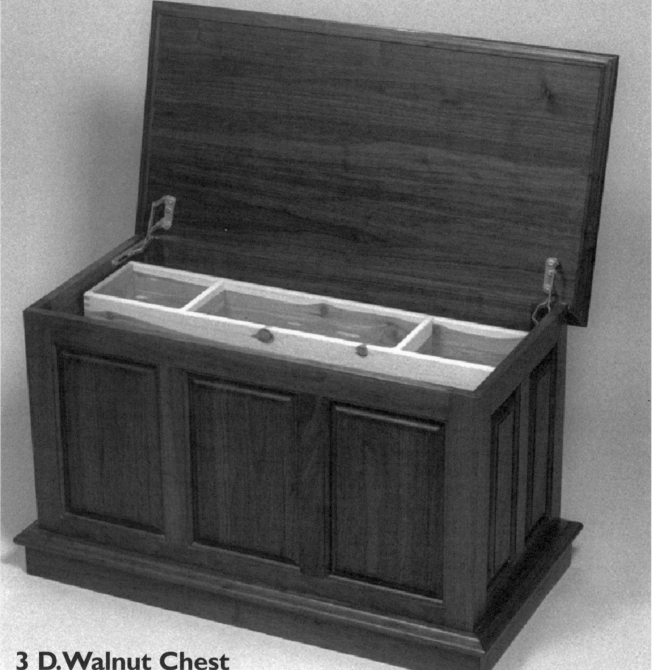

3 D. Walnut Chest

Figure 3-D-1

A chest is described in the dictionary as a box of considerable size. We are back to a basic box. What makes this chest different from the small boxes shown in previous projects? A chest can be a hope chest, a treasure chest, a blanket box, or a case to hold specific goods; tea, indigo, gold, treasure.

Hope chests are old fashioned. Many brides in years gone by had a hope chest in which they stored articles of clothing or house hold items for a home of their own.

Recently an 18 year old high school graduate requested a chest as a graduation present. When her parents went looking for this elusive piece of furniture, they found metal trunks, rough wooden boxes of various sizes but nothing that could be called a chest. This project incorporates the ideas from that 18 year old graduate and was built for her. Perhaps you have someone who would like a chest for what ever storage possibilities. This chest project incorporates box joints, rabbet dado joints, moldings, and panels. See figure 3-D-1.

Project Requirements

Recommended: Walnut

Material list:

Case panels (Walnut)
4 - 2"x20"x3/4" stiles (rabbet)
4 - 2 3/8"x20"x3/4" stiles (dado)
2 - 2 3/8"x12"x3/4" rails top
2 - 3 1/8"x12"x3/4" rails bottom
2 - 3 1/8"x29"x3/4" rails bottom
2 - 2 3/8"x29"x3/4" rails top
6 - 2 3/8"x13 1/4"x3/4" mullion centre
4 - 5 3/16"x13 1/4"x3/4" panel (side)
6 - 8 9/16"x13 1/4"x3/4"panel (Front Back)

Chest Lid (Walnut)
1 - 16"x33"x3/4" - laminated - trim to fit chest

Bottom Base: (trim to fit 45 angle)
2 - 2 1/2" x 20" x 3/4" ends
2 - 2 1/2" x 39" x 3/4" ends

Moldings for base and lid:

Cut from:
2 - 3 1/8"x22"x3/4"
2 - 3 1/8"x40"x3/4"

Moldings cut at 45° each end to fit:
2 - 1 1/4"x22"x3/4"
2 - 1 1/4"x40"x3/4"
2 - 1 5/8"x22"x3/4"
2 - 1 5/8"x40"x3/4"

Bottom (Cedar)
1 - 16"x33"x3/4"- laminated - trim to fit.

Material for Tray (Cedar)
2 - 4 1/2"x31 1/4"x1/2" sides
2 - 4 1/2"x6 1/2"x1/2" ends
2 - 4"x6"x1/2" dividers
1 - 6"x30 3/4"x1/4" bottom

Tray slides:
2 - 1 1/4"x14 1/2"x3/4" walnut or cedar

Skill Level

	Basic			Basic Plus
	Moderate		X	Advanced

Router Tools:
Table mounted router
Table fence
Panel Fence system
Spacer fences 1/4" and 3/8"

Router bits:
Stile and Rail Router bit
Panel Bit
Straight or Spiral Bits(1/4",3/8"and 1/2")
Slot Cutter 1/4"
Decorative molding bit
1/4" round over bit with pilot

Hardware:
Brass chest lid hardware or hinge and door stay hardware
22 - #6 x 1 1/4" - flat head wood screws

Construction details in:
The skills necessary to complete the projects in this book are presented in appendixes at the back. The following skills are used in this project. You may wish to review the following appendixes before you start.

Appendix I - Choosing and Sizing Material

Appendix II - Gluing and Clamping

Appendix III- B. Table fence set up

        D-b.Measuring

Appendix IV- B. Box joints

        D. Rabbet Dado joints

Appendix VI - A. Panel construction

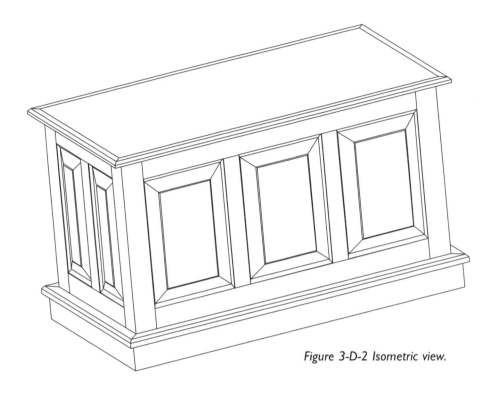

Figure 3-D-2 Isometric view.

How to build this project

Choose the wood for this project. Joint, plane and cut all materials to size according to the material list. Be sure all stock is cut square to the exact size listed. Appendix I contains instructions on choosing and sizing materials.

Familiarize yourself with the plans. See isometric view figure 3-D-2.

Glue up all pieces that require wider stock (chest lid, panels, chest bottom). Always glue these pieces ahead so you will not have to wait for the glue to set later. See Appendix II for assistance with CLAMPING AND GLUING.

Sort and lay out the following pieces: stiles, rails, mullions, and panels. Mark the face sides of all pieces. Remember the face side is the side that will be showing on the completed project, so pick the best side. Set up the router table with the panel system and run all the cope cuts using the stile and rail cutter. Lower the cutter and cut all the bead cuts. Change to the panel cutter and adjust the panel system to cut all the panels. See Appendix VI-A for assistance in cutting PANELS.

Rabbet dado joint

Using the 3/8" spacer fence on the table mount and a 3/8" spiral solid carbide bit run the combination joint (Rabbet/Dado) in the outside stiles. See figure 3-D-3 See Appendix IV-D.

Remember the dado is cut with the face side up and the rabbet is cut with the face side to the offset jig. Be sure that you run trial pieces first to get a good fit.

Figure 3-D-3 Rabbet dado joint

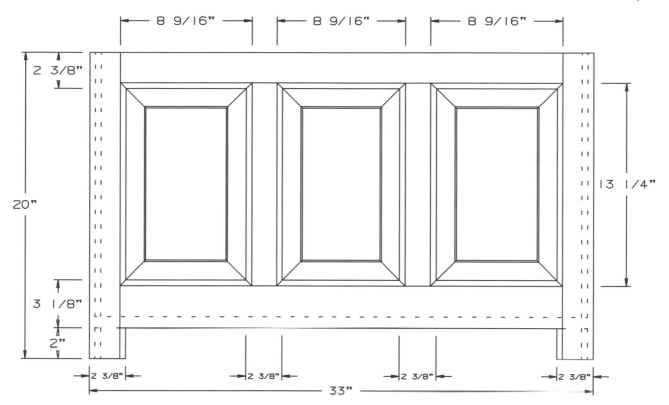

Figure 3-D-4 Front and back panel sections

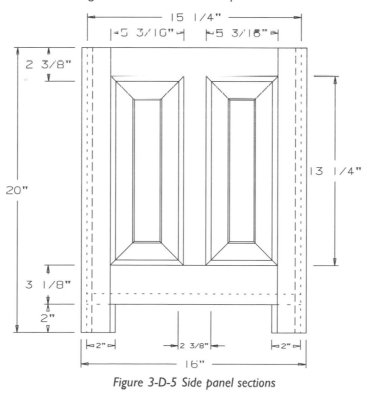

Figure 3-D-5 Side panel sections

Panel sections

Clean and sand all panel pieces for the chest. Dry fit each panel section. See figures 3-D-4 and 3-D-5.

Glue and clamp each panel section, being sure they are square. You should have four panel sections: One front, two sides and the back.

3-15

Moldings

Rough cut the base and lid moldings. Using the table-mounted router and a fence with the decorative molding bit, run the mold on both sides of the base/lid molding piece. Split the molding piece into two on the table saw. See figure 3-D-6. Joint the sawed edges.

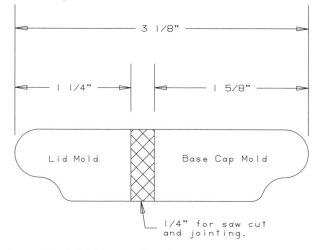

Figure 3-D-6 Split the molding piece in two.

Chest lid

Clean and sand the previously glued up walnut for the chest lid.

Pick a face side of the lid and ensure it has a scratch-free surface. When the project is complete, this will be the most visible part of the chest. Trim the lid to fit the chest size as shown in the plan.

Install a 1/4" slot cutter in the table-mounted router and position the table fence to cut a slot in the lid material. Rout this slot with the material face down against the table. Cut the "T" slot in the molding piece to match. See figure 3-D-7.

Cut a 45 degree angle on the moldings to fit all around the chest lid. Be sure the 45 degree cuts make a snug fit on all four corners. Glue and clamp the molding in place on the chest lid. See figure 3-D-8.

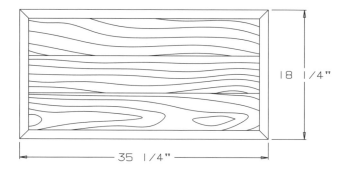

Figure 3-D-8 Laminated lid with molding.

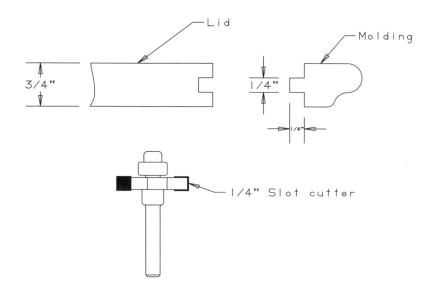

Figure 3-D-7 Groove and "T" slot with slot cutter.

The bottom

Clean and scrape the laminated cedar bottom. Choose a face side and cut to the chest size as specified in the material list. Unclamp the four raised panel sections (front, back and ends). Clean all the excess glue from the joints.

A 3/4" rabbet is required in the bottom inside surface of these panel sections to receive the 3/4" cedar bottom. Chuck up a 3/4" flat bottom bit in the table mounted router. Prepare the panel sections. Note that the stiles on these sections extend beyond the bottom rail. The rabbet for the bottom must be placed in the bottom of the bottom rail. To make it easy to run the required rabbet tack a strip straight across the bottom of the extended stiles. See figure 3-D-9. This stick will run against the table fence as the rabbet is being cut in the bottom of the bottom rail.

Set the depth of cut at 3/8" (use a brass set up bar). Position the table fence the proper distance from the cutter to rout a 3/4" rabbet in the bottom of the bottom rail.

Note: This cut may be a bit confusing as it is a rabbet in the bottom rails but a dado in the stiles.

Because of the 3/8" combination rabbet/dado joint used in the stiles of the panel sections, only the end sections can have the bottom rabbet run from edge to edge. The bottom rabbet in the front and back must start and stop. See figure 3-D-10.

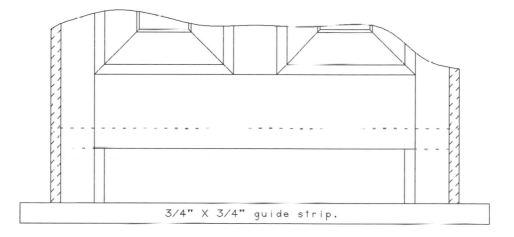

3/4" X 3/4" guide strip.

Figure 3-D-9 Strip tacked across bottom of panel section stiles.

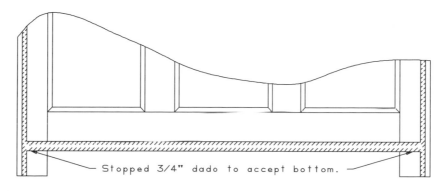

Stopped 3/4" dado to accept bottom.

Figure 3-D-10 Stopped dados in the front and back panel sections.

Assemble the project

Dry fit the panelled chest with the bottom in place. When you are satisfied with the dry fit, carefully take the chest apart and glue and clamp the chest together. Be sure the bottom is in place and the chest is square on all four corners. You should use a flat surface to assemble your project. If the assembling surface is not flat the project parts may twist in the gluing process.

Base moldings

Sort the four bottom base moldings. You should have the following: 2 - 2 1/2" x 20" molds and 2 - 2 1/2" x 39" molds. There should also be the following base cap molds: 2 - 1 1/4" x 22" x 7/8" molds and 2 - 1 1/4" x 40" x 7/8" molds.

Cut a 45 degree angle on one end of each of these moldings.

When the glue is set in the main chest clean and sand all excess glue from the surfaces. Turn the chest bottom side up on the assembling table. Cut the remaining 45 degree angles to fit the base mold in place on the chest. Glue, clamp and screw the moldings in place on the chest. See figure 3-D-11. Mount the screws through the back of the extended ends of the end and side stiles. This will hide the screws.

the parts are done. It is no fun just watching the glue dry.

When the bottom molding is set take the clamps off and clean the excess glue off. Turn the chest right side up on the assembling table.

Cut all the base cap mold with 45 degree corners and fit it over the base mold. See figure 3-D-12. Glue and clamp it in place. When dry remove the clamps. Clean and sand the entire chest and lid. See figure 3-D-13.

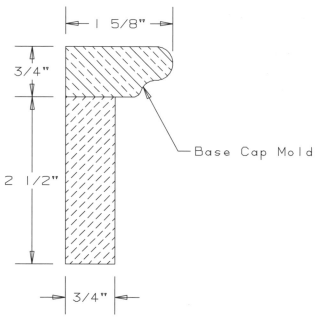

Figure 3-D-12 Position base cap mold.

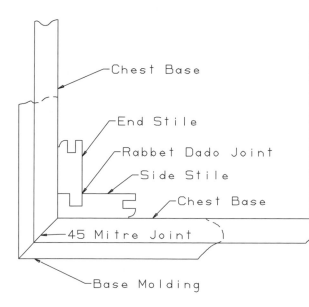

Figure 3-D-11 Base molding assembly.

While you are waiting for the glue to set you may wish to prepare the materials for the cedar tray. It does not matter in what sequence

Figure 3-D-13 Base mold installed.

Making the cedar tray

Finish cut the cedar materials for the tray. See figure 3-D-14. Set up the router table mount with a 1/4" spacer fence and a 1/4" spiral bit. Cut 1/4" box joints in the sides and ends of the tray pieces. For assistance in cutting box joints see Appendix III-A. See figure 3-D-15.

Figure 3-D-15 Cedar tray.

Cut 1/2" dados in the tray sides to receive the 1/2" dividers leaving about 7" compartments on each end of the tray. Chuck up a 1/4" spiral bit in the table-mounted router. Set the table fence to make stopped dados in the sides and through dados in the ends. See Appendix III-B-d. The 1/4" dados in the bottom of the sides and ends will receive the tray bottom. See figure 3-D-16. Cut the tray bottom to size and dry fit the tray. If it fits, glue and clamp the tray together. When set, clean excess glue and sand the tray.

We need to round over the top edges of the tray. Chuck up a 1/4" round over bit in the table-mounted router. Allow the bit pilot to follow the inside of the tray compartments to round over the top edges of the tray on the inside.

Install the table fence to isolate the bearing on the round over bit. Round over the outside top edges of the tray against the fence.

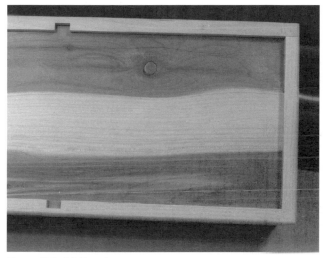

Figure 3-D-16 Tray bottom.

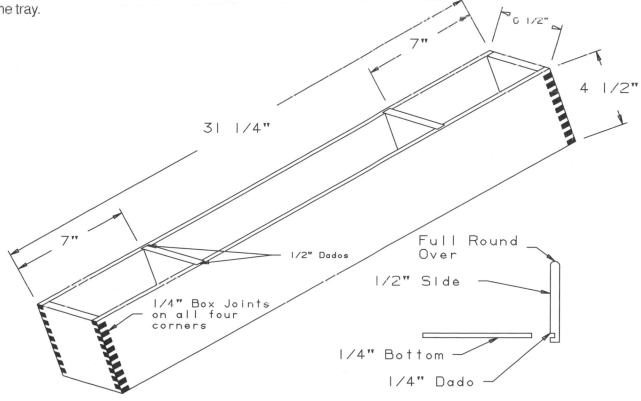

Figure 3-D-14 Tray parts.

Cut two support slides out of cedar and fasten the tray slides inside the chest at each end. Set them at least 1/2" deeper than the height of the tray. See figure 3-D-17.

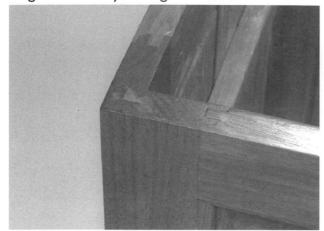

Figure 3-D-17 Support slide for the tray.

Figure 3-D-18 Lid hardware installed.

Install the lid hardware. See figure 3-D-18. Complete the project by finishing the wood according to your preference.

Note: Do not finish the cedar tray or bottom. This will keep a cedar smell inside the chest.

Notes:

Figure 3-E-1 Oak Cabinet

3 E. Basic Cabinet

All cabinetry is constructed with basic procedures. A cabinet is a box with a drawer and/or doors installed according to a plan or design. This basic cabinet is 24" x 32" x 11 7/8" deep. It is designed with two drawers and two doors. It could be used in a recreation room to store games, tapes, or discs. In the laundry room it could store soap, bleach and the iron. In the bath room it would fit over the toilet to store bathroom supplies. See figure 3-E-1.

Project Requirements

Recommended: Oak

Also suitable: Cherry, Walnut

Material list:

Panel doors:
4 - 2 3/8"x22 3/4"x3/4" oak stiles
4 - 2 3/8"x6 3/8"x3/4" oak rails
2 - 6 3/8"x18 3/4"x3/4" oak panels

Drawers:
2 - 4 3/4"x9 3/4"x3/4" oak fronts
  (mill with door material)
4 - 3 3/4"x11 3/8"x1/2" oak plywood
  sides
2 - 3"x8 1/4"x1/2" oak plywood backs
2 - 8 1/4"x11 3/8"x1/4" oak plywood
  bottoms

Basic cabinet:
2 - 3/4"x11 7/8"x32" sides oak plywood
3 - 3/4"x11 7/8"x23 1/4" top, bottom
  and shelf, oak plywood
1 - 1/4"x23 1/4"x24" back, oak plywood

Face Frame:
2 - 3/4"x2"x32" part A, oak
3 - 3/4"x2"x20" part B, oak
1 - 3/4"x2"x4" part C, oak
16 - 1/4"x1 1/8" part D, dowels

Hardware:
4 - cabinet hinges
4 - cabinet pulls

Skill Level

	Basic			Basic Plus
	Moderate		X	Advanced

Router Bits:
  1/4" Spiral bit
  1/2" Spiral bit
  1/2" Dovetail bit 14 degree
  1/4" Round over bit with pilot
  3/8" Rabbet bit
  3/4" Straight bit
  3/4" Bull nose bit
  Stile and rail cutter
  Panel cutter

Router tools:
  Table mounted router
  Table fence
  Mitre gauge
  1 " Brass Guide and ring nut
  Panel plate and fence system

Construction details in:
  The skills necessary to complete the projects in this book are presented in appendixes at the back.

Appendix I - Choosing and Sizing
           Material

Appendix II - Gluing and Clamping

Appendix III- B. Table fence set up
            D. Measuring

Appendix VI - A. Panel construction
            B. Mitre gauge
            C. Drawers

Construction details

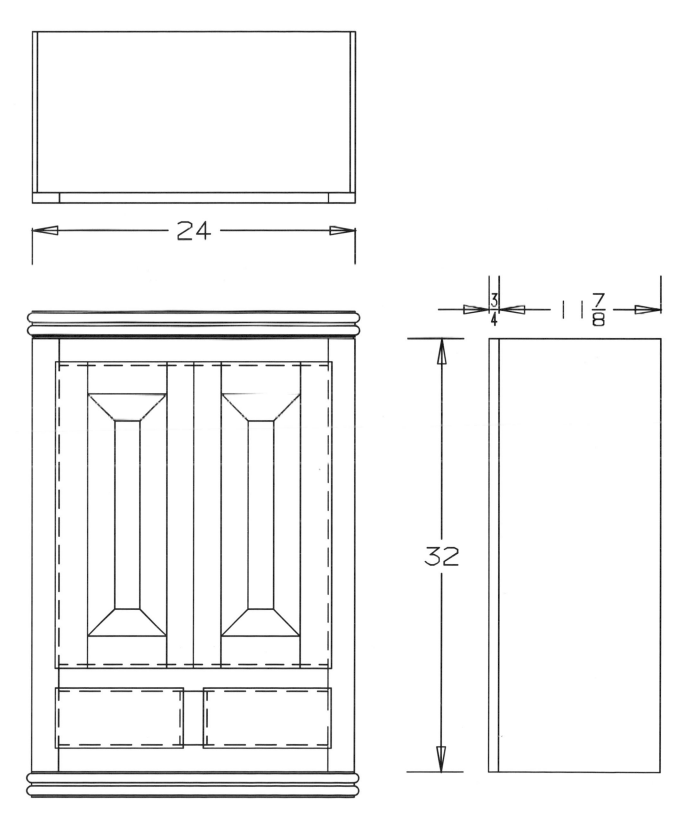

Figure 3-E-2 Cabinet drawing.

How to build the basic cabinet

Choose the wood for this project. Joint, plane and cut all materials to size according to the material list. Be sure all stock is cut square to the exact size listed. Appendix I contains instructions on choosing and sizing materials.

On the sides measure and mark the location for the following wood joints: a) Rabbet joints, b) Dado joints. Note: Choose the best surface for the outside of the cabinet and put the woodgrain direction pointing towards the top of the cabinet. Be sure this detail is consistent throughout the cabinet. See figure 3-E-3.

TOP

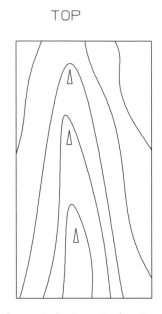

Figure 3-E-3 Arrows indicate grain direction and cabinet top.

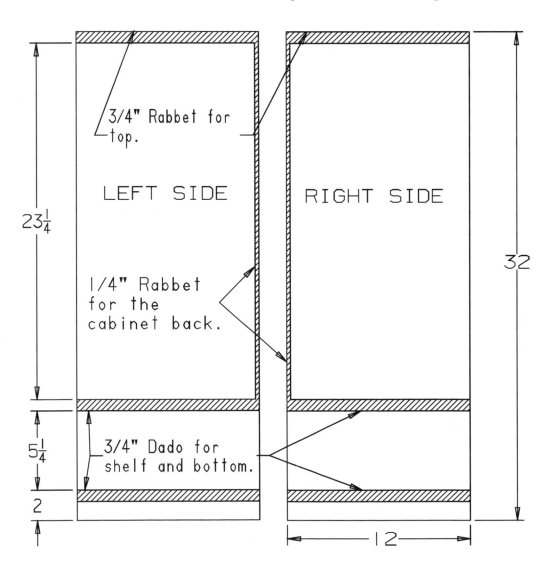

Figure 3-E-4 Left and right sides.

Using the router in the table-mounted position with a 3/8" Rabbet bit, cut the rabbets in the top and shelf for the back. Then cut the rabbets and dados in the sides of the cabinet. As a check, set up the router to make the wood joints and test this setup on scrap material first. Use a 3/4" Straight bit to cut the 3/4" dados. *Note: Before the rabbet is cut for the back, be sure that there is a left side and right side.* Place the two sides flat (side by side and dados up) and mark the rabbet for the back along the back edge of both pieces. This will ensure that the sides are left and right. See figure 3-E-4.

Cabinet assembly

Dry fit the sides, top, bottom and shelf to make sure that the pieces are milled properly. *Note: The dry fit process is a good practice and should be followed before every assembly process.* Using glue and 1 1/2" finishing nails, clamp and fasten the cabinet box pieces together with the blind nailing procedure. See figure 3-E-5. This will keep the fastenings unexposed.

Square and nail the back

The 1/4" back is used to keep the cabinet square and sturdy. Make sure that the 1/4" back is cut perfectly square as this will square up the assembled cabinet. Glue and nail the back into position using 1" finishing nails. This completes the basic cabinet. Next you require a face frame for the cabinet.

How to build the face frame

Cut all the pieces according to the face frame material list.

Mark the best sides of all pieces with a light "X" to indicate the face side of the material. These are the sides that will be exposed. On the work bench, lay the pieces in the proper position and mark corresponding joint parts. See figure 3-E-6.

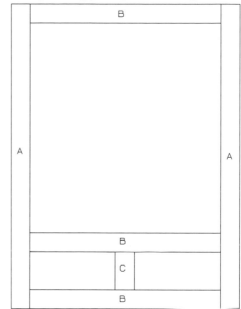

Figure 3-E-6 Face frame materials.

Check the outside dimensions of the frame to ensure that it will fit on the base cabinet.

Measure and mark the dowel locations (two dowels per joint). With a dowelling jig, drill the holes in the proper locations.

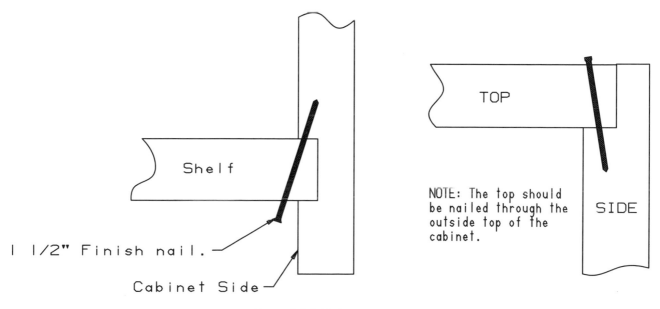

Figure 3-E-5 Nailing procedure.

Cut 1/4" dowel pins to the proper length and dry fit the frame assembly. Make sure that the dowel pins are not too long for the holes drilled in the face frame. See figure 3-E-7.

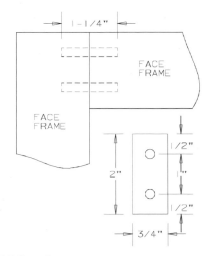

Figure 3-E-7 Dowel position.

Glue, assemble and clamp the face frame together. Be sure that the face frame is square before letting the glue set. See Appendix II. After the glue is dry, clean up and sand the face and back of the frame. Glue and clamp the face frame to the basic cabinet. Be sure the face frame is flush and even on the outside edges of the basic cabinet.

Cutting a vein

Using a 1/8" veining bit and your portable router with a router fence, cut a vein between the two sides of the cabinet and the face frame. This will give a decorative look to the cabinet and cover any minor irregularities between the base cabinet and the face frame. See figure 3-E-8.

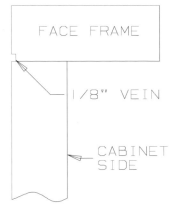

Figure 3-E-8 Veining on side of cabinet.

Material list (top and bottom molding):

2 - 3/4"x1 7/8"x23 3/4" Oak, front moldings
4 - 3/4" x 1 7/8" x 12 5/8" Oak, Side moldings

Note: These pieces are to be cut longer initially and fitted to the cabinet.

How to prepare the moldings:

Cut the parts to rough size as per material list. Using the table mounted router and the Bull Nose bit, mill the moldings needed for the top and bottom of the base cabinet. See figure 3-E-9 and 3-E-10 for milling details.

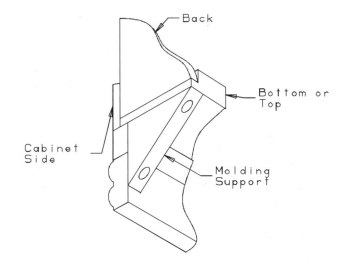

Figure 3-E-9 Molding parts.

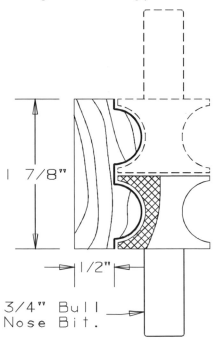

Figure 3-E-10 Bit and mold.

Material list for filler blocks

2 - 3/4"x1 1/2"x5" Pine, top blocks
2 - 3/4"x2 3/4"x5" Pine, bottom blocks

Cut and install the filler blocks to support the top and bottom moldings.

Cut and install the top and bottom moldings. Fasten the moldings to the filler blocks with 1 3/4" screws. See figure 3-E-11 and 3-E-12.

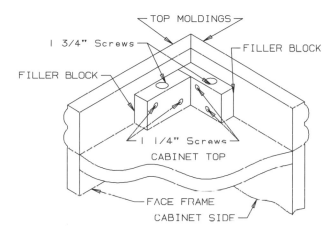

Figure 3-E-11 Top molding.

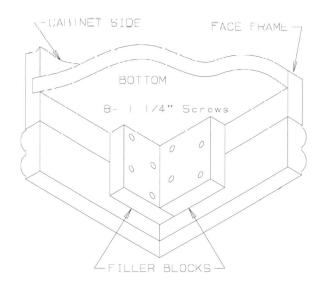

Figure 3-E-12 Bottom moldings

You now have a basic cabinet.

Use the drawer construction section to construct drawers to fit your basic cabinet. Use the drawer material list above. See Appendix VI-C.

Construct two panel doors. Use the material list above. See Appendix VI-A Panel construction.

Installing the doors

Install the raised panel doors following the instructions on the door hardware package. Align the drawer fronts with the panel doors. See figure 3-E-13.

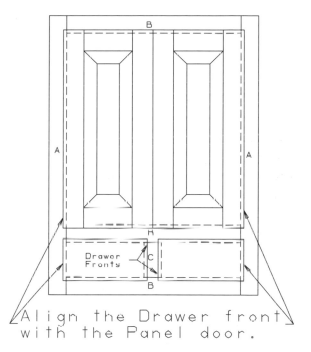

Figure 3-E-13 Aligning the drawer fronts with the panel doors.

Notes:

Figure 3-F-1 Plant stand

3 F. Plant Stand

We have labelled this a plant stand but with a few changes in the material list it could become a stand or small table for other purposes. The simple but sturdy construction makes it decorative for any room. See figure 3-F-1.

Project Requirements

Recommended materials: Oak

Also suitable: Cherry, Walnut

Material list:
- 1 - 12" x 12" x 3/4" oak top
- 1 - 3 1/2" x 22" x 3/4" oak upright
- 2 - 1 1/2" x 22" x 3/4" oak upright
- 2 - 1 1/2" x 14" x 1 1/2" oak legs

Router tools:
Table mounted router
Table fence
Jointer fence See Appendix III-C.
Mitre gauge
1" brass guide and ring nut
Shop made fixture for angle cuts and tapering See Appendix VII-J-a. fixture
(This fixture is used on the table saw)
Option: circle jig

Router bits:
5/32" roman ogee bit
3/4" straight bit
1/2" carbide spiral bit
Option: 1 1/4" plunge ogee bit

Skill Level

	Basic			Basic Plus
X	Moderate			Advanced

Hardware:
- 4 - #8 x 1 3/4" flat head wood screws
- 4 - #8 x 2 1/2" flat head wood screws
- 4 - tack on rubber feet for bottom of legs

Construction details in:
The skills necessary to complete the projects in this book are presented in appendixes at the back. You may wish to review the following appendixes before you start.

Appendix I - Choosing and Sizing Material

Appendix II - Gluing and Clamping

Appendix III- B. Table fence set up C. Jointer fence

Appendix VI - B. Mitre gauge

Appendix VII -J. Angle fixture

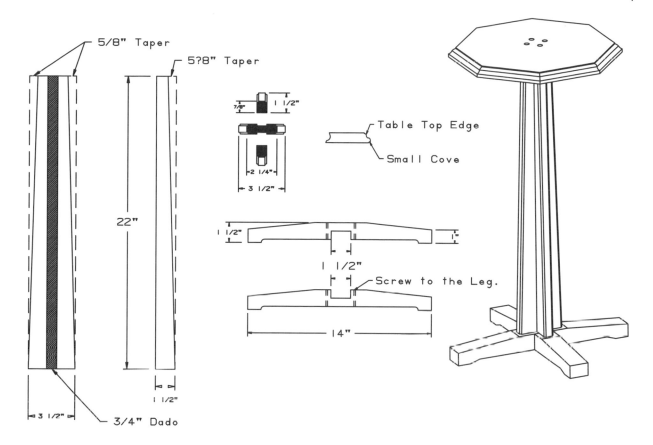

Figure 3-F-2 Stand plans.

How to build this project

Choose the wood for this project. Joint, plane and cut all materials to size according to the material list. Be sure all stock is cut square to the exact size listed. Appendix I contains instructions on choosing and sizing materials. See figure 3-F-2.

If necessary glue up pieces to make stock wide enough for the top.

Construct the taper fixture from Appendix VII-J. The cross lapped legs and the column are tapered but be sure you cut the cross laps in the legs and the two dados in the centre part of the column BEFORE the tapers are cut.

Chuck up a 3/4" flat bottom router bit in the table mounted router. Set the depth of cut to 1/4" (use the 1/4" brass set up bar). Adjust

the table fence so that a 3/4" dado will be cut down the exact centre of the 3 1/2" x 22" x 3/4" column. Check the setting with a sample piece before cutting your project stock. Run a 3/4" dado 1/4" deep on each side of the column. See figure 3-F-3.

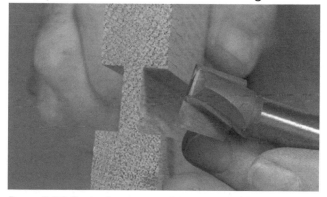

Figure 3-F-3 Dado the centre column.

Lay out and mark the location on the legs for the cross laps. Be sure they are centred and lapped flush. Chuck up a 1/2" spiral bit and install the one inch brass guide in the table mounted router. Position the mitre gauge over the guide and cut the cross laps on the legs. See Appendix VI-B. See figure 3-F-4 and 3-F-5.

Figure 3-F-4 Cut cross laps with the mitre gauge.

Figure 3-F-5 Cross laps in the legs.

Using the shop made Angle Fixture with the table saw, lock the column stock in the fixture and cut tapers on both sides of each column piece. See Appendix VII-J. Be sure not to end for end the column pieces as the tapers must all narrow to the top. See figure 3-F-6.

Reset the angle fixture and cut the tapers on the leg pieces. Mark the edges that need the taper to avoid a mistake. See figure 3-F-2.

Figure 3-F-6 Taper cut on taper fixture.

Octagon top

Lay out the octagon table top. See Appendix III-D-e. The angle fixture will also cut any angle you wish and works well to cut the octagon according to your lay out. See figure 3-F-7.

Figure 3-F-7 Octagon cut on angle fixture.

Reset the router table with a 1/2" spiral bit and a jointer fence with a 1/32" bite. Check the set up with a sample piece. See Appendix III-C. Joint all sawed tapers on the legs and column. Note: Be sure to joint down the grain on all tapers.

Glue and clamp the cross lapped legs.

Reset the router table with a 5/32" roman ogee router bit. Adjust the depth of cut to expose the full profile of the bit plus about 1/16". Check the set up on a sample piece. Run a mold around the eight sides of the octagon table top. Always use a table fence when the cut is straight. Isolate the bearing. See Appendix III-B-c. When the top mold has been completed lower the roman ogee cutter to expose only cove cut at the top of the cutter. Reset the table fence and isolate the bearing. Run a cove on the under side of the top. With this same cove set up, run a cove on all edges of the column.

Glue and clamp the column together. Be sure all pieces are square and flush.

Remove the clamps from the legs and clean the excess glue. Sand where necessary. Remove the table fence without changing the bit setting. Install the safety guide pin and run a cove on the top edge all around the cross lapped legs.

Sand all the parts. Locate and fasten the top on the column. See figure 3-F-8.

Drill and screw the column to the legs. See figure 3-F-9.

Figure 3-F-8 Octagon top attached to column.

Figure 3-F-9 Fasten column to legs

Finish as desired.

Notes:

Unit 4
THIS and THAT

The projects in this unit are small fun to do projects. Make a sliding book stand and then make some wooden books to display in it. The mug tree is a conversation piece. See if your friends can tell you how the dovetailing is done. Trivets and pot mats are always useful and these shaped ones are different and unique. Have fun making our THIS and THAT.

What you will learn in this section

This section contains a number of small projects which, besides being attractive in themselves, provide practice in router skills that is readily transferrable to other, larger jobs.

The small projects also provide excellent practice in producing inlay work. Inlays, when made of contrasting wood, are often the best way of dressing up other projects, from boxes to trays. The trick with inlays is that they have to be good, and the Oak Park accessories which were used to produce the inlays in these projects guarantee perfection every time.

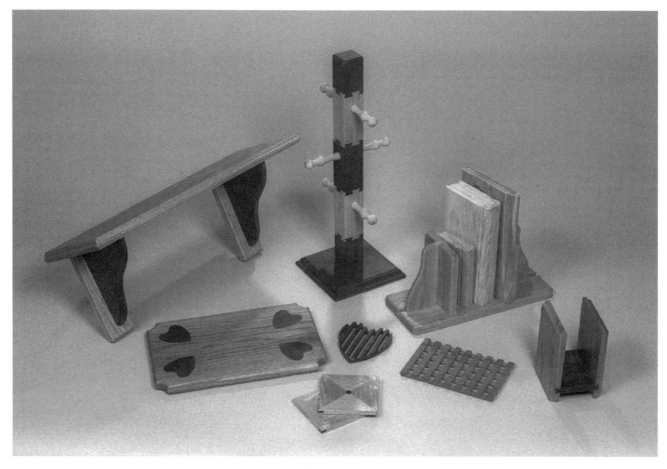

This and that.

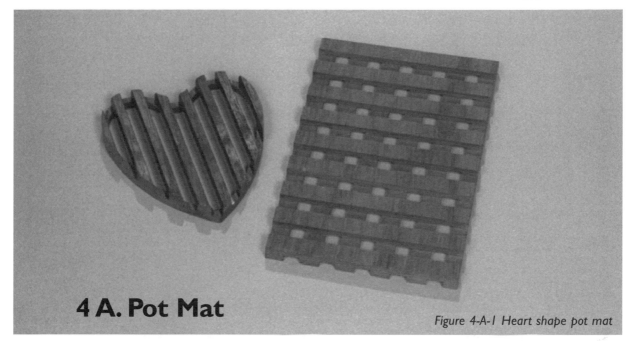

4 A. Pot Mat

Figure 4-A-1 Heart shape pot mat

Protect table and cupboard surfaces from hot pots, tea pots, or serving dishes by using a unique wood hot pot mat. The shape used to fashion this item is not important. It can be any shape. Make these pot mats for your home or for gifts. See figure 4-A-1.

Project Requirements

Recommended: Walnut

Also Suitable: Cedar

Material list:

  (For Trivet)
    2- 3/8" thick, any size from 4"x4" up.

  (For Mat)
    1- 5" x 6" 1/2" walnut

  (For Jig)
    1- 6" x 6" x 1/2" Polyethylene

Router tools:
  Table mounted router
  1/4" Spacer fence
  Heart pattern
  7/16" Guide
  1 1/2" Guide
  7" portable base plate
  .24" Inlay bushing (undersized)
  Pattern jig
  Double stick tape

Skill Level		
Basic	**X**	Basic Plus
Moderate		Advanced

Router bits:
  1/4" Spiral bit
  1/4" plunging round over bit
  1/4" straight carbide bit

Construction details in:
  The skills necessary to complete the projects in this book are presented in appendixes at the back. The following skills are used in this project. You may wish to review the following appendixes before you start.

Appendix I - Choosing and Sizing Material

Appendix IV - Spacer fence

Appendix V - D. Pattern cutting

How to build this project

Begin by gluing two squares of material so that the grains are at right angles to each other. In all cases the cuts are made along the grain, not across it.

First, the basic trivet.

Chuck up a 1/4" straight carbide bit, setting the depth at 3/8" so that it will just cut through one half of the glued-up stock. Set up a 1/4" spacer fence to produce even cuts with 1/4" spaces.

Run a series of cuts, with the grain, on one side of the stock. Turn the stock over and make similar cuts, also with the grain, on the other side. See figure 4-A-2.

Figure 4-A-2 Trivet on the square.

If the depth is right, you should get a criss-cross pattern with the holes providing just the right mesh to protect a sensitive surface from heat. Once cut, the trivet can be shaped in various patterns, or left square. Both options are attractive.

Using the 1/4" straight bit produces square edges. An attractive rounded-edge trivet can be produce by switching to a 1/4" plunge round over bit. This bit has a 1/4" end, and the curve that produces the round over effect, if used in a table mount, will produce an attractive rounded edge on each individual support stringer in the trivet.

If you want to produce a still more attractive trivet with its own base, just read on. . . .

A heart shaped-variation

Make a shop-made jig.

Chuck up a 1/4" spiral bit. Attach a 7" Base plate to the router and install a 7/16" guide with the ring nut. Fasten a .24" inlay bushing (under size) over the guide flange. Secure the polyethylene block in the pattern jig cavity with blocking and slide the heart pattern in place in the pattern jig. See figure 4-A-3. The pattern must be straight on the poly or the mat dados will not be straight.

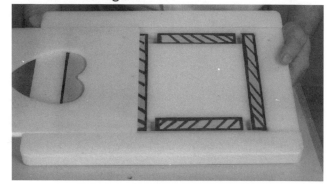

Figure 4-A-3 Polyethylene in the pattern jig

Cutting the pattern

Cut a hole out of the polyethylene following the pattern shape. The polyethylene square with heart cut out is your shop made jig.

The mat material

Fasten the same pattern over the mat material (walnut), with double stick tape. With the 1 1/2" guide and 1/4" spiral bit installed, set the depth of cut to one half the material thickness (about 1/4").

The cavity

Cut a cavity in the pot mat material in the shape of the pattern recessed to 1/4" all over. See figure 4-A-4. Be sure to clean the chips away periodically so they do not build up between the guide and the pattern. It is smart to make a final cut around the pattern shape at the end to ensure a smooth clean cut.

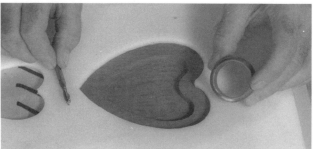

Figure 4-A-4 Walnut recessed heart shape

Cutting the shape

Install the 7/16" guide and set the depth of cut to cut through the pot mat material. See figure 4-A-5.

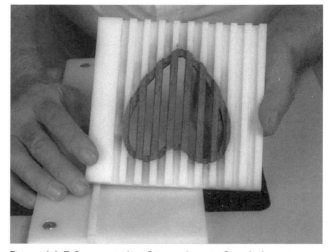

Figure 4-A-7 Bottom side of jig and mat after dado cuts.

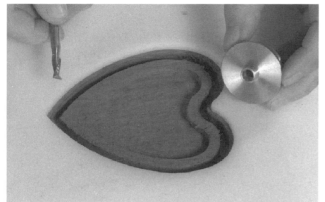

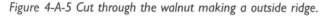

Figure 4-A-5 Cut through the walnut making a outside ridge.

It is important to plunge the router bit into the material with the guide tight against the pattern as we want to save the pattern shape piece. The material must also be secured to insure the heart shaped plug will not move when cut free. This can be accomplished with a sufficient amount of double stick tape. The pattern shape pot mat now will fit in our polyethylene shop jig.

Figure 4-A-6 Walnut in polyethylene jig.

Set up the jig

Chuck up the 1/4" plunge round over bit in the table mount router. Fasten the 1/4" spacer fence over the table. The plunge round over bit has a 1/4" tip which you can use to set the proper repeat.

Cutting the repeat grooves

Slide the pattern shaped pot mat material into the shop made jig with the cavity side up. Set the depth of cut to slightly more than half the thickness of the walnut material.

Cut repeat dados through the shop jig and the mat material in the desired direction. See figure 4-A-6.

Saftey first

Caution:The top of the router bit will be coming through the bottom of the cavity so make sure your hands and fingers are clear of the cavity bottom.

Continue to cut repeat dados all the way across the pot mat material. See figure 4-A-7.

Finish the mat

Remove the pot mat and sand it smooth. See figure 4-A-8. You now have a unique shaped pot mat. Make a variety of shapes for home or gifts.

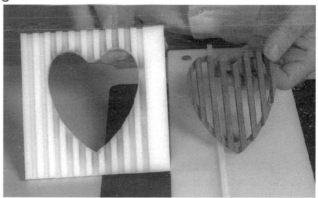

Figure 4-A-8 Heart pot mat and jig.

Figure 4-B-1 Book stand.

4 B. Sliding Dovetail Book Stand

We can never have too many book stands. Wherever books are stored, there is a problem with them falling over or being strewn here and there. With a place to hold them, the books can be organized and are easier to use. Use this stand to organize videos as well as books. See figure 4-B-1.

Project Requirements

Skill Level			
X	Basic		Basic Plus
	Moderate		Advanced

Recommended: Oak

Also suitable: Cedar

Material list:

    1 - 5" x 12" x 5/8" oak base A
    1 - 4 1/2" x 5 1/2" x 1/2" oak slide B cut into two, See diagram.
    2 - 4 1/4" x 5" x 5/8" oak ends C

Router tools:

    Table mounted router
    Table fence
    Brass insert and ring nut

Router bits:

    1/2" 14 degree dovetail bit
    1/4" round over bit
    1 1/4" plunging round over bit

Construction details in:

The skills necessary to complete the projects in this book are presented in appendixes at the back. The following skills are used in this project. You may wish to review the following appendixes before you start.

Appendix I - Choosing and Sizing Material

Appendix III- B. Table fence set up
             D. Measuring made simple

How to build this project

Choose the wood for this project. Joint, plane and cut all materials to size according to the material list. Be sure all stock is cut square to the exact size listed. Appendix I contains in depth instructions on choosing and sizing materials.

The perfect shape

Cut the book slide piece (B) in two. See figure 4-B-2. You will get two sliding pieces out of the one piece of stock and if cut right they will be identical.

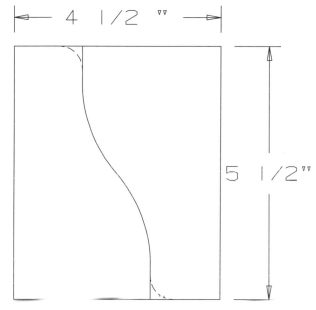

Figure 4-B-2 Cut B part into two equal pieces.

See figure 4-B-3 for the overall plan for the book stand.

Set up the dovetail bit

Mount the insert and ring nut in the plate of the table mounted router. Chuck up the dovetail bit and set the depth of cut at 5/16". See figure 4-B-4.

Do NOT change the height of the bit until all the dovetail slots and pins have been cut.

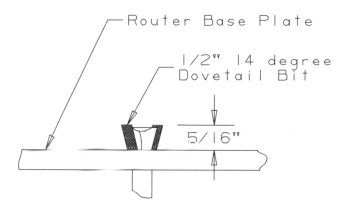

Figure 4-B-4 Set depth of cut for dovetails.

Mark the centre on the base and the end pieces. See Appendix III-D-f. Set the table fence to centre the dovetail bit on the base stock. Cut a linear dovetail down the centre of the base (A).

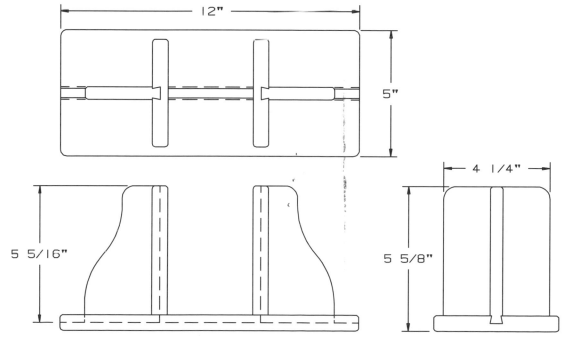

Figure 4-B-3 Book stand plan.

Do not feed too fast with a dovetail bit. There should be a steady stream of debri from the cut.

If the cuttings are not allowed to escape the cutter could jam and cause the stock to be pulled away or ruin the piece altogether. Reset the fence for the centre of the ends (C). Cut a linear dovetail slot down the centre of the ends. DO NOT CHANGE THE HEIGHT OF THE ROUTER BIT.

Making the pins

Adjust the table fence to cover most of the router bit. See figure 4-B-5. We want to put dovetail pins on the perpendicular side and end of B slide pieces. If we take just the small portion exposed in figure 4-B-5 it will leave a half inch dovetail pin in the 1/2" slide piece material. This is a trial and error operation so take a little at a time and try the pin in the base slot for fit. Remember you can cut more off but you cannot add material back on. Use your fine adjusting tool (Hammer) to tap the fence in or out to achieve a perfect dovetail pin. Put a dovetail pin on each straight side and the widest end of the two slide pieces (B).

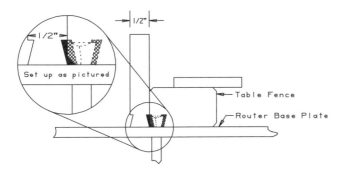

Figure 4-B-5 Set the bit for dovetail pins.

Radius the corners

Chuck up the 1 1/4" plunge round over bit, make a chip breaker with the table fence, and expose the full round over of the bit profile. See Appendix III-B-b and e. Round over the four base corners, two upper corners on the ends, and the corner away from the dovetail pins on the slide pieces. Hold the pieces on end against the fence with a backer block to prevent chip out. See figure 4-B-6.

Figure 4-B-6 Round corners of book stand pieces

Assemble the pieces into the sliding book stand. Mark the edges that will require rounding over.

Rounding the edges

Chuck up the 1/4" round over bit with a bearing in the table mounted router. Install the safety pin in the plate. See Appendix III-A-d. Round over both sides of the end pieces except the bottom. Do not run through the dovetail slots. Stop and start the round over where necessary. Be sure to use the safety pin as a starting point. Round over both top and bottom edges of the base being careful not to cut into the dovetail slot. Round over the top and side of the slide pieces away from the dovetail pins. Again stop and start to avoid cutting into the dovetail pins. See figure 4-B-7.

Figure 4-B-7 Book stand pieces rounded over.

Finish the book stand

Sand, clean, and finish the book stand pieces. Assemble the pieces and mark where the end (C) comes on the slide (B). Glue C onto B in this position. Allow the bottom dovetail pin to slide freely in the base dovetail slot. Your book stand is ready to hold children's books, receipt books, or any book of your choice.

Figure 4-C-I Wooden books.

4 C. Wooden Books

A wooden book has no other value than for decoration on a shelf or desk top. Wooden books can be constructed out of any kind of wood and painted with a variety of methods dependent on the end use of the book. See figure 4-C-I. This project goes well with the previous project, the sliding book stand.

Project   Requirements

Recommended: Coffee wood, Oak, Cedar

Material list:

I - 3 1/2" x 5" x 1" coffee wood
I - 4" x 7" x 1 1/2" oak
I - 4 1/2" x 9" x 3/4" cedar

Router tools:

Table mounted router
Table fence

Router bits:

3/8" round over bit
1/2" spiral carbide bit
3/4" V groove bit
1/8" round over bit

Skill Level

X	Basic			Basic Plus
	Moderate			Advanced

Construction details in:

The skills necessary to complete the projects in this book are presented in appendixes at the back. The following skills are used in this project. You may wish to review the following appendixes before you start.

Appendix I - Choosing and Sizing Material

Appendix III- B. Table fence set up

How to build this project

Choose the wood for this project. Because books can be any size and thickness the material you choose for this project can be a variety pack. Joint, plane and cut all material square and to the size you determine. Appendix I contains in depth instructions on choosing and sizing materials.

Grooves to look like books

Chuck up a 1/2" spiral bit in the table mounted router. Set the depth of cut to 1/8" (use the brass set up bar). Adjust the fence to centre the 3/4" stock thickness over the bit. Check the settings with a sample piece first. You may have to make more than one pass for thicker stock. Leave about 1/8" on both edges to represent the book cover.

Mount a stop block on the outfeed of the table fence to stop the cut 3/8" from the book spine. Mark the spine side of the book. See Appendix III-B-d. Cut both ends of all the stock stopping 3/8" from the uncut long side. See figure 4-C-2. Remove the stop block and run the 1/8" recess along one long side of all the stock. See figure 4-C-3. Run all the book stock you wish to make while it is set up.

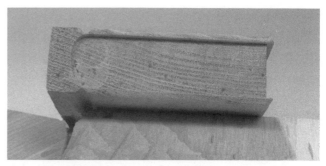

Figure 4-C-3 Make pages recess, ends and one side.

Spine sides with groove bit

Reset the table mount with a V groove bit. Set the depth of cut to 1/8" (use a brass set up bar). Mount the table fence so the centre of the bit is 3/4" from the fence. Caution: The fence is always mounted to the right of the bit when standing at the infeed side of the table. Run a V groove down along both spine sides of the book. See figure 4-C-4. Do this for all books being produced.

Figure 4-C-4 V groove on spine side.

Rounding over the book

Chuck up a 3/8" round over bit in the router. Install and use the safety pin. See Appendix III-A-d. Set the depth of cut to give a full quarter round. Check the set up with a sample piece. Put a quarter round on both sides of the spine. Do all the books. See figure 4-C-5.

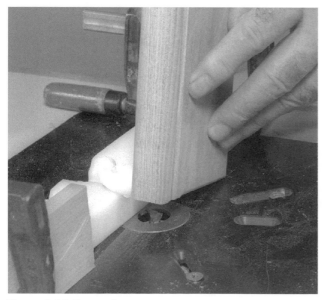

Figure 4-C-2 Stopped cut.

Figure 4-C-5 Round the spine edges

Reset the router table with a 1/8" round over bit. Install the safety pin and set the depth to just under the 1/8". Start this round over at the V groove. Do the end, the book side and the other end to the V groove. Round the cover on both sides of the book. Do this for all the books. See figure 4-C-6.

You could also use a table fence to round the spine edges and the cover edges because you are dealing with straight cuts. In this case you would isolate the bearing and run to the fence. See Appendix III-B-c.

Figure 4-C-6 Round the cover edges

Finishing the book

Sand the books and slightly round any sharp corners. Paint and decorate the books in any colour or decal configuration that you wish. Write many books with imaginative titles.

Notes:

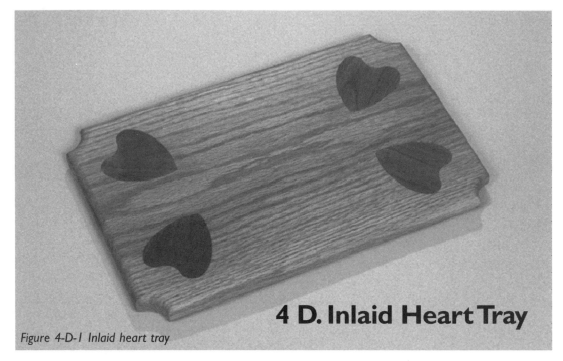

4 D. Inlaid Heart Tray

Figure 4-D-1 Inlaid heart tray

Many simple projects can be made fancy with an inlay design applied in a contrasting wood or other materials. The snack tray we have illustrated in this project is made of cherry wood with walnut hearts inlaid in the corners. See figure 4-D-1.

Project   Requirements

Recommended: Cherry, Walnut

Also suitable: Oak, White Ash

Materials list:
  1 - 8" x 12" x 3/4" - Tray material
  4 - 4" x 4" x 1/4" - Inlay material

Router Tools:
  Table mounted router
  Table fence
  Plunge router with 7" portable base Plate
  7/16" Guide
  1/4" Inlay bushing
  Heart pattern
  Shop made corner pattern jig
  Double-stick tape

Router bits:
  1/4" carbide router bit
  1/4" round over bit with pilot
  1/4" cove bit
  1/2" cove bit

Skill Level			
	Basic		Basic Plus
X	Moderate		Advanced

Construction details in:
  The skills necessary to complete the projects in this book are presented in appendixes at the back. The following skills are used in this project. You may wish to review the following appendixes before you start.

Appendix I - Choosing and Sizing Material

Appendix II - Gluing and Clamping

Appendix III- B. Table fence set up D. Measuring

Appendix V - B. Inlays

Appendix VII-B. Corner pattern fixture

How to build this project

Choose the wood for this project. Joint, plane and cut all materials to size according to the material list. Be sure all stock is cut square to the exact size listed. Appendix I contains instructions on choosing and sizing materials.

Inlays in the tray

The tray should be a hardwood as it may be used as a cutting board. The wood used for inlays should also be hardwood but of a contrasting colour. This enables us to fully appreciate the beauty of the corner inlays. Size four pieces to be used for the inlays. Make a corner fixture using the smallest heart pattern. See Appendix VII-B.

Chuck up a 1/4" Spiral bit in the portable plunge router with the 7/16" guide fastened securely with the ring nut. Attach the 1/4" inlay bushing over the guide flange. See figure 4-D-2.

Figure 4-D-2 For inlays you need a 7/16" guide and 1/4" bushing.

Position the heart pattern at a 45 degree angle, across the corner of the tray material using the shop made corner jig to hold it in position. See figure 4-D-3.

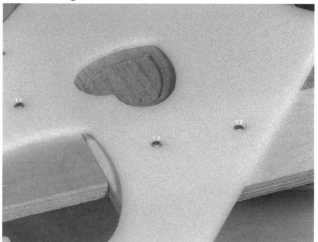

Figure 4-D-3 Corner pattern fixture.

Following the directions in Appendix V-B for making inlays, rout heart cavities in all four corners of the tray material.

Making inlay plugs

Double-stick tape the four inlay pieces to 1/2" plywood and position each piece (One at a time) in the corner pattern jig with the same heart pattern in place over the plug material. See figure 4-D-4. Remove the inlay bushing from the guide flange. Rout the inlay plugs being sure to stay tight to the pattern. Clean up and sand the four inlay plugs.

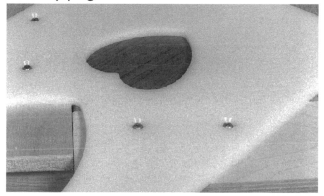

Figure 4-D-4 Cut inlays.

Decorating the corners

Glue the inlay plugs into the inlay cavities. Cut a radius on the four corners of the tray. This is accomplished by first tracing the radius from a template or using a compass to draw the radius on each of the four corners. Cut and sand the corners to the lines you have drawn.

Another way to achieve corner radii is to use a round over router bit or a cove bit in a table mounted router. Stand the tray on edge against the fence and round or cove all four corners. See figure 4-D-5. See Appendix III-B-e for coving corners.

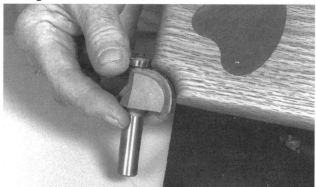

Figure 4-D-5 Cove the corners.

Install a 1/4" round over bit with a pilot in the table mounted router. Round the top edge of the tray being sure to use your safety pin. See Appendix III-A-d.

Some handles

Change to a 1/4" cove bit and cove the bottom edge of the tray. Use a 1/2" cove bit and a table fence with a stop block to cut finger coves in the two ends of the tray. See figure 4-D-6. For stopped cuts see Appendix III-B-d.

Finishing for food

You now have a handy snack tray which can be used for cutting cheese, serving snacks, or table serving of bread, cake, or dainties. The tray is decorative and pleasing to look at as well as serviceable.

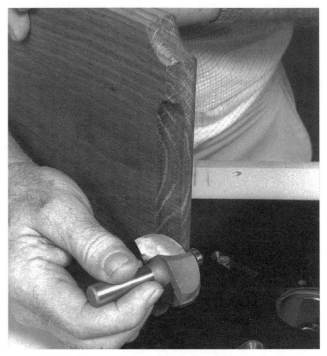

Figure 4-D-6 Finger coves in the ends.

Notes:

Figure 4-E-1 Holder

4 E. Letter or Napkin Holder

Use this small holder for letters or notes in the office. It works well to organize bills and memos by the telephone or on your desk. This small but unique project is both decorative and useful. If you have no need to organize letters, use it for a napkin holder in the dining room. See figure 4-E-1.

Project   Requirements

Recommended: Walnut

Also suitable: Cedar

Material list:
 2 - 4" x 5 1/2" x 5/8" cedar sides
 1 - 4" x 3 1/4" x 1/2" cedar divider

Router tools:
 Table mounted router
 Table fence
 Jointer fence See Appendix III-C.

Skill Level			
X	Basic		Basic Plus
	Moderate		Advanced

Router bits:
 5/32" roman ogee bit
 1/2" 14° dovetail bit

How to build this project

Choose the wood for this project. Joint, plane and cut all materials to size according to the material list. See figure 4-E-2.

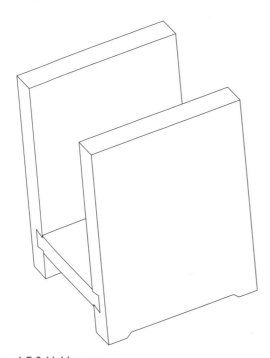

Figure 4-E-2 Holder parts.

Be sure all stock is cut square to the exact size listed. Appendix 1 contains instructions on choosing and sizing materials.

Linear dovetail on the sides

Chuck up a 1/2" dovetail bit in the table-mounted router. Set bit height at 3/8" (use a 3/8" setup bar). Secure the table fence over the table with 3/4" between the fence and the inside edge of the router bit. Check your setup with a sample piece. Run a dovetail across the grain of the piece. Run dovetails in both side pieces about 3/4" from the bottom. See figure 4-E-3.

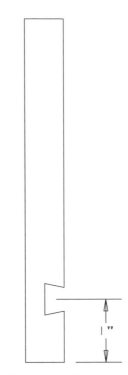

Figure 4-E-3 Dovetails in both sides.

Dovetail pins on both ends

Do not change the height of the dovetail bit. Move the table fence to expose a small shoulder of the dovetail bit. See figure 4-E-4.

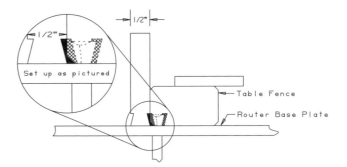

Figure 4-E-4 Position fence to make dovetail pins.

We want to put dovetail pins on both ends of the divider piece. If we take just the small portion exposed in figure 4-E-4 it will leave a half inch dovetail pin in the 1/2" divider piece. This is a trial and error operation so take a little at a time and try the pin in the side slot for fit. Remember you can cut more off but you cannot add material back on. Use your fine adjusting tool (Hammer) to tap the fence in or out to achieve a perfect dovetail pin. Put a dovetail pin in both ends of the divider piece.

Molding the sides

Install a 5/32" roman ogee bit and adjust the depth of cut to reveal the full profile. Adjust the table fence to isolate the bearing. See Appendix III-B-c. Run an ogee profile on the face side of both sides and the top of the side pieces.

Relief cuts with a router jointer fence

Install a 1/2" spiral bit and a jointer fence. Cut a 1/8" relief in the bottom of each side. Use a stop on the fence to ensure that the edge feet are the same. See Appendix III-C for jointer information. See figure 4-E-5.

Project finishing

Glue and clamp the divider into the dovetails in the sides. Make sure everything fits square and flush.

When the glue is set clean, sand, and finish the letter or napkin holder.

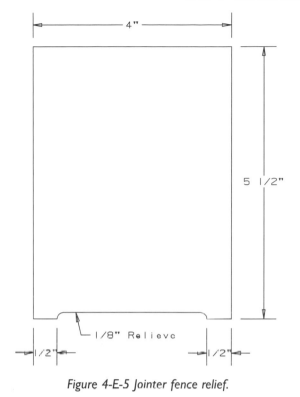

Figure 4-E-5 Jointer fence relief.

Notes:

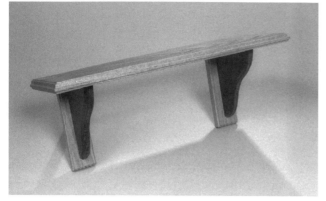

Figure 4-F-1 Wall shelf

Figure 4-F-2 Shelf pieces

4 F. Wall Shelf

A wall shelf can be used in many areas to hold figurines, plates or other collectables. The shelf in these plans can be taken apart. The mounting bases screw to the wall. The brackets fit into the mounting bases with linear dovetails. The shelf slides onto the brackets on linear dovetails. See figure 4-F-1 and 4-F-2. It is easily put together and taken apart for moving.

Project Requirements

Recommended: Oak

Also suitable: Mahogany

Material list:

1 - 7 1/2" x 20" x 3/4" oak shelf
2 - 2" x 7" x 3/4" oak wall mount
2 - 6" x 8" x 3/4" oak brackets

Router tools:

Table mounted router
Table fence
Mitre gauge
1" brass guide and ring nut
5/8" brass guide and ring nut
7" base plate
Shop made fixture See Appendix VII-C.

Router bits:

5/32" roman ogee bit
1/2" 14 degree dovetail bit
3/8" carbide spiral bit

Skill Level

Basic	**X**	Basic Plus
Moderate		Advanced

Construction details in:

The skills necessary to complete the projects in this book are presented in appendixes at the back. The following skills are used in this project. You may wish to review the following appendixes before you start.

Appendix I - Choosing and Sizing Material

**Appendix III- B. Table fence set up
D. Measuring**

Appendix V - D. Pattern cutting

Appendix VI- B. Mitre gauge

Appendix VII-C. Shelf bracket fixture

How to build this project

Choose the wood for this project. Joint, plane and cut all materials to size according to the material list. See figure 4-F-3 and 4-F-4. Be sure all stock is cut square to the exact size listed. Appendix I contains instructions on choosing and sizing materials.

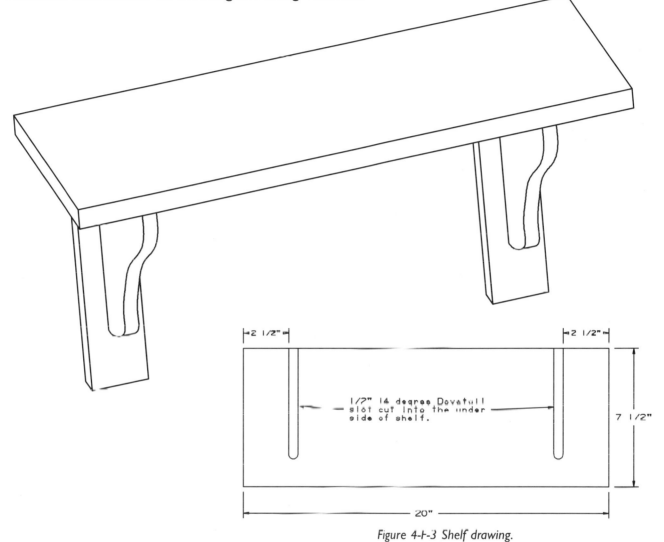

Figure 4-F-3 Shelf drawing.

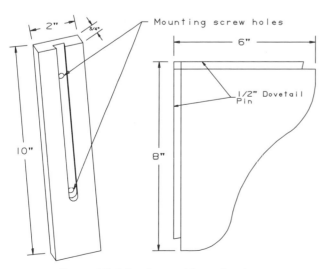

Figure 4-F-4 Bracket and base drawing.

Special requirement

The material for shelf brackets has a special direction of grain requirement. Please see Appendix VII-C. Shelf fixture before cutting and sizing the material for this project. Rough band saw the brackets to the fixture shape but leave an extra 3/8" to be trimmed with the router bit. Construct the shelf fixture at this time.

Cutting the brackets

Chuck up a 3/8" spiral bit in the table mounted router. Install a 5/8" guide to the base plate with a ring nut. Clamp each bracket piece securely in the shelf fixture and mold the designed edge. Be sure to start the cut with the pattern fixture against the guide flange. It is very important to secure the stock in this operation because the grain can be hard to cut. See figure 4-F-5.

Figure 4-F-5 Bracket material in shelf fixture

Making stopped dovetails

Chuck up a 1/2" dovetail bit. Install a one inch guide with the ring nut. Position the mitre gauge over the guide. Set the bit depth of cut at 3/8" (use a set up bar). See Appendix VI-B Mitre gauge. Check the set up with a sample piece of material.

The material receiving the dovetail pin is 3/4" thick, therefore you will use the pin fence on the right hand side of the gauge in order to centre the 1/2" pin in 3/4" material.

Refer to the plan and run stopped dovetails in the bottom of the shelf with the mitre gauge.

With the pin fence on the right hand side, run a dovetail pin on the top and back of each bracket. This must fit a stopped dovetail slot so it is necessary to cut a notch in each end of the pin. See figure 4-F-6.

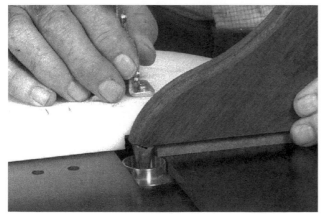

Figure 4-F-6 Notched dovetail pin

Wall mounting brackets

The wall mounting bases require that the mitre gauge be clamped to the table in a fence position. The distance between the bit and the mitre gauge head is half the width of the mounting base stock. Mark the end of the stock for centre and check the mark. See Appendix III-D. Set the dovetail bit centred over this mark and securely clamp the mitre gauge to the router table. See figure 4-F-7. Make stopped dovetail slots in each of the mounting bases. Run the dovetail into a stop (mark on the mitre head) and then turn off the router. Be sure the bit has stopped completely and then back out of the cut. Do this for both mounting bases.

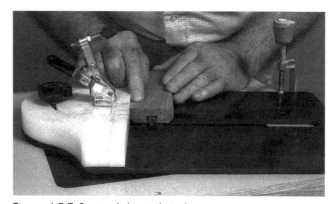

Figure 4-F-7 Stopped dovetails in bases

Molding the top shelf

Chuck up a 5/32" roman ogee bit in the table mounted router. Set the depth of cut to expose the full profile of the bit. Set the table fence to isolate the bearing on the bit. See Appendix III-B-c. Run an ogee mold on the end, the front, and the other end of the shelf top edge.

Lower the ogee bit to expose only the cove profile. Reset the table fence to isolate the bearing and run a cove on both long edges and the bottom end of both mounting bases. Remove the fence and with the safety pin in place put a small cove mold on both sides of the leading edges of the brackets. See figure 4-F-8.

Figure 4-F-8 Cove the brackets

Drill screw mounting holes in the dovetail slot of the mounting bases.

Finishing the shelf

Sand and finish all the parts for the wall shelf. Choose the position on the wall and screw the mounting bases to the wall. Slide the dovetail pin in the brackets into the base dovetail slot over the screws. Slide the shelf in place on the top dovetail pin of the bracket.

The shelf is complete.

Notes:

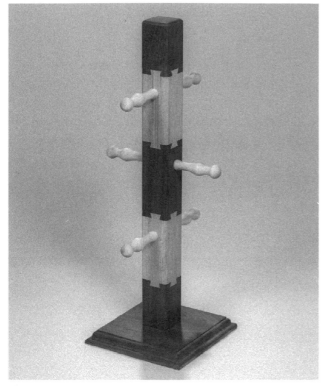

Figure 4-G-1 Mug tree

4 G. Mug Tree

This is a novel idea to keep that coffee cup close at hand. Hang it on a dovetailed tree. The blocks are fastened together with dovetails in a configuration that looks impossible.

Make a mug tree and let your friends puzzle over its construction. See figure 4-G-1.

Project Requirements

Recommended: Walnut, Oak

Also suitable: Other contrasting hardwoods

Material list:
   1 - 6" x 6" x 3/4" walnut base
   5 - 1 7/8" x 1 7/8" x 4" oak and walnut column blocks

Router tools:
   Table mounted router
   Table fence
   Brass insert and ring nut
   3/8" spacer fence
   Shop made holder Appendix IV-F.

Router bits:
   5/32" roman ogee bit
   1/2" 14 degree dovetail bit
   1/4" round over bit

Hardware:
   2 - #6mm x 1 1/2" flat head wood screws
   6 - shaker pegs

Skill Level

Basic		X	Basic Plus
Moderate			Advanced

Construction details in:

The skills necessary to complete the projects in this book are presented in appendixes at the back. The following skills are used in this project. You may wish to review the following appendixes before you start.

Appendix I - Choosing and Sizing Material

Appendix II - Gluing and Clamping

Appendix III- B. Table fence set up D. Measuring

Appendix IV- F. Sliding dovetail

How to build this project

Choose the wood for this project. Joint, plane and cut all materials to size according to the material list. It is important the 1 7/8" x 1 7/8" blocks are square on all corners and exactly 1 7/8" both directions. See figure 4-G-2. Be sure all stock is cut square to the exact size listed. Appendix 1 contains instructions on choosing and sizing materials.

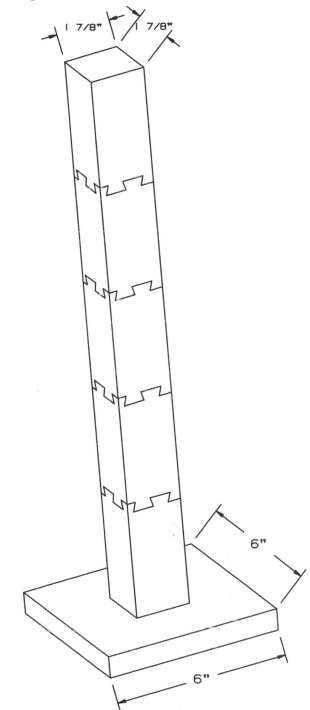

Figure 4-G-2 Mug tree plan

Sliding dovetails

Install the 1/2" dovetail bit in the table mounted router. Position the 3/8" spacer fence over the table to cut sliding dovetails. See Appendix IV for spacer joinery. Use scrap material to check the set up. Mark a face edge on all the blocks.

The corner holder

Make yourself a holder. Directions for the holder construction are in Appendix IV-F. Sliding Dovetails. See figure 4-G-3 and 4-G-4.

Figure 4-G-3 Two part holder to squeeze the block in position.

Figure 4-G-4 Bottom of the block in the holder

Clamp the blocks one at a time in the holder and cut sliding dovetails on both ends of three blocks and just one end of two blocks. Keep the marked edge to the fence and alternate the wood colours.

Gluing the column

Dry fit the column. Use a small brush to glue the dovetail column together alternating light wood and dark wood. Bar clamp it in place until the glue dries.

All surfaces smooth

You may note that the match is slightly off. This could be for a lot of reasons. Were the blocks perfectly square? Were they held square as they ran through the bit? Don't panic! When the glue is dry, joint two edges to get a square corner. Mark an "X" on the jointed sides. Plane the other two edges and they will automatically be square. The column should be 1 3/4" x 1 3/4" with all surfaces smooth. See figure 4-G-5.

Figure 4-G-5 Sliding dovetails

Larger for planing

Because the dovetail cuts come in at an angle there is lift out in the wood. Once glued and planed the chips are removed. With this operation it is best to make the stock 1/8" larger to allow for planing.

Molding the base

Install the roman ogee bit in the table mounted router. Set the depth of cut to expose the full profile. Secure the table fence in place to isolate the bearing. See Appendix III-B-c. Run an ogee mold on all four sides of the base. Be sure to start with a cross grain side.

Molding the column

Chuck up the 1/4" round over bit in the table mounted router. Expose the full profile and isolate the pilot with the fence. Round the four side corners of the column and the top four edges.

Shaker pegs in place

Drill six holes in the column to receive the shaker pegs. Sand both the column and the base.

Column mounted to base

Drill mounting holes in the centre of the base to fasten the column in place. Mount the base to the column with the wood screws. Sand and finish the mug tree.

Notes:

Unit 5
OFFICE and HOME

It has taken a veritable flood of cheap, plastic office and home knickknacks to produce a genuine appreciation for these items when they are made out of wood. Your router makes It easy for you to turn out accessories that can be a credit to any office, whether that office is located in a modern tower or in a room at home. Matching pen stand, pen case, in-and-out trays and organizer grow in beauty with age. Replicas make excellent gifts. Or, for a nostalgic experience, produce an old fashioned pencil box.

What you will learn in this section

This part of Router Projects and Jigs presents a good opportunity, with some of its simpler projects, to brush up on basic router skills. It also has items which will increase your ability to produce good sliding dovetail joints, and to make attractive angle box joints. Remember to let your good joinery show in your finished project. You may find the pencil box frustrating, but if you take your time and use scraps of wood to perfect the fit, your rewards will be great.

Office organizers.

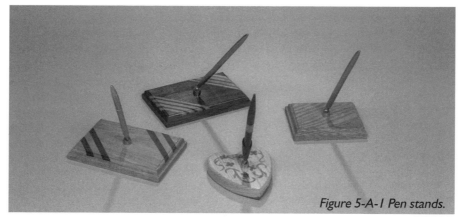

Figure 5-A-1 Pen stands.

5 A. Pen Stand

Sometimes a simple piece of wood can be fashioned into an exquisite gift for home or office with nothing more elaborate than a molded edge. Choose wood that has an interesting grain or texture. Shape the wood and apply painted decoration if desired. Whatever you do with this project idea, let your imagination dictate a project for those small pieces of material that are not large enough for anything else. See figure 5-A-1.

Project Requirements

Recommended: Oak, Walnut, Maple

Also suitable: Cedar, Mahogany

Material list:
 1 - 3 1/2" x 4 1/2" x 1" pen holder (rectangular)
 1 - 6" x 7" x 1" pen holder (heart)
 1 - 4" x 6" x 1" pen holder (corner inlay)
 material to make up an inlay strip of contrasting wood

Router tools:
 Table mounted router
 Table fence
 Shop made pattern fixture
 Heart pattern
 5/8" brass guide
 Brass ring nut
 7" base plate

Router bits:
 5/32" roman ogee bit with pilot bearing
 3/8" carbide spiral bit
 1/4" round over bit with pilot bearing
 1/2" 14 degree dovetail bit (for inlaid pen stand)

Skill Level

X	Basic		Basic Plus
	Moderate		Advanced

Hardware:
 3 - Pens and holders
 3 - Screws to fit holders

Construction details in:
 The skills necessary to complete the projects in this book are presented in appendixes at the back. The following skills are used in this project. You may wish to review the following appendixes before you start.

Appendix I - Choosing and Sizing Material

Appendix III- A-d. Safety Pin Use
 B-b and c. Table Fence
 D-b. Measuring

Appendix V - D. Pattern Cutting

Appendix VII- D. Pattern Fixture

Appendix VII- F. Sub Top

How to build this project

Because there is nothing to fit in this project, the wood chosen can be any size as long as it is large enough to support the pen and holder. Choose pieces for their unique characteristics: knots, grain and colour. The wood for the heart holder must be larger than the heart pattern.

Getting started

For the rectangular holder, chuck up the 5/32" roman ogee bit in the table mounted router. Set the depth of cut to expose the full bit profile plus 1/16" to give a nice profile line on the face of the project. Set the table fence to isolate the bearing and create a chip breaker. See Appendix III-B-b and c. Mold the four sides of the holder stock being sure to do the cross grain cuts first. Use a backer piece to prevent tear out. Mark and drill the screw hole for the pen holder in the stock. See figure 5-A-2.

Figure 5-A-2 Drill screw hole in holder

Sand and finish the pen holder. Attach the pen holder with the screw. Install the pen in the holder.

A heart shaped holder

Use the shop made pattern holder to cut the heart shape. See Appendix VII-D. In this project it is very important that the heart plug does not move even after it is cut free. Secure the shop made heart pattern fixture so it will not move during the cut. Fasten it to the sub top

positioned over your table. See Appendix VII-F. Slide the project stock into the fixture and secure with the hold down clamps. See figure 5-A-3.

Figure 5-A-3 Shop made pattern fixture

Chuck up the 3/8" spiral bit in the portable plunge router. Install the 5/8" guide with the ring nut on the 7" base plate bolted to the router. Set the depth of cut to cut through the 1" material. You want to secure the centre part of the stock with double stick tape to be sure the heart shape does not move after it is cut free. Or set the depth of cut to a depth that is almost through the material (1/32"). These last wood fibres will keep the heart in place and allow the back to be trimmed with a knife and sanded.

Cut the heart

Position the guide flange against one edge of the pattern and plunge the bit into the stock. Remember to keep the flange tight to the pattern because we wish to keep the centre heart. Move slowly, in a left to right direction (clockwise). If the stock is the right size, you can end up with a pen holder out of the plug and a picture frame from the outside part of the stock.

Round the edges

In the table mounted router, chuck up the 1/4" round over bit and set the depth of cut to give a smooth round over. We do not want a profile line so set the depth carefully. Check the setting with a sample piece. See Appendix III-A-d.

With the safety pin in place bear against the bit pilot to round the edges of the heart plug on both sides. Mark and drill a screw hole in the centre of the heart to receive the pen holder. Sand and finish the heart shaped pen holder. You may want to paint a design on plain wood or allow the wood grain to be the decoration and finish it clear.

Corner inlay pen stand

Cut materials to size. Construct a simple corner holder. See figure 5-A-4 and 5-A-5.

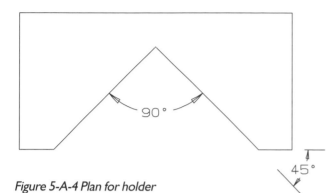

Figure 5-A-4 Plan for holder

Figure 5-A-6 Make first dovetail cut.

Figure 5-A-5 Corner holder.

Glue together the inlay material to make a variety of designs with different wood species. Maple and walnut make a great contrasting inlay.

Install the insert guide in the base plate to narrow the bit hole and chuck up a 1/2" dovetail bit. Adjust the height of the dovetail bit to the same thickness as the inlay material. See Appendix III-D-b.

Clamp the base material in the holder and adjust the table fence so that the corner will be 1" from the edge of the bit. See figure 5-A-6. Make the first dovetail cut. Move the fence out and make repeat cuts until the inlay width is cut. It is important that this width is measured at the widest part of the dovetail. Remember to cut a little at a time. You can do just one corner of the pen stand or two corners.

Dovetail inlay piece

Remove the holder and set the fence over to expose a small corner of the dovetail bit. See figure 5-A-7 and 5-A-8.

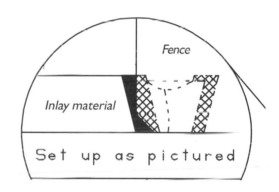

Figure 5-A-7 Dovetail bit setting.

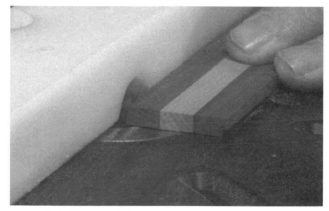

Figure 5-A-8 Dovetail the inlay.

Run a dovetail on each side of the inlay stock. Slide the finished inlay into the dovetail slot in the pen stand. See figure 5-A-9. Glue the inlay in place. Trim and sand excess inlay material even with the pen stand stock.

Figure 5-A-9 Inlay slides into recess.

Mold the edges

Chuck up the 5/32" roman ogee bit and mold this stand as you did for the solid pen holder above. Drill the screw hole for the pen holder in the stand. Sand and finish the pen holder. Install the holder and insert the pen. Let your creativity take hold and have fun with this idea.

Notes:

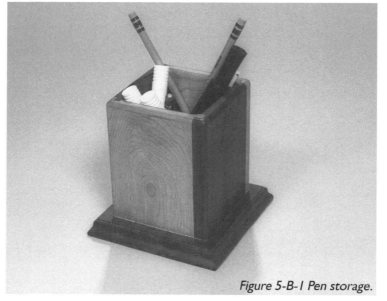

Figure 5-B-1 Pen storage.

5 B. Desk Pen Storage

When the phone rings, can you quickly find a pen to write with. Build this pen storage for your desk. Pencils, pens, and rulers will always be at your finger tips. See figure 5-B-1 and 5-B-2.

Project Requirements

Recommended: Maple, Walnut

Also suitable: Cedar

Material list:
    1 - 5" x 5" x 3/4" walnut base
    2 - 3 1/2" x 4 3/4" x 1/2" walnut sides
    2 - 3 1/2" x 4 3/4" x 1/2" maple ends

Router tools:
    Table mounted router
    Table fence
    1/4" spacer fence

Router bits:
    5/32" roman ogee bit with pilot bearing
    1/4" round over bit with pilot bearing
    1/4" carbide spiral bit

Hardware:
    4 - #4 x 1 1/4" flat head wood screws

Skill Level			
X	Basic		Basic Plus
	Moderate		Advanced

Construction details in:
    The skills necessary to complete the projects in this book are presented in appendixes at the back. The following skills are used in this project. You may wish to review the following appendixes before you start.

Appendix I - Choosing and Sizing Material

Appendix II - Clamping and Gluing

Appendix III- A-a. Direction of Feed
          -b. Order of Cut
          -d. Safety Pin Use

Appendix III- B-c. Table Fence

Appendix III- D-a. Measuring

Appendix IV- D. Rabbet Dado Joint

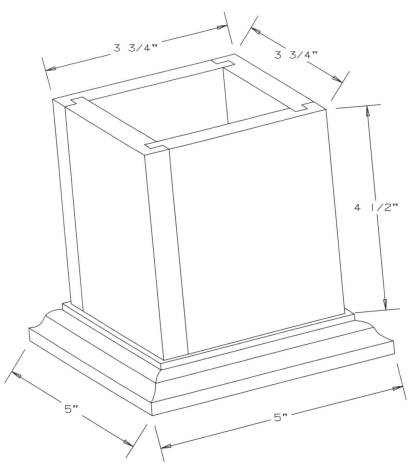

Figure 5-B-2 Pen storage plan.

How to build this project

Choose the wood for this project. Joint, plane and cut all materials to size according to the material list. Be sure all stock is cut square and to the exact size listed. Appendix I contains instructions on choosing and sizing materials.

Install the 5/32" roman ogee bit in the table mounted router. Adjust the depth of cut to expose the full profile of the ogee bit. Set up the table fence and isolate the bearing. See Appendix III-B-c.

BEFORE YOU PLUG IN THE ROUTER

Any time a fence is installed on the router table, hand turn the chuck to be sure the bit is NOT touching the fence.

Start the router and run a test piece of stock to check the depth and fence settings for the full roman ogee profile. See figure 5-B-3. Adjust the settings if necessary. Cut a full profile roman ogee on the base piece being sure to follow the direction of feed and cross/straight grain instructions. See Appendix III-A-a and b.

Figure 5-B-3 Mold the base piece.

Rabbet dado joint

Install the 1/4" spiral bit and set up the 1/4" spacer fence on the table mounted router. Set the depth of cut to half the thickness of the side and end material. See Appendix III-D-a.

Note: In order for this joint to work it is very important that all side and end material is exactly 1/2" in thickness.

All four pieces used to form this box are the same size and thickness. In the rabbet dado joinery, you will have a rabbet on one edge facing out and a dado on the opposite edge facing in. See figure 5-B-4.

Figure 5-B-4 Each side has a rabbet and dado.

Note: Both the rabbet and dado cuts are made along the straight grain 4 1/2" edge of each piece. Cut test pieces with a rabbet dado joint and check the fit. See Appendix IV-D. When you are satisfied with the fit, cut all the rabbet dado cuts in the side and end material. Dry fit the box pieces. See figure 5-B-5.

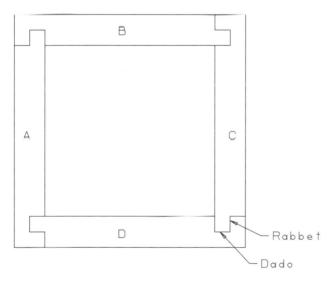

Figure 5-B-5 Fit the rabbet dado joints.

This box does not need a bottom because it will be attached to the base piece. Glue and clamp the box together, being sure it is square. See Appendix II for clamping and gluing information. When the glue is set, clean and sand the box.

Round the edges

Install a 1/4" round over bit with a bearing in the table-mounted router. Set the depth of cut to produce a smooth round over with no profile line. Place the box opening over the bit and allow the bearing to bear against the inside edge of the box opening to round over the inside top of the box piece. Install the safety pin in the proper location and round over the outside top of the box. Leave the bottom square to be attached to the base. See Appendix III-A-d. Round the outside corners of the box if desired.

Center the box

To center the box on the edge molded base, line up the box edges in one corner of the molded base on the profile line. Mark on the base where the other two sides of the box extend. Divide in half the distance this mark is from the adjacent profile line on the base on the two sides. See figure 5-B-6. Move the box to these new marks. You will have centered the box on the base. Mark and drill screw holes in the base. Using the four wood screws, fasten the box to the base.

Sand and finish the desk pen storage. There you have a handsome storage place for your pens, pencils or whatever is needed in a handy place.

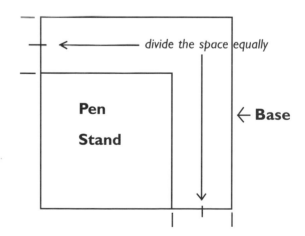

Figure 5-B-6 Center the box on the base.

Figure 5-C-1 Pen cases.

5 C. Pen Gift Case

We all use storage regardless of what we choose to keep in it. These simple cases with sliding dovetail lids are easy to construct and make decorative storage for a variety of items. They make excellent cases for presentation pen or pen/pencil sets. Outside the office they can be used to hold jewelery or any number of other small items. Try a variety of woods for decoration. We have pictured a single pen case and a pen/pencil case in the instructions for this project. See figure 5-C-1.

Project Requirements

Recommended: Walnut, Oak

Also suitable: Cedar, Mahogany

Material list:
Single pen case
1 - 1 1/2" x 6 1/2" x 3/4" oak base
1 - 1 1/2" x 6 1/2" x 3/8" walnut lid
Pen/pencil case
1 - 2 1/4" x 9 3/4" x 3/4" oak base
1 - 2 1/4" x 9 3/4" x 3/8" walnut lid

Router tools:
Table mounted router
Table fence
Pattern jig
Blank pattern piece
1" brass guide
Ring nut
7" base plate

Skill Level				
	Basic			Basic Plus
X	Moderate			Advanced

Router bits:
1/4" round over bit with pilot bearing
1/2" 14 degree dovetail bit
5/8" flat bottom core box bit

Construction details in:
The skills necessary to complete the projects in this book are presented in appendixes at the back. The following skills are used in this project. You may wish to review the following appendixes before you start.

Appendix III- A-a. Direction of Feed

Appendix III- B-b. Table Fence Chip Breaker

Appendix V - D. Pattern Cutting

How to build this project

Choose the wood for this project. Joint, plane and cut all materials to size according to the material list. Be sure all stock is cut square to the exact size listed. Appendix I contains instructions on choosing and sizing materials.

Make a pattern

We will begin by cutting the cavity in the base. Using the blank pattern piece make a pattern for the cavities for one or both of the cases. See Appendix V-D. It is possible to do both cases in the pattern jig at one time.

Cut the cavity

Centre and secure the base stock inside the pattern jig with furniture blocks on one end and one side. Use pattern bolts on the other end and side to tighten the stock in place. Slide the pattern over the stock in the pattern jig and lock it by inserting the pin.

Install the 7" base plate, 1" guide and ring nut on the router. Chuck up the 5/8" flat bottom core

box bit and set the depth of cut to 5/8". See figures 5-C-2 and 5-C-3. Cut the case cavities moving from left to right inside the pattern. The guide flange will follow the pattern as the bit cuts below.

Figure 5-C-2 Rout cavity in piece.

Before removing the pattern be sure the cavity cut is smooth. Chips and saw dust tend to clog up the pattern and may need to be cleared. There should be very little sanding if this cut is done properly.

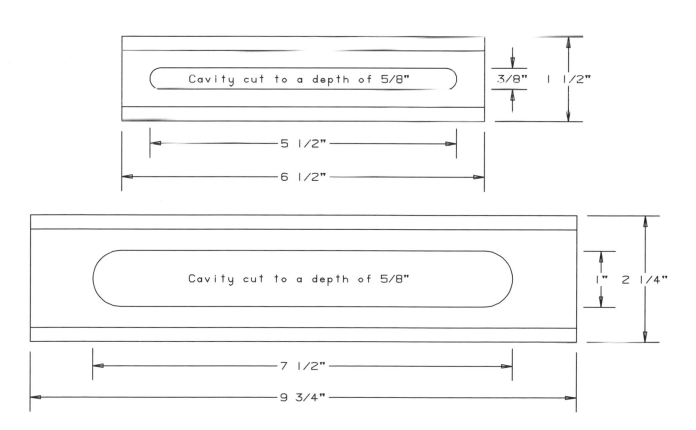

Figure 5-C-3 Single pen or two pen cavity.

Dovetails

Install the 1/2" dovetail bit in the table mounted router. Adjust the depth of cut to 3/16" using brass set up bars. See figure 5-C-4. Mount the table fence to the table, leaving 1/4" between the top corner of the dovetail bit and the fence. See figure 5-C-5.

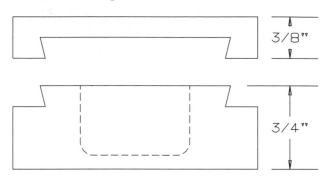

Figure 5-C-4

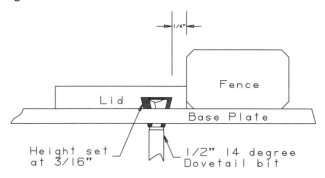

Figure 5-C-5 First cut wide case.

Cutting the lid slides

We will put the dovetail slide on the wide case first. With the edge of the lid stock against the fence run a dovetail slot through the stock. Be sure to use a push stick for these operations to enable you to exert pressure down on the stock. End for end the stock and make the second cut. See figure 5-C-6.

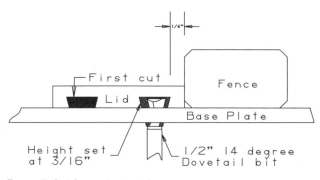

Figure 5-C-6 Second cut wide case.

Note: Direction of feed is very important when using a router. As long as the bit is cutting in wood on both sides you can expect an easy operation, as in the first two cuts. When cutting on only one side of the bit, you must exercise a little caution and be sure the material being cut is on the cutting side of the bit. You are moving into the cut and not with the cut. CAUTION: Be sure not to trap the material between the bit and the fence. Always feed into the cutting side of the router bit. See Appendix III-A-a.

Adjust the table fence to the right to split the remaining material in two passes. See figure 5-C-7. Always feed the work piece into the rotation of the cutter. See figure 5-C-8. With the lid material against the fence make the third cut. End for end the stock and make the final cut. The lid should be cleanly cut with dovetail slide edges.

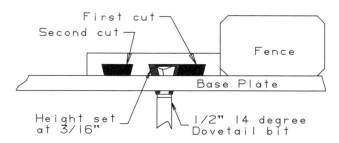

Figure 5-C-7 Split the remaining material for two cuts.

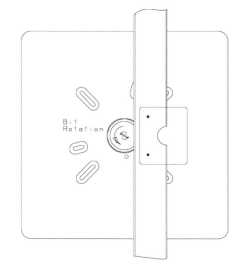

Figure 5-C-8 Rotation of cutter.

Small case

For the first pass on the small case, set the table fence 1 1/4" from the top left corner of the dovetail bit. See figure 5-C-9. Make the first cut with the small case lid stock against the fence. End for end the stock putting the other side of the lid stock against the fence for the second cut. See figure 5-C-10. This set up will ensure that you feed the work into the router bit in the right direction.

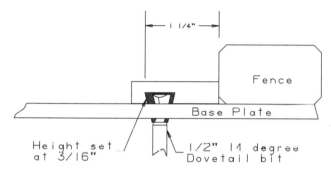

Figure 5-C-9 First cut small case.

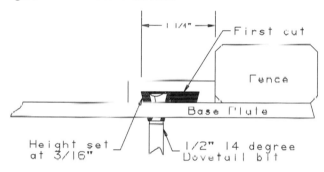

Figure 5-C-10 Second cut small case.

DO NOT CHANGE THE HEIGHT OF THE ROUTER BIT.

Base slide

Reset the table fence to cut the dovetail slide in the base stock pieces. Clamp one end of the fence to the table. Start the router and slowly swing the fence into the cutter until the dovetail bit sinks completely into the fence. This fence now acts as a chip breaker and will prevent stock tear out. See Appendix III-B-b.

Back the fence off to expose no more than 1/8" of the dovetail bit. Secure the fence in this position. With cavity side down cut a dovetail along each side of the base stock. See figure 5-C-11.

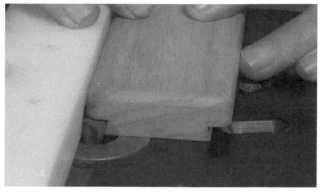

Figure 5-C-11 Dovetail the base stock.

The fit of this slide is a trial and error procedure. Use your fine adjusting tool (hammer) to move the fence slightly to the right and make successive cuts on each side of the base stock until the lid slide fits your base slide. See figure 5-C-12.

Figure 5-C-12 Check the fit.

You will be surprised how easy this trial and error method works if you remember to take small cuts and check for fit after each cut. Be careful, you can't add material, if you take off too much.

Trim and round over

Slide the lids on the respective case bases. If necessary trim the ends and joint the outside edges while both lid and bottom are slid together. Jointing may eliminate any tear out that might have occurred during the dovetailing.

Install a 1/4" round over bit in the table mounted router and position the safety pin. Set the depth of cut to expose the full 1/4" round over. Check the setting on a sample piece. When you are satisfied with the set up, round all the ends of the cases first then all the long edges. You may wish to tape the case together to prevent the lid from sliding during the rounding operation on the ends. Sand the cases and stain or finish as you desire.

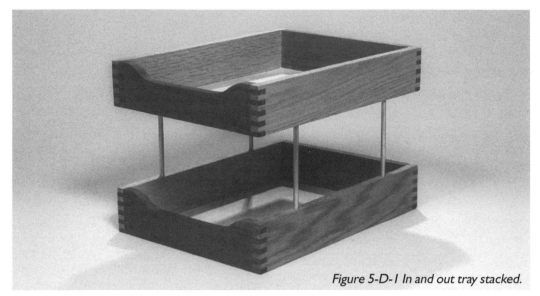

Figure 5-D-1 In and out tray stacked.

5 D. In and Out Tray

Decorate your desk with a classic wooden in and out paper tray. Match it to other desk accessories. The tray featured in this picture is constructed of two common hardwoods, Black Walnut and Red Oak. You may prefer to use the same species of wood throughout, depending on the decor of your office. The trays can be used as individual bins or can be stacked by using brass dowels to space them for easy access. See figure 5-D-1.

Project Requirements

Recommended: Oak, Walnut, Baltic Birch plywood

Material list:
2 - 2 1/2" x 13 1/4" x 1/2" oak sides
2 - 2 1/2" x 10" x 1/2" walnut ends
1 - 9 3/4" x 13" x 1/4" baltic birch ply bottom

Router tools:
Table mounted router
Table fence
1/4" spacer fence
5/8" brass guide
Brass ring nut
Shop made fixture for front end scallop

Router bits:
1/4" carbide spiral bit
1/4" carbide rabbet bit with pilot bearing
3/8" carbide spiral bit

Hardware optional:
4 - 1/4" diameter brass rods 6" long

Skill Level

	Basic			Basic Plus
X	Moderate			Advanced

Construction details in:
The skills necessary to complete the projects in this book are presented in appendixes at the back. The following skills are used in this project. You may wish to review the following appendixes before you start.

Appendix I - Choosing and Sizing Material

Appendix III-D-b. Measuring

Appendix IV-A. Box Joints

Appendix VII-G. Scallop Fixture

Appendix VII-K. Drill Fixture

How to build this project

Select the materials for this project. Joint, plane, and cut pieces to size according to the material list. Be sure all stock is cut square and to the exact size listed. Appendix I contains instructions for choosing and sizing materials.

The sides

Chuck up a 1/4" solid carbide router bit and fasten the 1/4" spacer fence over the table mounted router. Be sure the router is unplugged before changing bits or set ups. Adjust the depth of cut to slightly more than the material thickness of the sides and ends (1/2"). See Appendix III-D-b. Cut box joints in two scrap pieces and adjust the set up until you get the desired fit. See Appendix IV-A. Mark the top on each side and end piece. Clamp the two sides together and cut box joints in both ends of the sides being sure the marked side is against the fence. To prevent chipping use a push stick behind the stock. See figure 5-D-2.

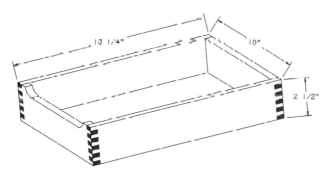

Figure 5-D-2 Box joint the ends and sides.

The ends

Fasten the off set block in place over the spacer fence. Be sure this off set block is securely clamped to the table whenever the router bit is moving. Clamp the end pieces together and with the marked (top) side against the off set block, make the first box joint slot in both ends of the end stock. Shut off the router and when the bit comes to a stop remove the off set block. Cut the remaining box joints in the ends with the top marks against the spacer fence. Dry fit the four pieces together with the marked edge up on all pieces.

Figure 5-D-3 Scallop in front of tray.

Scallop the fronts

In the front of the in and out tray there is a relief or scallop to allow easy access to the papers it holds. See figure 5-D-3. This operation entails a lot of marking, sawing, and sanding. If more than one tray is being made it is worth while to make a fixture to hold and mold these scallops. See figure 5-D-4. Directions for making this fixture are found in Appendix VII-G. The fixture is designed to allow the router bit to always

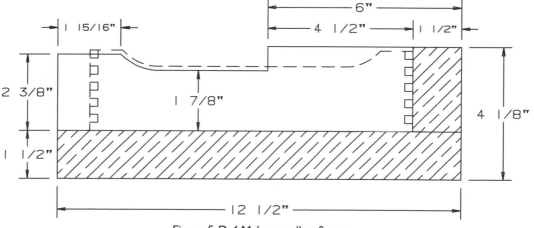

Figure 5-D-4 Make a scallop fixture.

cut with the grain of the wood. By cutting one half scallop at each pass both halves will match. This same fixture can be used to make reliefs for trays of different widths.

Choose one end piece to be the front of the tray. Mount this front piece in the scallop fixture. Make sure it is snug against the stop block at the right and the fixture back. Secure the stock with the hold downs.

Note: Be sure the hold downs are adjusted to exert good pressure on the work piece. Ensure that the lock nuts on the clamps are tight and will not vibrate loose during the cutting operation.

Mount a 3/8" solid carbide spiral bit in the table mounted router and install a 5/8" brass guide and ring nut. Set the depth of cut to cut through the thickness of the material. Turn the router on with the tail of the fixture tight against the brass guide. See figure 5-D-5. Move the fixture from left to right up to the notch in the fixture keeping pressure against the back.

Figure 5-D-5 Cut half the scallop.

Note: You may want to stop the router and then back out of the cut. End for end the work piece and secure the stock in the fixture. See figure 5-D-6. Repeat the above process to finish the scallop. The scallop pattern in the fixture will follow tight against the guide while the 3/8" bit will make a clean, smooth scallop design in the tray front. Always cut with the grain.

Figure 5-D-6 End for end the piece in the jig.

Sand the surfaces. Glue and clamp the four tray pieces together being sure the corners are square. Appendix II gives step-by-step information on clamping and gluing. Allow the glue to dry prior to proceeding.

The bottom

Chuck up the 1/4" rabbeting bit in the table mounted router. Adjust the depth of cut to the thickness of the ply bottom (1/4"). Turn the router on and allow the bit pilot to ride against the inside of the glued tray sides and ends. This will result in a clean cut 1/4" rabbet in the bottom of the tray to receive the ply bottom. The rabbeting bit leaves four rounded corners. Round the corners on the ply bottom to match the rabbet in the tray. Glue the bottom in place. Carefully sand the entire tray and apply the finish of your choice.

Stacking trays

To make stacking trays, construct a second tray and drill four 1/4" holes about 2 1/2" in from each corner in the top sides of one tray and in the bottom sides of the other tray. Install brass rods (1/4") in the tray holes to set one over the other in a stacking configuration. See figure 5-D-7. Use a drilling jig to get these just right. See Appendix VII-K.

Figure 5-D-7 Drilling jig for stacking tray.

5 E. Desk Set

Figure 5-E-1 Desk set.

A desk may quickly gather a lot of clutter. Organized storage for office necessities like pens, pencils, paper clips and note pads can eliminate the clutter and yet assure needed articles are readily at hand. This desk set provides for two pens in holders with a magnified paper clip tray and a note pad holder. See figure 5-E-1. The whole unit may serve as a paper weight.

Project Requirements

Recommended: Walnut

Also suitable: Oak

Material list:
1 - 6" x 10" x 3/4" walnut base
2 - 3" x 2" x 1/4" walnut ends
2 - 3" x 6" x 1/4" walnut sides

Router tools:
Table mounted router
Table fence
1/4" spacer fence
Small oval pattern
1" brass guide
Brass ring nut
7" base plate

Router bits:
1/4" carbide spiral bit
5/32" roman ogee bit with pilot bearing
5/8" flat bottom core box bit
1/8" round over bit with pilot bearing

Hardware:
2 - matching desk pens and holders
4 - #4 x 1" flat head wood screws

Skill Level

	Basic			Basic Plus
X	Moderate			Advanced

Construction details in:

The skills necessary to complete the projects in this book are presented in appendixes at the back. The following skills are used in this project. You may wish to review the following appendixes before you start.

Appendix I - Choosing and Sizing Material

Appendix III- A-a. Direction of Feed
A-b. Order of Cut

Appendix III- B-b. Chip Breaker
B-c. Isolate Bearing

Appendix III- D-b. Measuring

Appendix IV- A. Box Joints

Appendix VII- F. Sub Top

How to build this project

Choose the wood for this project. Joint, plane and cut all materials to size according to the material list. Be sure all stock is cut square to the exact size listed. See figure 5-E-2. Appendix I contains instructions on choosing and sizing materials.

The oval cavity

Secure the base block to the sub top with corner blocks. See Appendix VII-F. The sub top provides a work surface that can be nailed or routed without damage to the router table top. Secure the small oval pattern to the base block with double stick tape. Be sure the pattern is centred lengthwise on the base and about 15/16" from the front edge. See figure 5-E-3.

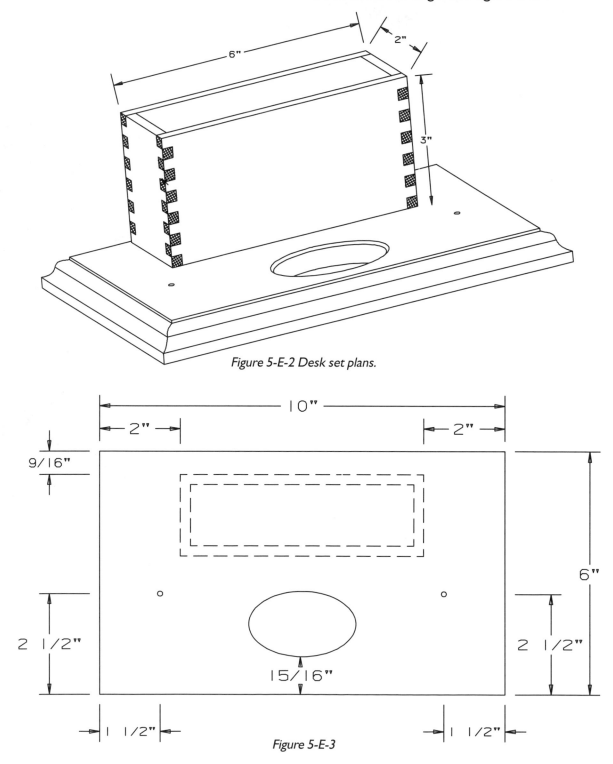

Figure 5-E-2 Desk set plans.

Figure 5-E-3

Cut the cavity

Chuck up the flat bottom core box bit with a 7" base plate on the router. Install the 1" guide with the ring nut to the base plate. This operation is an internal pattern rout and works best with a plunge router. Set the depth of cut to 5/8" (use brass set up bars). Moving from left to right, plunge the bit into the cut with the guide flange against the edge of the pattern. Moving slowly, cut out the oval shape. Stop periodically to clear the cut of debris. Continue to rout the oval cavity until the bottom and sides are smooth. This will leave a 1/8" thick bottom in the oval. Do not remove the pattern until you are satisfied with the cavity. There should be little or no sanding to do.

Molding the base

Set up the table mounted router with a 5/32" roman ogee bit. Adjust the depth of cut to expose the full profile of the bit and about 1/16" more. Set the table fence to isolate the bearing and provide chip breaking. See Appendix III-B-b and c. Test the set up by running a sample piece. See figure 5-E-4. Cut a roman ogee mold around the base stock. Remember direction of feed and always cut across the grain first. Making the final cut with the grain will clean up the cross grain cuts. See Appendix III-A-a and b.

Figure 5-E-4 Mold base.

Box joints

Chuck up the 1/4" spiral bit in the table mounted router. Position the 1/4" spacer fence over the table. Set the depth of cut to the thickness of the material (slightly more than 1/4") being used to make the note paper storage bin. See Appendix III-D-b. Check the settings by making a box joint in two sample pieces. When you are satisfied with the fit, run box joints in the sides

and ends of the note storage bin. Because the sides and ends are different sizes they will have to be routed in pairs. See Appendix IV-A. Dry fit the pieces. Glue and clamp the bin pieces together. Be sure it is square. It will not require a bottom as it will be fastened to the base.

Round the edges

Chuck up the 1/8" round over bit in the table mounted router and set the depth of cut to pick up the full round. Use a test piece to check the setup. Put the oval cavity in the base over the bit and cut a 1/8" round on the top face of the oval. See figure 5-E-5.

Figure 5-E-5 Round top edge of oval.

Using the same bit, set up and cut a round over both inside and outside the top edge of the bin. See figure 5-E-6. When making the outside cut remember to install the safety pin.

Figure 5-E-6 Round top of bin.

Locate and drill holes in the base for the pen holders. Drill screw holes in the base to mount the bin according to the plan.

Sand and finish the desk set.

A finishing tip: Screw the bin to the base before applying the finish but mount the pen holders after the project is completely finished.

5 F. Old Style Pencil Box

Figure 5-F-1 Pencil box.

Project Requirements

Recommended: Oak

Also suitable: Other close-grained hardwoods

Material list:
3- 2 1/2" x 10" x 3/4" exactly sized
1- 2 1/4" x 10" x 3/16" lid size

Router tools:
Table mounted router
Pattern jig
Pencil box pattern
Double stick tape
Ring nut
1" guide
3/4" guide

Router bits:
1/2" straight bit
1/2" 14 degree dovetail bit
5/8" flat bottom bit(optional)

Furniture blocks:
We need to make some blocks which will hold the pencil box material tight in the jig. Here is a list of the necessary blocks. They can be made out of any kind of wood. Hardwood is ideal as it will last longer when making more boxes.
2 - 1/4" X 12" X 3/4" exactly
3 - 2 1/2" X 2" X 3/4" exactly

Skill Level			
Basic			Basic Plus
Moderate		X	Advanced

One other thing which comes in handy when making the pencil box is a plywood support block. This is a piece of 1/4" plywood cut to fit between the slats on the bottom of the pattern jig. This will support any block in the jig which does not reach across the slats. Note: Make sure that the plywood does not stick out past the pattern jig slats or the jig will not fit into the table top. Here is the proper size.
1 - 7 3/4" X 10 7/8" X 1/4" plywood

Pencil box material:
This pencil box uses dovetail slides and needs material which will wear nicely. This eliminates soft woods because they do not wear as well.

Construction details in:
The skills necessary to complete the projects in this book are presented in appendixes at the back. The following skills are used in this project. You may wish to review the following appendixes before you start.

Appendix V - D. Pattern Cutting

Before the development of zippers and plastic, pencils were stored and carried in wooden boxes. The basic pencil box consisted of two blocks with pockets cut in them to hold the pencils. The top block had a dovetail sliding lid with the top block being allowed to swing to the right for access to the bottom block when the lid was open. In some cases a third block was added on the bottom with a dovetail slide. See figure 5-F-1.

This is a three-block pencil box. It will be 2 1/2" x 10" x 1 7/8" when assembled. The bottom block will slide open on a dovetail. The top block will have a sliding dovetail lid and will swing to the right to allow access to the middle block. The top block will have three pockets, the middle block two and the bottom block one.

A note of challenge

This project is not an easy one. Because of the close tolerances needed between compartments and the thin webs of wood left, the woodworker must be very precise in stock sizing and use of jigs and cutters.

How to build this project

The first step is to place the plywood support block into the top then place the pattern jig in the table plate hole. The plywood is now trapped under the pattern jig. Now place the furniture blocks into the pattern jig as shown in the diagram below. Then put the pencil box material into the jig as shown in the same diagram. See figure 5-F-2. Now slide the pencil box pattern into the pattern jig. See figure 5-F-3. Lock the pattern into place with the safety guide pin in position B.

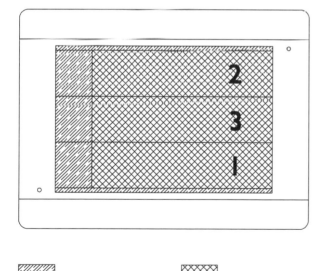

Figure 5-F-3 Slide pattern over stock.

Getting started

The numbers on the blocks shown in figure 5-F-2 relate to the number of pockets in each block. They will also serve to identify the blocks when discussed in this text. Therefore when we are talking about the block with three pockets, this would be the block pictured with a 3. Marking these numbers on the blocks with a pencil may help to keep track of them.

Set up the router with a 1/2" straight bit and a 1" guide. Make sure that the 1/2" bit is centred in the guide. Set the depth of cut to leave a bottom in each compartment. You may want to use a 5/8" flat bottom core box bit instead of the 1/2" router bit. If you use this bit, care should be taken when cutting multiple pockets as there will be less material left between the pockets.

Furniture Blocks   Pencil Box Material

Figure 5-F-2 Block material in pattern jig.

Note: Although the stock is 3/4" thick, you want to cut to a depth of only 5/8". It is best to do this in three cuts, cleaning out the cavity several times while making each cut. Make the first cut 1/4" deep, then add another 1/4" in depth for the second cut and a final 1/8" in depth for the last one. See figure 5-F-4. Rout out three compartments as shown.

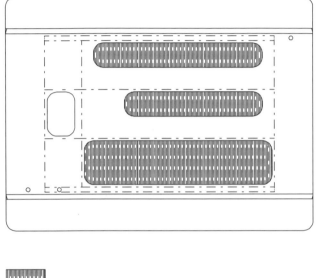

Cut these pockets.

Figure 5-F-4 Rout out three compartments.

Use a vacuum

A vacuum is a helpful tool to clean the chips out of the pencil pockets. The wood chips created by the router will clog the pattern so the guide may not be following tight to the pattern. Therefore you should rout around the pattern once after vacuuming the wood chips from the pencil pockets. This will ensure that the pattern was followed tightly by the guide. See figure 5-F-5.

Slide the pencil box pattern out of the jig. Now move the pencil blocks to the positions shown in figure 5-F-6. Slide the pencil box pattern back to the previous position. Using the same method as before cut the pencil pockets shown in figure 5-F-7.

Figure 5-F-5 Completed parts ready for assembly.

Note: The pockets that have been cut are indicated on the diagrams.

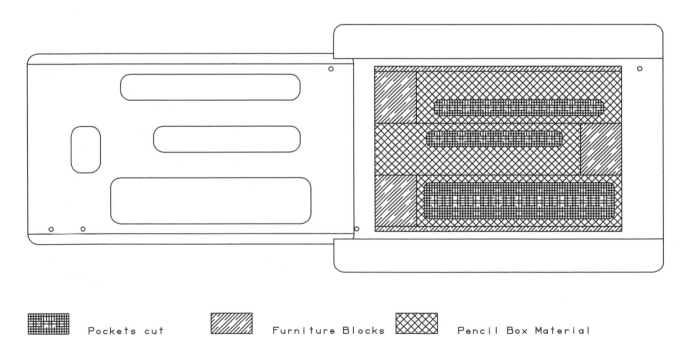

Pockets cut   Furniture Blocks   Pencil Box Material

Figure 5-F-6 Rearrange blocks in the jig.

Again slide the pencil box pattern out of the jig. Move the pencil blocks to the positions shown in figure 5-F-8. Slide the pattern to locking hole A in the pattern. See figure 5-F-9. Cut the last pencil pocket. All the compartments are now routed.

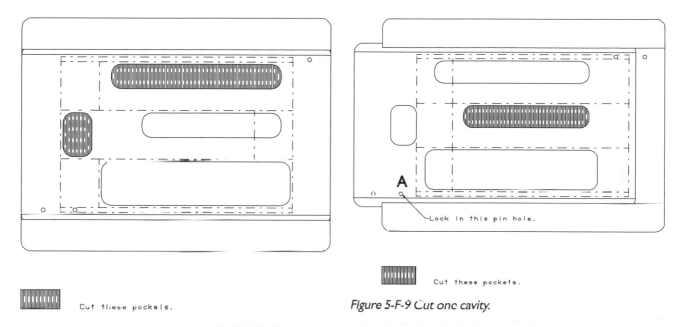

Cut these pockets.

Figure 5-F-9 Cut one cavity.

Cut these pockets.

Figure 5-F-7 Rout two cavities.

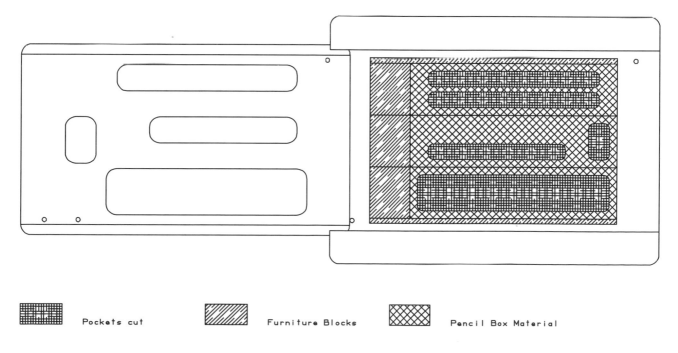

Pockets cut   Furniture Blocks   Pencil Box Material

Figure 5-F-8 Rearrange the blocks in the jig.

Cutting   dovetails

Leaving the jig set, change the bit in the router to the 1/2" dovetail bit. Now change the 1" guide to the 3/4" guide and again make certain that the bit is centred in the guide. Set the depth of cut to 3/16".

Note: You may have to adjust the height of the bit until you get a good fit. Use a scrap block of wood to test your height adjustments before you cut your good material.

Remember that the dovetail bit is not a plunge type bit therefore you will have to start the routing from a pocket. Cut and clean the area shown in figure 5-F-10. You will be cutting one of the furniture blocks but keep in mind that it is only necessary to clean the pencil box material. In other words we have to cut the furniture block in order to clean the pencil box material out that end.

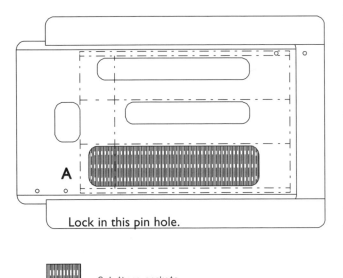

Lock in this pin hole.

|▓▓▓▓▓▓▓| Cut these pockets.

Figure 5-F-10 Clean with dovetail bit.

Now unlock the pencil box pattern and slide it in to the locking hole A. Lock the pattern in place and cut and clean the same pocket. You should now have a dovetail ledge on three sides of the pencil box block. The ledge should be about equal on all three sides. This ledge creates a hole which will accept the lid or another level of the box.

Changing   blocks

Slide the pattern out of the pattern jig. Now exchange the pencil block which has the three pockets (number 3) with the block we just cut the dovetail in (number 1). Slide the pattern to the locking hole A and cut and clean this block the same as before. Then move to locking hole B and again cut and clean as before.

The pencil pockets have now been cut into the pencil blocks. The next step is to cut a dovetail groove on the bottom of the second block. This is so the third block will slide onto the second. The same process will be used to make a lid for the top block.

Dovetail   groove

This next process will be done with the router set up in a table. Set up the table mounted router with the 1/2" dovetail bit. Then mount the 3/4" guide making sure that the 1/2" dovetail bit is centred in the guide. Now set the depth of cut to 3/16". Remember that there will be a 1/4" pattern on the bottom of the material. Again it is important that the depth of cut be 3/16".

Make set up blocks

If you plan to make other boxes of similar design in the future, cut some set up blocks for the depth of cut. This will make the set up a lot faster next time.

The next step requires the pencil lid pattern and some double stick tape. Take the block with two pockets and stick the lid pattern on the bottom using the tape. It is important that the pattern be centred with the distance at the round end the same as the two sides. Therefore the distance from the edge of the pattern to the edge of the block is equal on the three sides. See figure 5-F-11.

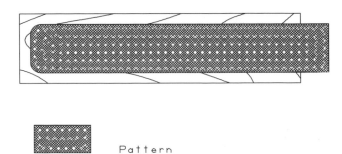

|▓▓▓▓| Pattern

Figure 5-F-11 Lid pattern attached to 2 compartment block.

Note: It is advised that this step be done on a scrap block first in order to set the proper depth of the bit.

To cut the dovetail in the bottom of the block, place the pattern on the table. See figure 5-F-12. The pattern will now follow the guide in the base plate. The dovetail bit will cut a dovetail on the three sides which have wood exposed around the pattern. If the height of the bit is correct this block will fit in the dovetail slide in the bottom block of the pencil box (number 1). Therefore you should try cutting this dovetail on a scrap block to get the fit right first.

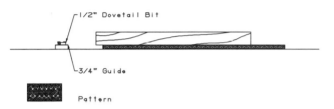

Figure 5-F-12 Cut dovetails in block bottom.

Checking the fit

Remember if the block slides tight or is a tight fit the bit was too high. Therefore if you lower the bit the fit gets looser. AGAIN cut a scrap block to fit first then cut the pencil box block after you know it will fit. It is harder to make a new pencil box block than to use a piece of scrap.

You make the pencil box lid the same way only you use a block that is 3/16" thick. You would mount the lid on the pattern the same way as the block. Then once mounted follow the same actions to produce the lid. The lid slides in the dovetail slide of the block with the three pockets (number 3).

A thumb pull

To complete the pencil box lid we need a thumb pull. This is so we have some way of getting a hold of the lid to slide open the box. What we have found to work nicely is to use a large drill bit (1/2" drill bit). Chuck the bit into a drill press and drill a divot in the lid.

Note: Remember do NOT drill a hole. Just drill to the edge of the drill bit. This will create a smooth divot or thumb pull. This thumb pull can be drilled in the lid at a convenient location.

The mitre cut

The top pencil block must be made to swing open after sliding the lid back. This is so we can gain access to the second pencil block pockets (number 2). In order to do this we are going to cut a compound mitre in the top pencil block (number 3). See figure 5-F-13. Be sure to use a thin-kerf blade (a Japanese hand saw is good) to make the cut. With a compound mitre the block will wedge shut before the lid slides across to lock it from swinging open.

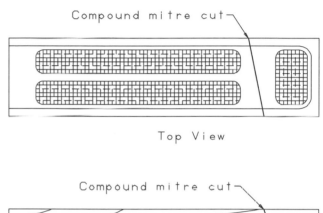

Figure 5-F-13 Cut a compound mitre.

The pivot hole

We now have to drill a pivot hole in the top pencil block in order to swing the block open. This hole should be large enough to allow a 1" flat head screw to slide through snugly. Then we must counter sink the head of the screw below the surface to allow the lid to slide freely. See figure 5-F-14. The hole should be located at the end of the two pockets opposite the compound mitre and centred.

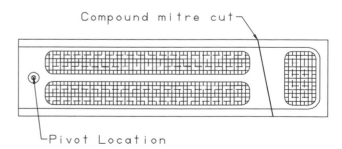

Figure 5-F-14 Drill the pivot hole.

Assembly

The small piece of the top block with the one pocket is glued to the top of the second block. See figure 5-F-15. Set the small block on the top of the second block and lightly draw a line on the second block. This line will now indicate where the glue should be applied. Apply the glue to the top of the second block. If you apply the glue to the bottom of the small block you would glue over the pockets of the second block. This would be hard to clean. See figure 5-F-16.

The next step is to screw the other top block (the large piece) to the second block. Start by sliding the top block tight at the compound mitre. Flush the top block and the second block. Now using a smaller drill bit than the screw to be used, drill a pilot hole. Screw the top block to

the second block. Make sure that the top block is free to swing open.

Slide the lid into the top block when it is swung shut. Slide the bottom block onto the second block. Sand the box as necessary to flush the sides and for a smooth finish. Your pencil box is now complete.

This pencil box can be used for other purposes such as a jewelery box. One could add as many blocks as wanted to the bottom of the box or use a block for the sliding lid. This would give you a box with the middle block swinging open for access to the bottom block. The top block would form the lid for the middle block with the sliding lid to open it. The box is only limited to your imagination.

Finish the item with the method of your choice.

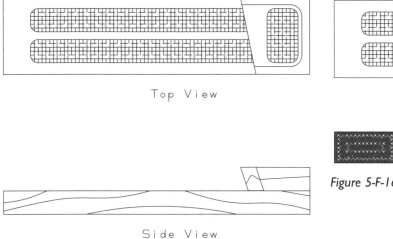

Top View

Side View

Figure 5-F-15 *Position the mitred compartment over the 2 compartment block.*

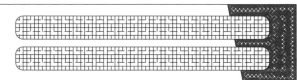

Glue

Figure 5-F-16 *Apply glue to compartment block.*

Notes:

Figure 5-G-1 Angle clock.

5 G. Clock

Simple contrasting wood pieces fastened with decorative joinery can produce an exciting project with very little work. This unique clock idea incorporates two contrasting materials such as Walnut and Maple with 30 degree box joints. See figure 5-G-1. This same procedure could be used to produce a table picture frame with either an oval or heart shape opening. What ever you wish to do with this idea, follow the directions to make the clock pictured here. If only one kind of wood is available the project is still attractive.

Project Requirements

Recommended: Walnut, Maple

Also suitable: Cedar

Material list:
 2 - 4 7/8" x 5 7/16" x 5/8" one piece walnut and the other maple

Router tools:
 Table mounted router
 3/8" spacer fence
 Table fence

Router bits:
 3/8" carbide spiral bit
 1 1/4" plunging round over bit
 1/4" round over with pilot bearing

Hardware:
 Clock face with works

Skill Level

	Basic		Basic Plus
X	Moderate		Advanced

Construction details in:
 The skills necessary to complete the projects in this book are presented in appendixes at the back. The following skills are used in this project. You may wish to review the following appendixes before you start.

Appendix I - Choosing and Sizing Material

Appendix III- A-d. Safety Pin

Appendix III- B-e. Table Fence

Appendix IV- C. Angle Box Joint

How to build this project

Choose, joint, and plane the material. See Appendix I. Cut the pieces to width according to the cut list.

Cut a 30 degree angle on one end of each piece of stock using the radial arm saw. Now cut both pieces to length. See material list.

Lay out the centre of the stock that will receive the clock face and drill the round hole to fit the clock works.

Angle box joints

Set up the router table with a 3/8" spacer fence and a 3/8" solid carbide spiral bit. Following directions for box joints make angled box joints in the angled end of each piece of stock. See Appendix IV-C. Use a shop designed push stick to hold your pieces during this operation. Remember to offset the pieces. Always mark the fence side of the pieces before you cut. See figure 5-G-2.

Figure 5-G-2 Fence side marked.

Round corners

Set up the router table with a 1 1/4" plunge round over bit and the table fence. Set the depth of cut and the fence to expose a smooth round over.

Round the four corners opposite to the box joints cut previously. See figure 5-G-3. Use a push stick to keep the material perpendicular to the fence and prevent tear out. See Appendix III-B-e.

Figure 5-G-3 Round the corners.

Dry fit

Dry fit the 30 degree box joint. Mark the project for the stopped 1/4" round over process. You do not want to round over into the joint.

Set up the router table with a pilot bearing 1/4" round over bit. Set the depth of cut to make a smooth round over. Install the safety guide pin in the router plate. See Appendix III-A-d. See figure 5-G-4.

Figure 5-G-4 Round over edges using a safety pin.

Round all exterior corners following the marks indicating the stopped round overs. Do not round into the box joints. Round the back rim of the clock hole.

The finishing touches

Glue and clamp the box joint. Clean away the glue and finish sand the project. Finish the wood surface with the procedure of your choice. Install the clock face and works. You now have an attractive clock for your desk, on a table or over the TV.

Unit 6
KIDS CORNER

These projects are for kids, big kids and little kids. Things to ride in, things to play with, and things to look at. Make something for the grandchildren or get them to help you make a wagon. Sturdy basic construction is a must to ensure that the play things are safe and will last past the first ride. Make a monkey finder and turn it on yourself. Above all have fun making unique, wooden products that are sturdy and beautiful.

What you will learn in this section

When you build the projects listed in Kids Corner, you will be practicing, on a larger scale, many of the skills you have honed by constructing other, smaller items. Even the initial monkey finder is more difficult than it appears at first glance. By building on a larger scale, you will gain confidence and satisfaction with your work. The wheel barrow is both attractive and practical, as are the table and stools. You may wonder if the wagon is strong enough to stand up to everyday use. It is. Your reward for these projects will be found in the eyes of the recipients.

KIDS
CORNER

6A Monkey finder.

6B Wheel barrow.

6C Table and stools.

6D Wagon.

Figure 6-A-1 Monkey finder.

6 A. Monkey Finder

This is just a novelty. We are not sure who named it a monkey finder but rightly so. Just look in the little mirror. See figure 6-A-1. This item needs a well constructed fixture to accomplish the external guide cut necessary for quantity production.

Project Requirements

Recommended: Walnut

Also suitable: Cedar

Material list:
  1 - 2 1/4" x 2 7/8" x 1/4" any wood blank

Router tools:
  Table mounted router
  5/8" brass guide and ring nut
  Safety pin
  Shop made jig See Appendix VII-E

Router bits:
  1/2" spiral bit or 1/2" thumbnail bit

Hardware:
  1 - 1" diameter mirror
  Double stick tape

Skill Level			
	Basic		Basic Plus
X	Moderate		Advanced

Construction details in:
  The skills necessary to complete the projects in this book are presented in appendixes at the back. The following skills are used in this project. You may wish to review the following appendixes before you start.

Appendix I - Choosing and Sizing Material

Appendix V - D. Pattern Cutting External

Appendix VII-E. Monkey Finder Fixture

The challenge here is the fixture and how to use it. It is not advisable to start external routing with this project. Practice with a larger fixture like the mirror frame.

How to build this project

Choose the wood for this project. Joint, plane and cut all materials to size according to the material list. Be sure all stock is cut square to the exact size listed. See figure 6-A-2. Appendix I contains instructions on choosing and sizing materials. Construct the needed external guide work fixture. See Appendix VII-E.

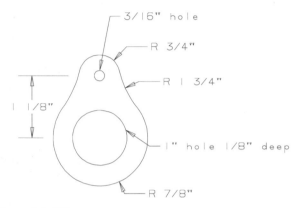

Figure 6-A-2 Plan.

Cut the blank material to the size required. Prepare the stock by putting a 3/16" hole right through the stock in the position indicated. Make a 1" diameter recess 1/8" deep with a forstner bit where indicated. See figure 6-A-3.

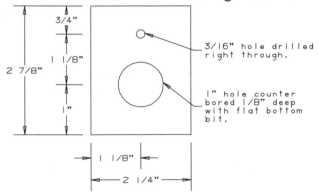

Figure 6-A-3 Blank preparation.

Chuck up the 1/2" spiral or thumbnail bit in the table mounted router. Install the 5/8" brass guide securely with the ring nut. Mount the prepared stock in the monkey finder fixture. Adjust the depth of cut to slightly above the stock material for the 1/2" spiral. If you wish to round the

piece while cutting the shape use a thumbnail bit. See figure 6-A-4. Centre the thumbnail on the blank material.

Figure 6-A-4 Thumbnail bit.

With the safety pin in place start with the largest diameter of the fixture and blank facing the bit and the right side snug against the safety pin. Make sure your hands are above the guard on the fixture. Cut the excess material off allowing the fixture to follow the brass guide completely around the fixture. See figure 6-A-5.

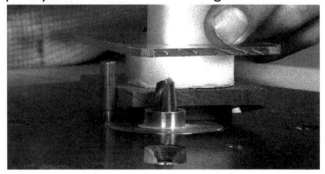

Figure 6-A-5 Pattern of fixture used against the guide.

Remove the monkey finder from the jig. Sand and stain or finish as you wish. Fasten the 1" mirror in the recessed cavity with double stick tape. Look in the mirror and see the monkey! Great for kids.

Put another blank in the fixture and rout one after the other until you have a dozen. See figure 6-A-6.

Figure 6-A-6 Fixture and blank part.

Figure 6-B-1 Wheel barrow

6 B. Wheel Barrow

The wheel barrow may be used for what it is designed for, or as a toy or display item. Kids will have fun learning to haul things in their wheel barrow. It is a good place to display plants, since it can be moved easily from one part of the house or yard to another. See figure 6-B-1.

How to build this project

Choose the wood for the project. Joint, plane and cut all materials to size according to the material list. Be sure all stock is cut square to the exactly size listed. Appendix I contains instructions on choosing and sizing materials.

Most materials are listed in rough measurements because they have to be cut to shape.

BE SURE TO COMPLETE ANY LAMINATING OR EDGE GLUING FIRST.

Some of the cuts in this project require the use of a framing square. Refer to Appendix III-D-h to make sure your framing square is really square.

Project Requirements

Recommended: Maple

Also suitable: Cedar

Material list:
    1 - 14"x14"x7/8" maple wheel
    2 - 1 3/4"x46"x1" maple handles
    2 - 4"x11"x1" maple legs
    2 - 4"x4"x1" maple leg brackets
    2 - 5"x 13 5/8"x1" maple stretchers
    1 - 19"x20 3/4"x1/2" plywood bucket bottom
    1 - 10"x13 3/4"x3/4" maple bucket front
    2 - 6 3/4"x21 1/2"x3/4" maple bucket sides
    1 - 3 3/4"x19 5/8"x3/4" maple bucket back

Router tools:
    Table mounted router
    Table fence
    Brass insert and ring nut
    3/8" spacer fence
    1" brass guide and ring nut
    12" standard wheel jig
    Sub top for table
    7" base plate

Router bits:
    1/2" 14 degree dovetail bit
    1/4" round over bit with pilot bearing
    1" bull nose bit
    3/8" spiral bit
    1/2" spiral bit
    3/8" rabbeting bit with pilot bearing

Skill Level

	Basic		Basic Plus
	Moderate	X	Advanced

Hardware:
    1 - 1/4" x 4 1/2" machine bolt
    4 - 1/4" x 2 1/2" machine bolts
    5 - 1/4" hex nuts
    12 - 1/4" flat washers
    2 - #8 x 1 3/4" wood screws
    16 - #6 x 1 1/4" wood screws

Construction details in:
    The skills necessary to complete the projects in this book are presented in appendixes at the back. The following skills are used in this project. You may wish to review the following appendixes before you start.

Appendix I - Choosing and Sizing Material

Appendix II - Gluing and Clamping

Appendix III- B. Table Fence Set Up
            D. Measuring

Appendix IV - Box Joints

Appendix V - C. Wheel Jig

Appendix VII- F. Sub Top

The handles

Although this assembly may look complicated it is not. Start with the handles themselves. Refer to figures 6-B-2a and 6-B-2b. The end of each handle used to form the wheel bracket is cut as shown in these figures, using the framing square to get the right angle. After making the cut simply reverse the short piece and glue it, using clamps, in the position shown.

Before gluing you will probably want to round over the front edge of the longer handle piece, as shown in figure 6-B-2b. Shown in the figure is a 7/8" round over which can be cut using a band saw and then sanded smooth. This could also be done using a round over bit. After gluing you will want to drill the holes for mounting the wheel and to attach the leg assembly to the handles. The locations are shown on the drawings.

To finish off the handles, chuck up a 1" bull nose bit and, using the table mount with the full half round of the bit exposed, run in about 8" of the handle ends to make the handle grips. If you do not have a bull nose bit use a 1/2" quarter round bit and round all four corners. This cut is shown in a cross section in figure 6-B-2a.

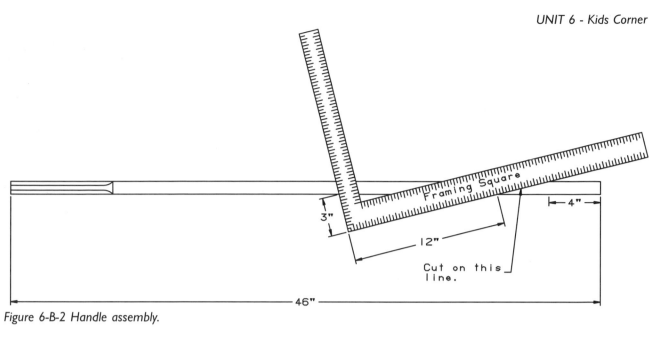

Figure 6-B-2 Handle assembly.

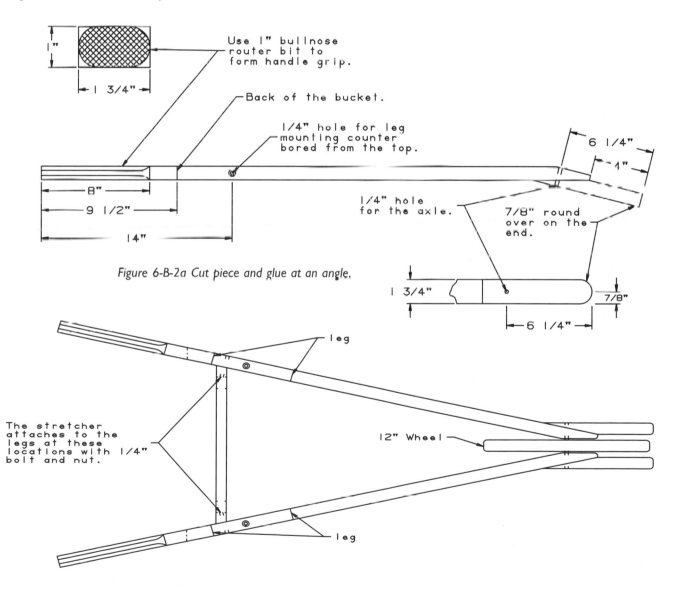

Figure 6-B-2a Cut piece and glue at an angle.

Figure 6-B-2b Handle and wheel assembly.

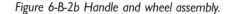

Legs and stretcher

To complete the handle assembly you will need legs, supporting brackets and a stretcher to separate the handles.

First, rough cut the legs and the support brackets to the size indicated on the material list. Cut the dovetail joints before cutting these pieces to the shape as indicated in the plan.

Chuck up a 1/2" dovetail bit in the table mounted router. Install the insert and ring nut and position the table fence to the right of the bit with 1/2" between the centre of the bit and the fence. Using a brass set-up bar, set the depth of the cut to 3/8".

Cut dovetail slots along one long edge of each leg, making the cuts just long enough to accommodate a bracket.

Cut the brackets to fit into this slot. Remember, DO NOT CHANGE THE HEIGHT OF THE DOVETAIL BIT. Make sure the cut is made on the side of the bracket where the grain will provide the most strength. See figure 6-B-3.

Reset the table fence to expose a small portion of the dovetail bit.

Cut the dovetail pins on the brackets by cutting first one side and then the other. Using this method will create a dovetail pin centred on the bracket.

Start by cutting the pin too large, (make just a small cut on each side) and then, tapping the fence with your fine adjustment tool (a hammer) to expose more of the bit, make the pin smaller. See figure 6-B-4.

Remember when using this method that you can always cut deeper but there is no way you can add back if you cut too deep.

When you get the fit you want, glue and clamp the bracket to the legs. When the glue has set cut each leg to the shape indicated on the plans. See figure 6-B-5.

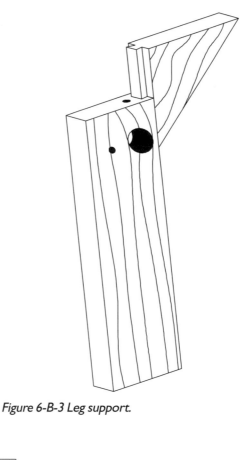

Figure 6-B-3 Leg support.

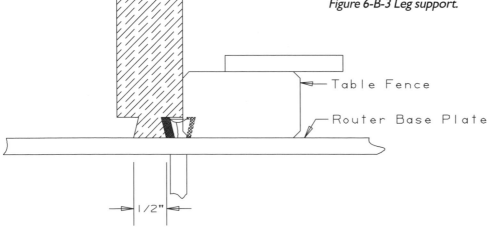

Figure 6-B-4 Setup to cut dovetail pins.

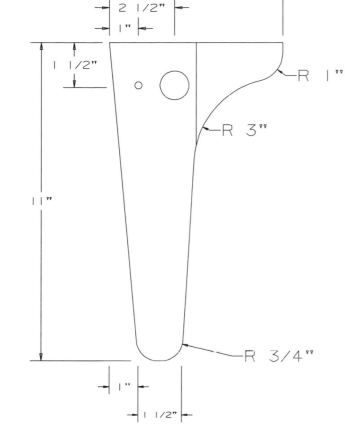

Figure 6-B-5 Leg bracket.

The stretcher

This is straight forward. The angle cuts on the ends can be determined by using your framing square to make the same 3" x 12" angle you used to cut the handles. Perhaps you made yourself a little jig when you determined this cut on the handles. The holes that are indicated are designed to accept the assembly bolts. See figure 6-B-6.

Assembly

Before assembly it is a good idea to round over exposed edges, using the same method described later in the finishing of the bucket. Then simply bolt the leg assembly to the handles and bolt the stretcher in place. See figures 6-B-7 and 6-B-12 on page 6-12.

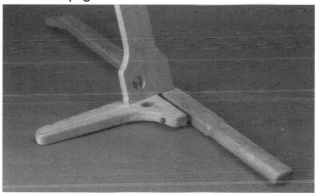

Figure 6-B-7 Leg, handle and stretcher.

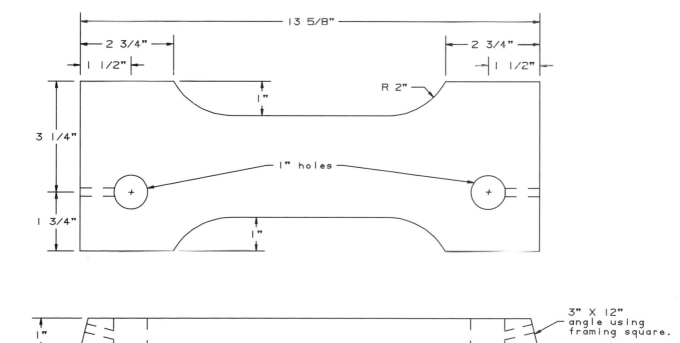

Figure 6-B-6 Shape the stretcher.

Making the wheel

Use the sub top over the router table, secure the wheel stock to this sub top and position the wheel jig over the stock on the centre pin. Chuck up a 1/2" spiral bit in your portable, plunge router. Install the 7" base plate with a 1" guide secured with a ring nut. Check to make sure the bit is centred in the guide. Refer to Appendix V-C for instructions on producing a wheel. Cut the spoke holes first and finally the outside of the wheel. To finish, use a 1/4" round over bit with bearing and safety pin to round over the outside of the wheel, and then, without the safety pin, round over all inside edges of the spoke cavities.

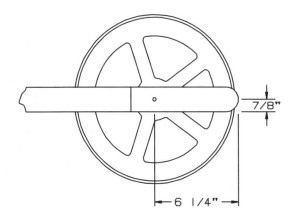

Figure 6-B-8 Wheel.

Mounting the wheel

The wheel is mounted as shown in figure 6-B-8. Use a machine bolt and be sure to use spacer washers, tightening just enough to allow the wheel to turn freely.

The bucket

Look at all the pictures and drawings carefully on pages 6-12 and 6-13. The bucket is not a regular shape. Its irregularity makes it more attractive. See figure 6-B-9. Because the back is wider than the front the required box joints will have to be cut on an angle. Begin by standing each piece on your work bench and noting (and marking) how the angles will be cut.

Figure 6-B-9 Bucket.

Making angle box joints is covered fully in the appendix section IV-D. It is always a good idea to practice on scrap wood before making the final cuts.

To construct the bucket you will need a support block, 1 1/2" thick, cut to the same angle as the pieces on one end and the reverse of this angle on the other end. This will guide you in making both left and right hand pieces. Make this support block first and mark the ends so that you will know which end makes which joint. Check the accuracy of your support block on scrap wood.

Remember, the box joints are NOT cut all the way on all ends. Mark your pieces with a pencil to remind yourself of this when you are cutting. Also mark in pencil the bottom of each piece as a guide to where all the cuts begin. See Appendix IV-D.

How it works

FRONT PIECE - cut box joints on each end up to 6" from the bottom.

BACK PIECE - cut box joints all the way along each end.

SIDES - cut box joints all the way along the front ends but only 3 3/4" up on the back ends.

If this is not entirely clear study the drawing 6-B-12 on page 6-12 until you understand what you are about to do.

Making the cuts

Chuck up a 3/8" spiral bit in the table mounted router. Install the insert, ring nut and the 3/8" spacer fence. Set the depth of the cut to slighty more than the thickness of the material, using set-up bars. In each case, CHECK WITH SCRAP MATERIAL before making actual cuts. Make the cuts in the sides first, then the front and back paying particular attention to the stop marks you have put on the pieces. Test fit the pieces, then dry fit and clamp, checking to make sure your bucket is the same shape as the bottom.

Adding the bottom

The dimensions of the bottom is shown in the drawing . See figure 6-B-11. However, to get the best fit, first cut the rabbet inside the bottom of the bucket before finishing the bottom to exact size.

Chuck up a 3/8" rabbeting bit in the table mounted router. Set the depth of cut to match the thickness of the bottom material. Place the dry fit and clamped bucket on the router table bottom down and using the pilot bit, rout a recess cut to accept the bottom piece. Caution: make sure the clamps are secure.You might want to complete this cut by doing it twice, once with the depth about half the thickness of the bottom and the second time with the depth exactly right.

Make the straight cuts to bring the bottom to size first.The corners can be cut accurately by chucking up a 5/8" round over bit in the table mounted router. Adjust the fence until the bit cuts just a round over, but no profile, in a scrap piece cut to the same angle as the bottom piece. Then, using a backing block and the fence for a guide, stand the bottom on edge and feed it through the round over bit. The resulting cut should fit exactly into the rounded corner left by the 1/2" rabbetting bit used to cut the recess in the glued up box.

Glue and clamp the sides of the bucket together. Then screw the bottom in place.

Finishing off

Chuck up a 1/4" round over bit in the table mounted router. Adjust the depth to the full profile, but do not leave a profile line. Using the safety pin, round over all the outside edges of the wheel barrow parts. Sand all parts.

Screw the bucket to the handle assembly. Sand again and stain. Happy wheel barrowing.

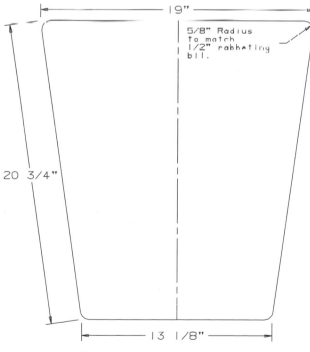

Figure 6-B-11 Bottom in bucket.

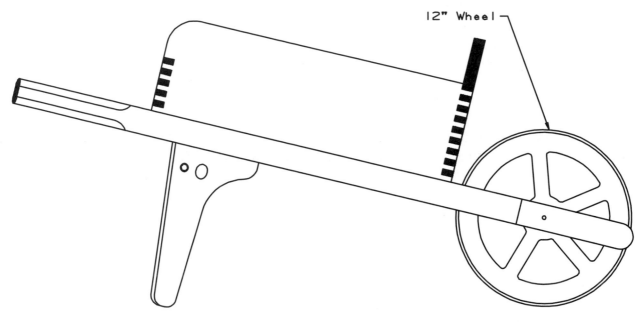

12" Wheel

Figure 6-B-12 Wheel, leg and handle assembly.

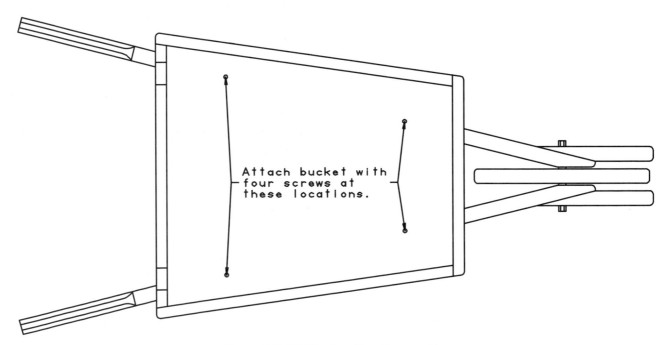

Attach bucket with
four screws at
these locations.

Figure 6-B-13 Wheel and handle assembly.

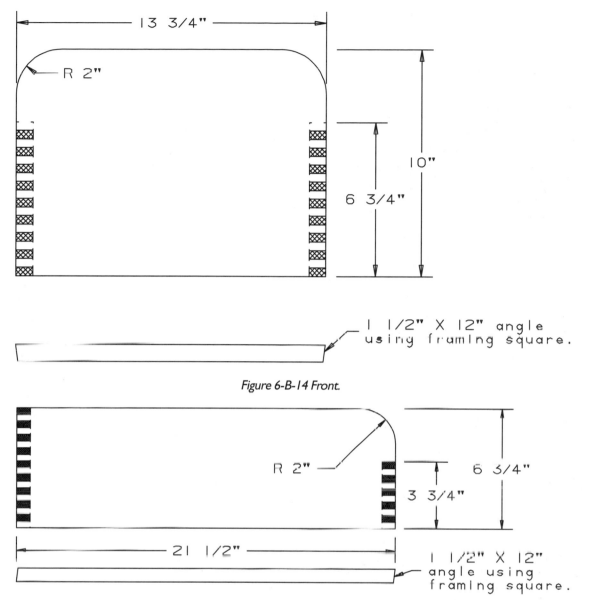

13 3/4"

R 2"

10"

6 3/4"

1 1/2" X 12" angle using framing square.

Figure 6-B-14 Front.

R 2"

6 3/4"

3 3/4"

21 1/2"

1 1/2" X 12" angle using framing square.

Figure 6-B-14a Sides.

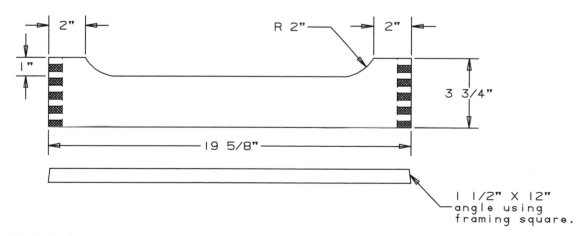

2"

R 2"

2"

1"

3 3/4"

19 5/8"

1 1/2" X 12" angle using framing square.

Figure 6-B-14b Back.

6 C. Table and Stools

Children need a place to play games, draw pictures, and talk with their friends. This set is built to their special size needs. This table and stool set is sturdy, aesthetic, and sized just right. See figure 6-C-1.

Figure 6-C-1 Table and stools.

How to build this project

The stools in this project are really just small sized tables. Adjust your measurements accordingly and follow the directions given for the construction of the table. In fact, you may want to build the stools first to get the practice that you can benefit from when building the table.

Choose the wood for this project. Appendix I contains in depth instructions on choosing and sizing materials.

Cut the legs to size. Be sure they are square and all the same length.

Cut the rails to the exact length but make them 1/8" wider than required. These will be jointed to exact size later. Choose the face side and mark them.

Project   Requirements

Recommended: Cherry

Also suitable: Any durable hardwood

Material List:
Stools
16 - 1 5/8" x 1 5/8" x 11" legs
16 - 2 3/8" x 6 3/4" x 3/4" rails
16 - 2 3/8" x 4 1/4" x 3/4" cross brackets
4 - 11" x 11" x 7/8" stool seats
Table
4 - 1 5/8" x 1 5/8" x 19 3/4" legs
4 - 2 5/8" x 18" x 3/4" rails
4 - 2 5/8" x 4 1/4" x 3/4" cross brackets
1 - 24" x 24" x 7/8" top

Router tools:
Table mounted router
Table fence
Mitre gauge
1 " brass guide and ring nut

Router bits:
1/4" round over bit with pilot bearing
1/2" 14 degree dovetail bit
1" 45 degree V bit
1 1/4" plunge round over bit

Skill Level

	Basic			Basic Plus
X	Moderate			Advanced

Hardware:
20 - 5/16" x 3" hanger bolts
20 - 5/16" flat washers
20 - 5/16" wing nuts
24 - #8 x 1 1/2" round head socket wood screws

Construction details in:
The skills necessary to complete the projects in this book are presented in appendixes at the back. The following skills are used in this project. You may wish to review the following appendixes before you start.

Appendix I - Choosing and Sizing Materials

Appendix III- B. Table Fence

Appendix VI- B. Mitre Gauge

Cutting the cross brackets

Cut the corner blocks to length. These will also be jointed to exact width after the dovetail pin is cut on each end so they should be a little wider than specified. The jointing removes any chipping that may occur during the cutting of the dovetails.

With the 45 degree V bit in the table mounted router and the table fence positioned to expose the full angle, cut a 45 degree miter on each end of all the corner blocks as shown in the drawing or use your miter saw to cut the pieces to size. See figure 6-C-2.

Figure 6-C-2 Mitered corner block.

Install a 1/2" 14 degree dovetail bit in the table mounted router. Install a 1" brass template guide in the base plate. Position the mitre gauge over the guide. Use sample pieces of stock to experiment with to obtain a good fit on the dovetail joint. Appendix VI-B contains directions on mitre set up.

Cut a dovetail slot on each end of all the rails 1 5/8" centred from each end as shown in the drawing. Be sure to use the stop block and hold down clamp.

Using the pin fence of the mitre gauge in the 45 degree position, cut dovetail pins on each 45 degree end of the corner blocks. This is a dovetail fastening system. See figure 6-C-3.

Joint 1/16" off each side of each rail and corner block to clean up the chipping. Drill a 11/32" hole in the centre of each corner block.

Rail and leg detail

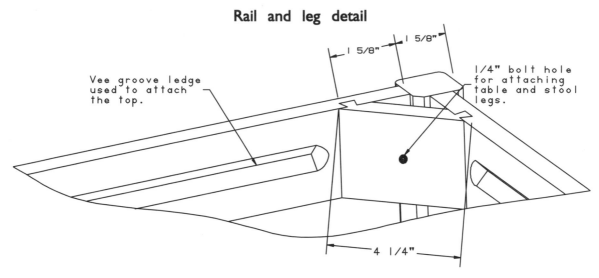

Vee groove ledge used to attach the top.

1 5/8"

1 5/8"

1/4" bolt hole for attaching table and stool legs.

4 1/4"

The rail ledge

Install a 45 degree V groove bit in the router positioned in the table mount. Set the table fence a suitable distance away from the cutter to make a ledge in the stool and table rails to enable you to secure the top to the leg system with 1 1/2" wood screws. See figure 6-C-4. Set the cutter depth to one half the rail thickness.

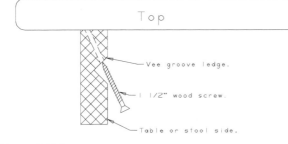

Figure 6-C-3 Dovetail fastening system.

Top

Vee groove ledge.

1 1/2" wood screw.

Table or stool side.

Figure 6-C-4

The legs

Install a 1/4" rounding over bit in the router table mount. Use the fence and isolate the bearing so the stool leg will be against the fence. Round all the corners of all the legs. Remove the fence.

Use the safety pin and round all four edges of the bottom end of each leg. The legs will have to stand upright on the table to make these cuts. You will note that the bearing will follow the rounded edge of the sides and will produce clean round cuts on all the bottom edges.

Using a 45 degree V groove bit in the table mounted router, chamfer cut the 45 degree to create a flat surface for the length of 2 1/4" on the inside top of each leg. (This will provide an easy surface to install the wood threaded end of the hanger bolts). See figure 6-C-5 on page 6-16.

In the flat surface just made, predrill a centred 9/32" pilot hole 1 1/4" from the top of each leg piece. Use a vise grip wrench or double lock nut to install the hanger bolts into the legs.

Leg assembly

Dry fit the corner blocks into the rails to ensure a snug fit. Glue the corner blocks in place with the rails. Be sure they all fit snug. Be sure the pieces are square. Let the glue set.

Tighten all the legs in place with the washers and wing nuts. No glue is needed on

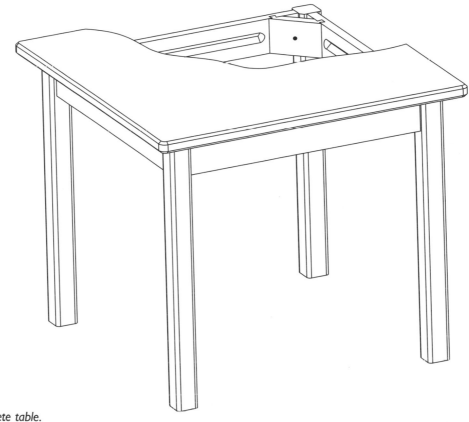

Figure 6-C-6 Complete table.

these legs. See figure 6-C-6. Take all the legs off the rails and round the exposed edge of the rails and corner blocks on the bottom, with a table mounted round over bit. When complete, sand and reinstall the legs.

Figure 6-C-5 Angle surface for hanger bolts.

Stool and table tops

Chuck up the 1 1/4" plunge round over bit. Set the depth of cut for the full round over. Use the table fence to make a chip

breaker (See Appendix III-B.) and expose the full round over. Check the setting with a sample piece. Stand the stool tops on edge and cut the corners off round with this table set up. Clamp a backer piece to the stock to prevent chipping. Round the corners of the table top in the same way.

All corners rounded

With the 1/4" round over bit in the table mounted router and the safety pin in position, rout the top and bottom of all the stool and table tops. You do not want a profile line so be sure the depth of cut leaves a round cut. Center the tops on the leg systems and install the wood screws through the screw ledge in the rails.

Finishing

Sand and finish four stools and the table. Perfect for the grandchildren at Christmas or for a birthday.

Figure 6-D-1 Wagon

6 D. Wagon

Kids have played with wooden toys for years. A prize possession these days is a wood toy that is hand made. Even if no children are involved this wooden wagon will be handy to use for display of potted plants or just for show.

Project Requirements

Recommended: Birch, Maple

Material list:
- 2 - 3 1/2" x 32" x 3/4" box sides
- 2 - 3" x 14 1/4" x 3/4" box ends
- 1 - 14 1/4" x 32" x 1/2" baltic birch plywood bottom
- 1 - 3" x 16" x 1 1/2" rear axle
- 2 - 3 1/2" x 7" x 1 1/2" rear axle brackets
- 1 - 3" x 16" x 1 1/2" front axle
- 1 - 2 1/2" x 12" x 1 1/2" axle bracket
- 1 - 5" x 12" x 3/4" front reach
- 1 - 1 3/4" x 30" x 3/4" tongue (centre)
- 2 - 3" x 7" x 3/4" tongue (sides)
- 1 - 1 1/4' x 7" x 1/4" spline in tongue
- 4 - 11" x 11" x 1 1/8" wheel blanks

Router tools:
- Table mounted router
- Table fence
- Brass insert and ring nut
- 1" brass guide
- 10" star wheel jig
- Heart pattern
- Mitre gauge
- 5/8" brass guide
- Sub top for router table
- 7" base plate

Router bits:
- 1/2" 14 degree dovetail bit
- 3/8" spiral bit
- 1/4" round over bit with pilot bearing
- 3/8" rabbeting bit
- 1/4" spiral bit

Skill Level

Basic			Basic Plus
Moderate		X	Advanced

Hardware:
- 14 - # 6 x 1" flat head wood screws
- 4 - 1/4" x 2" lag bolts
- 4 - 3/8" x 3" lag bolts
- 4 - 1/4" x 3 1/2" carriage bolts
- 2 - 1/4" x 4 1/2" continuous thread rod
- 6 - 1/4" hex nuts
- 2 - 1/4" lock nuts
- 14 - 1/4" flat washers
- 8 - 3/8" flat washers
- 1 - 3" x 1/4" poly washer

Construction details in:

The skills necessary to complete the projects in this book are presented in appendixes at the back.

Appendix I - Choosing and Sizing Material

Appendix II - Gluing and Clamping

Appendix III - B. Table Fence Set Up
     D. Measuring Made Simple

Appendix V - D. Pattern Cutting
     E. Wheel Jig

Appendix VI - B. Mitre Gauge

How to build this project

This is a project that looks more complicated than it is. However, it is one that requires careful study, particularly of the plans, before proceeding. Choose your wood first. Joint, plane and cut all materials to size according to the material list. Be sure all stock is cut square and to the exact size listed. Appendix I contains instructions on choosing and sizing material.

The sizes provided allow for laminating and edge gluing, and wherever this is required it should be done first.

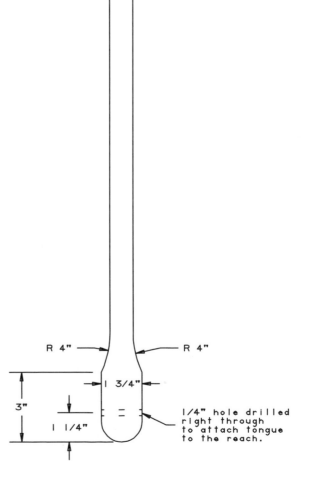

Walnut spline.

The tongue

First, laminate the materials for the tongue to the rough size shown in the illustration. Then chuck up a 1/4" spiral bit in a table mounted router. Set the depth of the cut to 1/2" and position a fence to leave 1/4" between the fence and the bit. This set up is for the first cut of the slot needed to receive the spline, which in turn will strengthen the handle.

Stand the tongue lamination on end with the wide end on the table. Cut a 1/4" slot in the end. Reset the depth of cut to 1" and run the piece through again to complete the recess for the spline.

Cut the spline, preferably from a piece of contrasting hardwood, to its dimensions of 1 1/4" wide, 7" long and 1/4" thick. Glue and clamp it in place. Set it aside until dry. (You may want to proceed with the box or wheels in the meantime.)

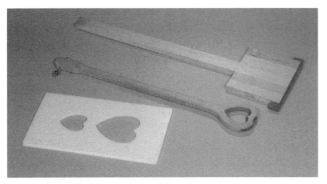

Figure 6-D-1 Tongue piece and heart pattern.

After the spline is dry, double stick tape the heart pattern to the splined tongue piece. Take care to centre it on the stock. See figure 6-D-1.

Chuck up a 3/8" spiral bit in a portable plunge router. Install a 5/8" guide in the 7" plate, secure it with a ring nut, and centre the bit in the guide. Set the depth of the cut to slightly more than the thickness of the tongue and clamp the tongue to the workbench, making sure that the routed parts will hang off the edge to prevent any damage to your workbench. Keeping the guide flange tight to the pattern, plunge the bit into the heart hole and, working from left to right, cut out the pattern. Details of pattern work can be found in Appendix V-D.

Then draw an outside heart shape on the tongue stock about 3/4" outside the hole. Cut this with a band saw or jig saw. See figure 6-D-2. Shape the other end of the handle according to the drawing, using a band or jig saw.

Figure 6-D-2 Heart shaped handle.

All that is left to do with the handle is to round over exposed edges, including the inside of the heart. You may wish to do this now, or leave it until you have other parts of the wagon ready for rounding over. How to round over is detailed later in this project.

The box

First, cut the sides and ends of the box to the dimensions indicated on the plans. Box details can be found on pages 6-24 and 6-25. Drill all the holes in the located points. Where these holes are countersunk, do the counter boring first and then drill the smaller holes through the stock.

The dovetail joints

Chuck up a 1/2" dovetail bit in a table mounted router. Install a 1" guide secured with a ring nut. Position the mitre gauge over the guide. Set the depth of the cut at slightly less than 3/8". Check the setup by running a slot and pin in some scrap stock.

Cut the dovetail slots in each end of the box sides first, then cut the dovetail pins on the ends of the two box sides. Appendix V-B contains details on mitre gauge work. Dry fit the box together. See figure 6-D-3.

Figure 6-D-3 Dovetail joint in box.

The bottom rabbet

Chuck up a 3/8" rabbeting bit in the table mounted router. Secure the fence in place and isolate the bearing. How to do this can be found in Appendix III-B. Set the depth of the cut to the thickness of the plywood bottom. Run a rabbet in the bottom edge of each side. The ends fit on top of the bottom and do not need to be rabbetted.

Rounding over

This is a good time to round over the box and the tongue. If you have decided to build your wheels ahead of this point they can be rounded over at the same time. Chuck up a 1/4" round over bit in a table mounted router and set the depth to expose the full round over but not to leave a profile line. Be sure to use a safety pin in rounding over outside edges. Remove the safety pin when rounding over inside edges, such as the inside of the tongue and the inside of the spokes on the wheels.

Figure 6-D-5 Wheels.

Assembling the box

Dry fit the box to test the accuracy of your work. It is now time to glue and clamp the dovetail joints and to glue and screw the bottom into place. See figure 6-D-4.

Figure 6-D-4 Wagon box.

The wheels

To make the wheels use a sub top over your router table. Secure the wheel stock to the table and position a star wheel jig over the stock on the centre pin. Chuck up a 1/2" spiral bit in a portable plunge router. Install the 7" base plate with a 1" guide secured by a ring nut. Centre the bit in the guide. Cut the spoke holes first. Refer to appendix V-C for instructions on producing a wheel. After the spoke holes have been cut, cut the outside of the wheel as described in the appendix. Repeat for all four wheels.

Finish off by rounding over all exposed edges. Use a safety pin when rounding over the outside edges, but remove the pin when rounding over the inside edges of the spokes. See figure 6-D-5.

The axle assembly

Before starting to assemble the axles study the drawings on pages 6-26 and 6-27.

To accurately drill the holes for the bolts that hold the wheels you will need to construct an axle drilling jig. See figure 6-D-6.

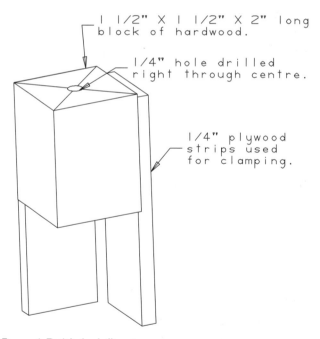

Figure 6-D-6 Axle drilling jig.

Use this jig to centre and align the holes for the bolts in the ends of the axles.

To make the axle assemblies simply cut the parts to the size and shape shown on pages 6-26 and 6-27. Drill the holes as shown on the detailed drawings.

The rear axle assembly

After drilling the ends of the axles, bolt the axle brackets to the axles using 1/4" x 4 1/2" threaded rod. Locate the rear axle assembly on the back underside of the wagon box. Secure it with 2" lag bolts.

NOTE - The two mounting lag bolts are used in the rear bracket centre in the box end. The front of the bracket is secured by wood screws from inside the box bottom into the bracket. See figure 6-D-7.

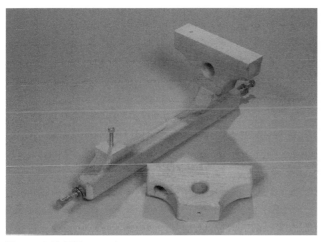

Figure 6-D-7 Rear axle parts.

The front axle assembly

Insert the front pivot bolt through the tongue holder, marked 'B' on the detailed plans and fasten this tongue holder to the axle support (C on the plans.) Lay the 3" diameter poly washer over the bolt and insert the bolt through the piece marked 'A' which in turn is fastened by two lag bolts to the front end of the wagon box. See figure 6-D-8.

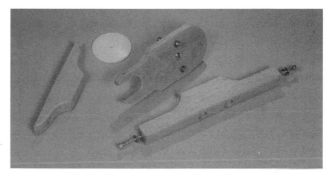

Figure 6-D-8 Front axle parts.

Finishing off

Install the four wheels. Be sure you have a washer on each side of each wheel and tighten only enough to allow the wheel to turn freely. Attach the handle to its bracket.

The wagon should be sanded and then stained or painted as you wish.

Notes:

Wagon Box Details

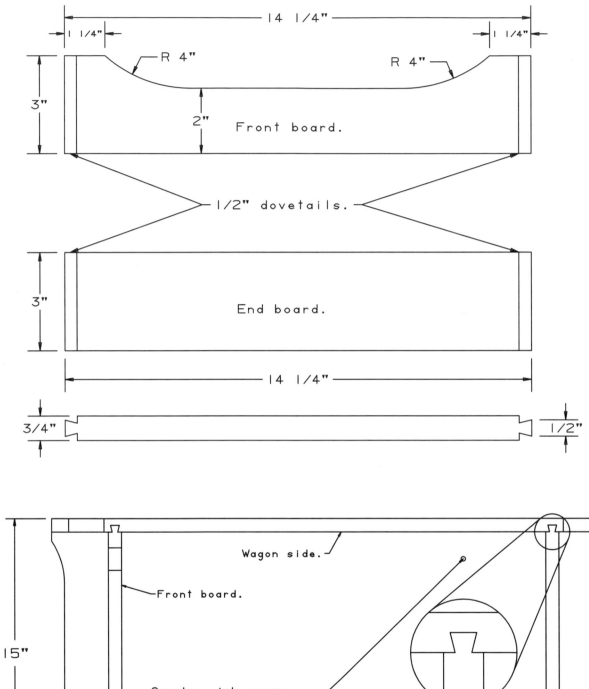

14 1/4"

1 1/4"   1 1/4"

R 4"   R 4"

3"

2"   Front board.

1/2" dovetails.

3"

End board.

14 1/4"

3/4"   1/2"

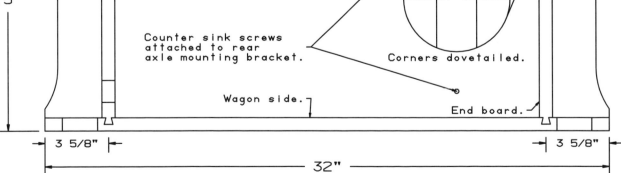

15"

Wagon side.

Front board.

Counter sink screws
attached to rear
axle mounting bracket.

Corners dovetailed.

Wagon side.

End board.

3 5/8"   3 5/8"

32"

Wagon Box Details

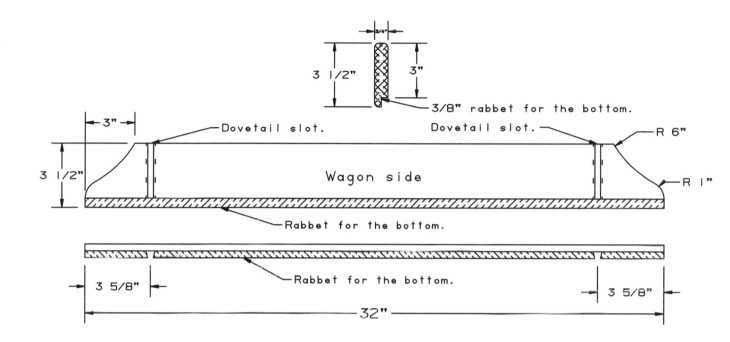

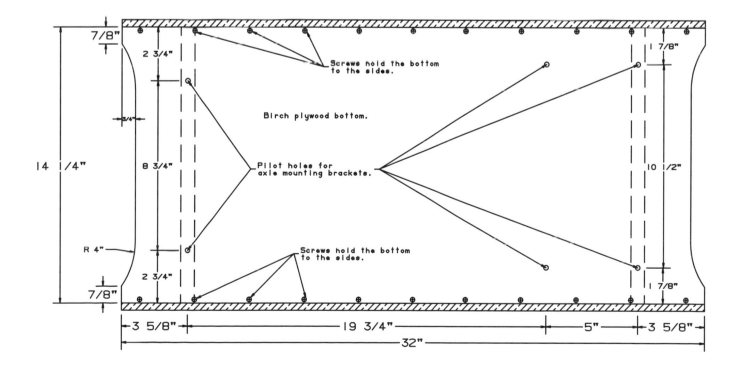

Rear Axle Assembly

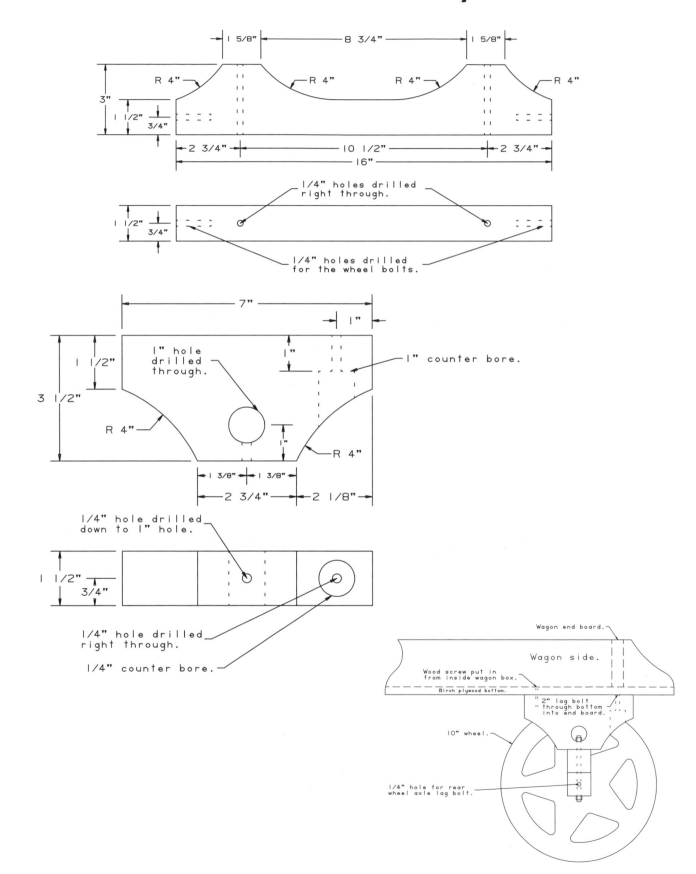

1 5/8"   8 3/4"   1 5/8"

R 4"   R 4"   R 4"   R 4"

3"

1 1/2"

3/4"

2 3/4"   10 1/2"   2 3/4"

16"

1/4" holes drilled
right through.

1 1/2"

3/4"

1/4" holes drilled
for the wheel bolts.

7"

1"

1 1/2"

1"

1"

1" counter bore.

3 1/2"

R 4"

1" hole
drilled
through.

R 4"

1"

1 3/8"   1 3/8"

2 3/4"   2 1/8"

1/4" hole drilled
down to 1" hole.

1 1/2"

3/4"

1/4" hole drilled
right through.

1/4" counter bore.

Wagon end board.

Wagon side.

Wood screw put in
from inside wagon box.

Birch plywood bottom.

2" lag bolt
through bottom
into end board.

10" wheel.

1/4" hole for rear
wheel axle lag bolt.

Front Axle Assembly

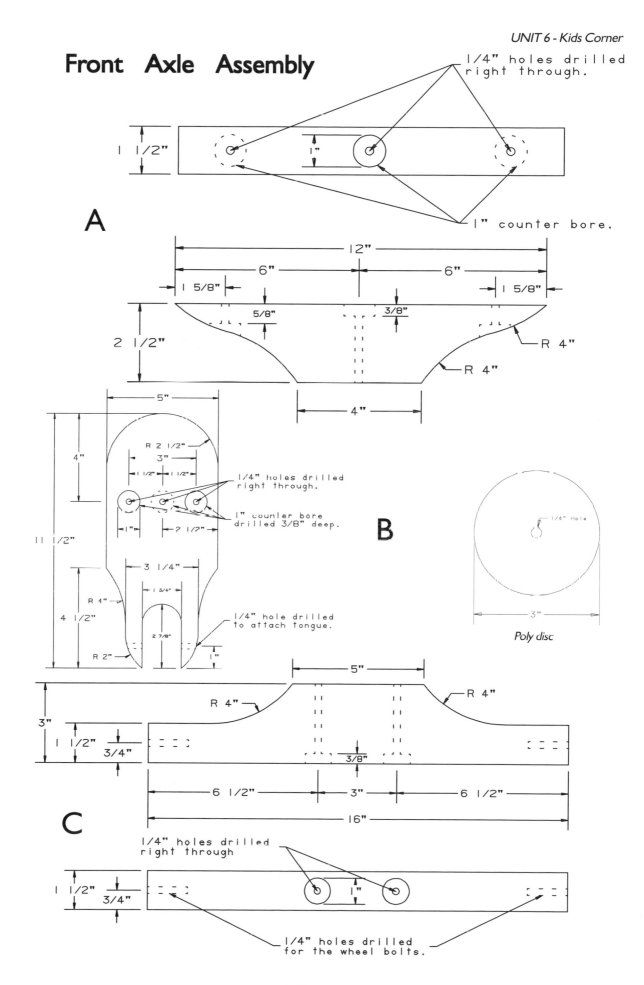

1/4" holes drilled right through.

1 1/2"

A

1" counter bore.

12"

6"   6"

1 5/8"   1 5/8"

5/8"   3/8"

2 1/2"   R 4"

R 4"

4"

5"

R 2 1/2"

3"

1 1/2"   1 1/2"

4"

1/4" holes drilled right through.

1" counter bore drilled 3/8" deep.

B

11 1/2"

1"   2 1/2"

3 1/4"

1 3/4"

R 4"

4 1/2"

2 7/8"

1/4" hole drilled to attach tongue.

R 2"   1"

1/4" Hole

3"

Poly disc

5"

R 4"   R 4"

3"

1 1/2"

3/4"   3/8"

6 1/2"   3"   6 1/2"

16"

C

1/4" holes drilled right through

1 1/2"

3/4"   1"

1/4" holes drilled for the wheel bolts.

6-27

Appendix   Introduction

As a reader and a woodworker, the authors and publisher hope you will both enjoy this book and find in it some valuable information.

After you have browsed through the book, take the time to read all of the appendix material first. The appendix contains the core information for most of the projects and by reading it you will get some idea of the skill level needed to accomplish the operations that are described.

Each project has been graded according to the skill level required. The authors believe it would be a good idea to begin with a project or two at the basic level before proceeding to the more advanced work that is part of some of the other projects. Doing so will avoid a lot of frustration.

Just a word of explanation about some of the photographs in the book. The primary aim of these photographs is to show, as clearly as possible, the operations required. Most are shown with the router stopped. In some, the angle may give the impression that the operators' hands are closer to the router bit than they actually are.

The basic thing to remember is that fingers and router bits do not mix well. Read carefully the sections on the use of push sticks and other devices to make sure that your fingers never even come close to a spinning bit. Remember to be careful even after you shut off the power to the router. If you have to brush away the shavings around the bit, wait until it has stopped completely, then use a brush and not your hands. Although generally noisy, routers are safe woodworking tools, provided they are treated with respect and common sense.

The authors have always stressed safety first through their demostrations, seminars and workshops.

Appendix I
Choosing and Sizing Materials

The rules to use when choosing wood for a project are simple. Look at the piece and imagine it, if you can, in place as part of the finished project.

Don't automatically reject a piece because it has a flaw such as a knot. Consider whether the rest of the piece justifies its use and if the flaw can be hidden where it will not be seen.

Quality is important. It is false economy to pick a piece of wood simply because it is cheap and then spend more hours working on it than you would on a more suitable piece.

Quality and processing

To size the wood you have picked you have to consider both the quality and the method of processing. If you can adopt a consistent plan, sizing will quickly become second nature.

One of the first facts you will discover is that every piece of lumber has its own natural beauty and that no two pieces are exactly alike. Here are some questions you should ask yourself when you are figuring out how much you will need:

* How do the boards you have selected match in (a) grain and (b) colour and how important is it that they do?

* How straight are the boards you have picked? If they are not straight can you get what you want out of them by working around the twists or warps?

This is all part of developing, within yourself, a selection system that works without having to think about it.

Do you have enough material

A good rule of thumb is to buy about 10 to 15 per cent more than you think you will need. This will allow for a few mistakes, and it is better than having to go back and try to match what you have already finished.

Familiar with the material list

Know which pieces will be visible in the finished project and where these pieces fit into the finished job. It is a good practice to start looking for the most visible pieces first. For example, a dresser should have the best material on top because that is the part that is most visible. Pick the exposed pieces first and you will then have the luxury of selecting the less visible parts, knowing that they can have flaws which will not be seen.

What is a face

Actually, each piece of wood has six faces. It is good to start thinking of them in order of importance, such as the number one face, the second face, the number one end, the second end and the number one edge and the second edge. Decide which faces are most important to the project and size accordingly. See figure I-1.

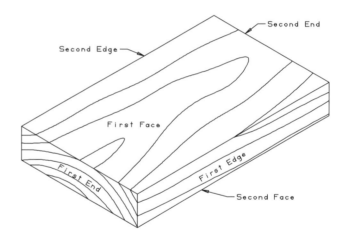

Figure I-1 The six faces of each piece of material.

You may realize that all this selection process takes place away from power tools. It is always a good idea to separate your thinking time from your cutting time. You should not try to make selection decisions while you are cutting. While cutting concentrate only on the marks you have made and your overall safety.

The condition of the wood

Temperature and moisture content of the wood are important in any processing operation. If you live in a cold climate, let your wood reach room temperature before you start cutting. If you live where it is hot, don't take wood directly out of the hot sun and start working on it. Those living in a humid climate should keep their wood in the driest place to avoid shrinkage or warping after cutting. Ideally, hardwood should have a water content in the range of six to ten per cent. You can measure this content with a moisture meter, which you can buy at a good hardware supply store. When ever possible, long-term storage should be in a cool, dry place.

Equipment needed

Accurate sizing requires equipment other than your router. A tablesaw and a planer are necessities. A 6" or larger jointer is handy, as is a radial arm, cutoff or sliding compound saw.

The first operation should be to rough cut the pieces to length. It is always a good practice to allow an extra 1 1/2" on each piece AFTER cutting off between four and five inches of the ends of rough boards. This eliminates shrinkage cracks on the ends.

Planing and jointing

The line of surface planers available today provide an excellent method of producing PARALLEL smooth faces. Remember that a surface planer will not straighten a board, or take a warp or bow out of it. It will simply make the two surfaces parallel.

Setting the depth of cut on the jointer

The jointer has a split table. The in feed table is adjusted to give you depth of cut. We recommend to joint about 1/16" at one time. Too fine a setting will allow the stock to slip on top and have a tendency to ride the knife rather than cut.

Check to see if the stock is straight. If there is a bow, it is possible to eliminate this by jointing.

Joint a bowed board

Place the bowed board as in figure I-2. Starting from the centre, joint out toward the ends. Reverse the stock and starting again in the centre, joint the opposite end. Continue alternating stock ends until the bow is eliminated. Make one final cut starting at one end going towards the other. Check the direction of grain. Always joint with the grain.

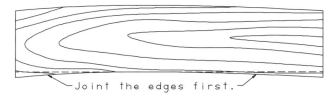

Figure I-2 Eliminate a bow in stock.

If the bow is too great in this flat surface you may be wise to choose a different piece. In most cases the pieces with the most bow can be cut for shorter stock required in the project. This cuts down on a lot of jointing.

Next the planer

Once you have the one smooth, straight face you want, you can switch to the surface planer to get the piece to the required thickness. Once both surfaces are level alternate the surface faces as you use the surface planer. Plane all the pieces you intend to join at the same time. It is always better to remove several small thicknesses rather than trying to take off too much too fast.

Tip: To make sure that the planer has consistent material thickness. See figure I-3 Go no go jig. This handy jig is made of a hardwood and has the grooves made by the router that are the desired thickness. To check to see that the planer is making the proper thickness use the gauge and the pieces either fit in the gauge or not. This will check the accuracy of your planing.

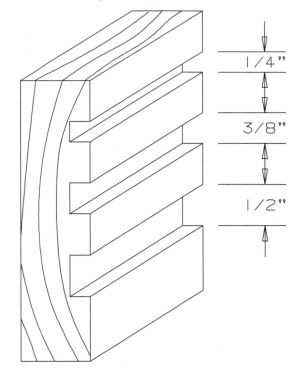

Figure I-3 Go-no-go jig to check the material thickness.

Once you are satisfied with the surfaces you have planed to the required thickness, it is time to joint one straight edge.

Joint one straight edge

Follow the same procedure as you did jointing the first flat surface. The importance of sharp jointer knives cannot be over emphasized. Be sure the jointer fence is exactly 90 degrees to the bed. Feed slowly to avoid "mill marks".

Ripping stock to width

It is always a good practise to rip the stock 1/8" wider than required and then joint 1/16" off each edge. Be sure to watch the direction of grain on these jointed edges. This practice will ensure straight edges.

Cutting to length

The final operation in sizing material is cutting to length. Our rough cuts are 1" to 1 1/2" longer than our finished piece. If you have a number of pieces to cut to the same length cut one end first and then put a setup block, or stop block to guarantee that all will be the same length when the final cut is made. When sliding the work piece to the stop block watch that saw dust does not build up between the stock and the stop block. Do not jam the stock against your stop block as you may move it and end up with a longer piece than you intended.

Notes:

Appendix II
Clamping and Gluing

Gluing

Most of the projects included in this book contain the phrase, "assemble and glue." It is important to understand glue, how it works and how to use it. You will have spent a lot of time cutting, routing and sanding your project and you don't want to ruin it by a sloppy glue job.

The thing to remember about glue is that a properly glued joint is stronger than the wood it is holding. This is important since pieces that are properly glued cannot be easily separated.

Generally speaking, wood that is jointed glues better than wood that is simply sawn. Sawn edges are not as smooth as those that are jointed, and the glue works better the smoother the joints it is used to fasten.

Another important thing to remember is that glue will only hold where the pieces are touching. Those who attend Bob Rosendahl's demonstration will hear him referring to 1/4" glue to fix mistakes, but that is only a figure of speech. To get glue to hold properly, the pieces must fit properly.

Also, most glues require proper clamping. It is just not good enough to slap glue on both edges of a joint and hand press them together.

The secret of good gluing

1. Get the edges to be glued as smooth as possible.

2. Make sure all the surfaces to be joined touch each other.

3. Use enough, but not too much of the RIGHT KIND of glue.

4. Plan your clamping to insure that pressure is even along the joint.

The first requirement is made easy when routed joints are to be glued. The router produces better fitting joints than most other power tools, and the joints produced usually require little or no sanding.

If you make proper use of fences and jigs the joints you want to glue should fit exactly.

Kind of glue

Check the kind of glue you are using. Most glue containers have instructions telling you what the glue is designed to do. Care must be taken in storing glue. If you leave it at the summer cottage during the winter months don't expect to be able to use it next season.

The right amount of glue

Using the right amount of glue is important. All the surfaces to be joined should be covered with just enough glue so that a bit squeezes out when the joint is clamped. Too little, and no glue will appear as the clamps are tightened. Too much, and you will have yourself a dickens of a time cleaning it up.

One of the drawbacks to glue is that the excess must be cleaned off before any finish is applied. Believe us, there is no better way of finding glue that you missed cleaning than to put the first finish on.

Excess glue is best removed with a scraper or putty knife. Never use a wet cloth or sand paper. All a cloth does is spread a fine film of glue, usually invisible, on the wood around the joint. Unfortunately, this film appears like invisible ink when the finish is applied.

Clamping pressure

Finally, a general word about clamping. It is always a good idea to use support blocks between your steel clamps and your finished projects. If these support blocks are the same size as the sides being clamped, something easy to make on small projects, they distribute the pressure of the clamps evenly and produce a good result.

Always test clamp your pieces together before gluing. Doing so will give you an indication of where the clamps should go. It will also indicate just how much pressure is required. Getting the right pressure is a matter of practice. Too little and the joint won't hold properly. Too much and there is a real danger of damage.

Gluing specific joints

To glue the rabbet dado combination joint, put glue where the pieces will touch. Clamp so that the pressure is applied in one direction, between what are really two dado joints. See figure II-1

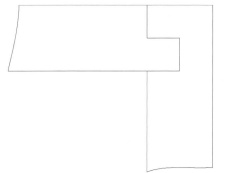

Figure II-1 Rabbet dado joint.

Box joints

Since these joints usually fit snug, it is important not to put on too much glue. Using a small brush helps. It also helps to apply masking tape to the inside of the joints to prevent glue from squeezing out. Cleaning glue from the inside of a box joint is a difficult task. Remove the tape, and the glue that is on it, before the glue is fully set. See figure II-2

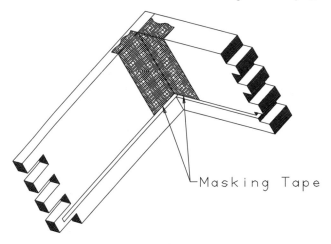

Figure II-2 Masking tape on the joint.

The cope and bead joint

Used in constructing raised panel doors, side panels on cabinets, mirror frames and other work, this joint must be square. Provided the pieces have been cut square and correctly routed, the joint can be squared by using proper pressure when positioning the clamps.

Take time to understand how this construction works. The panel itself is not glued in, but rather "floated" inside the frame, to prevent cracking due to age, shrinkage or humidity change.

It is essential to put glue on the rails avoiding the corner where the panel fits.

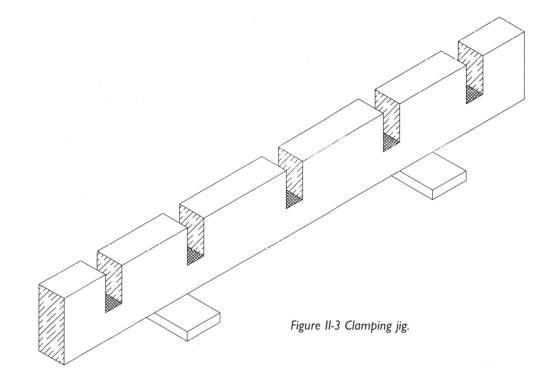

Figure II-3 Clamping jig.

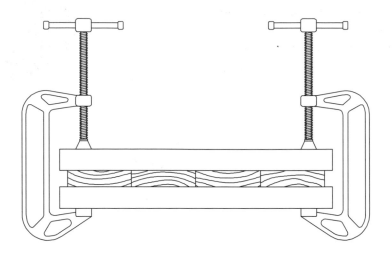

Figure II-4 Preventing cupping.

It is a good idea to pair up your clamps when assembling these joints. Bar clamps produce a good, even pressure between the jaws. Be sure when using bar clamps that the clamps are placed square to the work piece. It is important to assemble the project on a flat surface, and it is a good idea to produce a simple jig out of 2" x 4" wood, notched to position the clamps. See figure II-3

Remember to protect your project from direct injury by the steel clamps and from the chemical reaction produced between steel and the glue. This can be accomplished by putting blocks (called shoes) and plastic sheet (big plastic garbage bag) between the clamps and the finished wood of the project. Wood can be used for these blocks but if you have poly you will find that glue does not stick to this material the way it does to wood.

The right pressure

As stated before, it is more important that pressure be even rather than too heavy. It is a good idea to put a bit of pressure on and then check again to be sure the project is level and square. Then the pressure can be increased. It is preferable to leave the project until the glue is completely dry, but if it has to be moved, make sure to move it to another flat surface. Make sure the screw thread of the clamping bolt is centred on the edge of the stock.

Edge gluing

This is often necessary to get the width you want for a drawer front or a table top. Watch for the way the pieces fit together before you apply glue. Check that the pieces are square and straight, and this is the time to match things like colour and grain.

Again, it is a good idea to pair your clamps so that the pressure remains even. Here is another place where a jig to hold the clamps comes in handy. Apply an even coating of glue to the surfaces to be joined, and check, after applying a bit of pressure, to insure that the pieces are flush, even and not warped.

Handling cupping and warping

Often wood becomes cupped because of the milling process, the width of wider boards and the position of growth rings. If the clamping pressure tends to increase this condition, clamp two solid pieces of material across the width to supply support while the glue is drying. See figure II-4

When edge gluing start with two end clamps and slight pressure. Add additional clamps where they are needed to insure an even finished product. If you are working with long stock, start with one end and apply clamps as needed toward the other end. This will allow for adjusting the pieces, and keeping them even as you go down the length.

Gluing a box with two clamps

Isn't it always the way, you start gluing a project and you need one more clamp. There are thirty clamps on the project already. How can the project be glued with only two clamps? Lets follow this step by step process and see what is needed. The first item needed is a way to make clamping pressure on the box even. To do this, plywood pieces are cut which are 3/4" smaller than the box sides and top/bottom. There are four pieces for each box.

Layout the pieces

The first process is to layout the pieces and dry fit the parts. If the box fits, put the glue in the rabbet joints and put together. Take one clamp and place on the box ends. This is a temporary clamp to make sure that the ends are in the rabbet joint properly. See figure II-5.

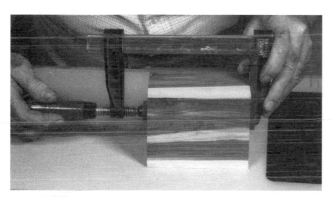

Figure II-5 Temporary clamping on the ends.

Using the blocks cut to match the top and bottom, place one on the top of the box and one on the bottom of the box. With the plywood pieces in place use the second clamp and tighten the top and bottom together. See figure II-6.

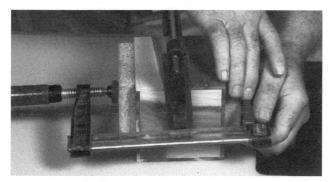

Figure II-6 Put the blocks and clamp into place on the top and bottom.

Remove the temporary clamp and line the plywood block to the two sides. See figure II-7.

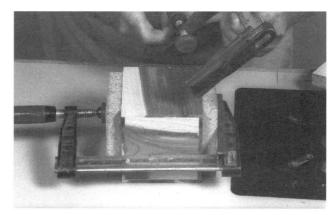

Figure II-7 Remove the temporary clamp.

Place the second clamp into position and put even pressure on the box. See figure II-8.

Figure II-8 Set the blocks and clamp the sides.

Check to see that the glue is squeezing out of the wood joints all around. Put aside to let dry and clamp the next box.

Appendix III
Router Basics

Safety

As always the first consideration is the safety factor. To work safely with your router the following points should be observed.

1. Always wear eye protection.

2. Unplug the router before making adjustments or changing router bits.

3. Keep your work area clean. Do not leave loose pieces of stock or tools on the router table.

4. Keep all router bits, cutters and chuck parts clean and in good working order. Do not use damaged router bits and avoid the use of dull bits and cutters.

5. Be sure the bearings on all router bits roll free with no rough spots. Change any damaged bearings. Do not try to relubricate the old bearing.

6. Let the router come up to full speed before feeding the stock into the cutters. Always have control of the router or work piece. Note: When free hand routing make sure the stock is firmly clamped in place and do not rely on router mats as a method of securing the stock.

7. Use a dust pick up whenever possible and be aware of the health hazzards when milling exotic woods. Be sure to remove all of the cuttings and excess material from an internal pattern rout.

8. When using polyethylene as a jig material remember that the cuttings come out as long strings and not as chips. Never grab or pull these strings from the moving cutter as this could pull your hand into the cutter.

III-A. Router Basics

The router was originally designed as a versatile, hand held shaper. Its speed produced cuts that required little or no sanding.

Not long after the router appeared, people started building table mounting devices, so that the material could be pushed against the router, rather than moving the router along the stock. Most of these tables, including many still on the market are awkward to use because they require unbolting the router to change a bit.

A good table mounting workstation should allow you easy access to the router when changing bits. Using a router, hand held or mounted in a table, requires an understanding of some basic characteristics of this unusual power tool.

a. Direction of feed

Probably the most important thing to understand when using the router is the correct direction of feed. Take a minute to examine your router upside down on the workbench, so you can see the bit. Routers generally run clockwise when hand held, and counter clockwise when mounted upside down in a table. IT IS IMPORTANT TO ALWAYS MOVE THE ROUTER OR THE STOCK SO THAT YOU ARE WORKING INTO THE CUT, RATHER THAN WITH IT. See figure III-A-a-1.

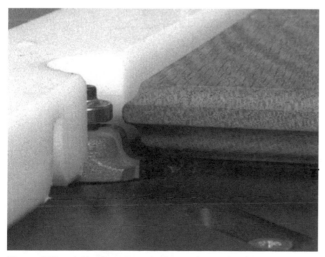

Figure III-A-a-1 Feeding the wood into the router bit.

The easiest way to make sure you are doing things right, especially if the router is mounted in a table, is to get your eye at table level and look at the bit. You will want to push the stock into that bit so that the carbide cutting edge hits the material first. When you are looking at the bit at table level notice where the carbide edge is and make sure you push the stock toward that edge, and not toward the back of the bit. See figure III-A-a-2.

Figure III-A-a-2 Showing the cutting edge of the router bit. Feed the stock into the cutter.

You will probably make the odd mistake. That is why we stress the safe operation of the router, by using push sticks and a fence whenever possible. The worst thing that can happen if you are feeding on the wrong side of the fence with a push stick is that the router will grab the material and shoot it away from you. The up side of making a mistake is that you are unlikely to repeat it.

When hand holding a router remember to move from left to right, or counter clockwise around an irregular shape if cutting an outside edge. Just to complicate things, if you are cutting an inside edge of an irregular shape, such as a picture frame or circle, you should move clockwise.

It is all a matter of control. If you are on the wrong side of the cutter, you are really cutting on the side that is pulling away from you. The router is controlling you, rather than you controlling the router.

You will soon get the hang of whether you are right or wrong just by the feel of the machine as it cuts into the wood. Moving into the wood gives you a feeling of control which you will soon recognize. See figure III-A-a-3.

Figure III-A-a-3 Direction of cut is important with a hand held router.

b. Order of cutting

One of the characteristics of any router is that, when cutting across the grain, it leaves some tear out visible at the end of the cut. This can be minimized by using a push block, but an easier and better way is to cut the pieces in the right order. This order (when using a table mount) is ALWAYS cut an end grain first, then turn the piece counter clockwise to cut the adjacent long grain. Follow this by the next end grain and finally the last long grain. You should have no visible tear out.

c. The bit

When you look at the diagram notice the profile line. This profile line is the part directly below the shape of the cut and is important because it can help hide imperfections in the wood. Using the profile line, for example, allows any warp or cup imperfections to be moved to the vertical line, getting rid of many flatness problems and making the molded edge more attractive.

You can use different parts of the router bit to produce different types of molding. This is known as STACKING THE PROFILE. This is useful in producing different appearances with the same cutter. For example, it is possible to round over the top face of a board and put a cove on

the bottom of the same board. See figure III-A-c-1 .

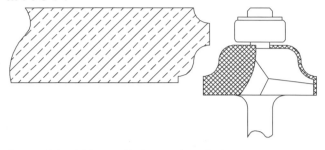

Figure III-A-c-1 The profile line and stacked cutter.

Understanding what a bit will do is essential in deciding what is best for your project. Looking at a bit and translating that bit into what the cut will look like takes practice. There is an easier way. Put the cutter on a piece of paper and trace the profile outline. This produces the reverse of the bit, and represents what the cut will look like. When you get the hang of it, you will be able to skip the tracing part. However, it is a good procedure to use as a start.

d. The safety pin

Besides being exactly what its name says, the safety pin is essencial when using bits that have pilot bearings, when the router is table mounted. The safety pin makes it possible to feed the stock into the bit in the correct manner, without having to worry about the bit grabbing the stock and shooting it away. See figure III-A-d-1 The safety pin must positioned between the operator and the cutter. Oak Park's table mounting base plates have the saftey pin hole pre drilled in the proper location.

Figure III-A-d-1 Cutting with the safety pin in place. Keep your fingers away from the cutter.

To use the safety pin just position the stock against the pin and rotate it into the cutter. It is not necessary to keep the stock in contact with the safety pin at all times, but it is essential to use the pin when starting the cut.

What the safety pin does is to provide a support for the stock when starting the cut. It allows the operator to control how quickly the stock is fed into the bit and, as its name says, provides a margin of safety that is not present if such routing tasks are attempted without the pin in place.

Using a guard over the safety pin just adds that extra margin of safety. See figure III-A-d-2.

Since the cutter is larger than the bearing, any small imperfections that are in the shape will be transfered to the mold by the bearing. The pilot bearing can be used to follow irregular cuts, but keep in mind the correct direction of feed and make sure that the surface is smooth. When making a straight cut it is better to use a fence.

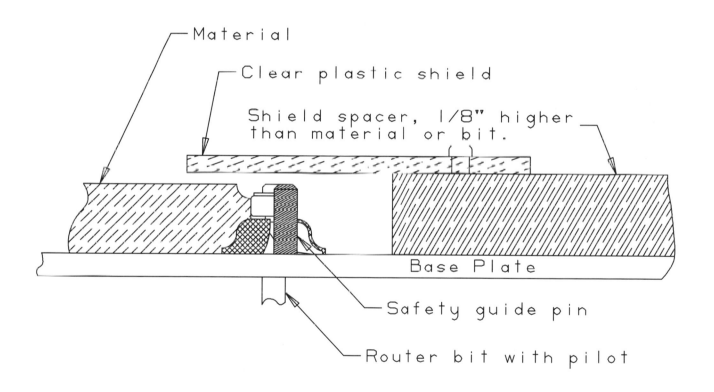

Figure III-A-d-2 The guard for the exposed router bit.

III-B. Router Table Fence

a. Design of Table Fence

The fence is an important accessory when using a table mounted router. The fence should be about 2" wide by 1" thick. All four edges should be chamfered. It should be no longer than necessary to clamp it securely to the table. Too long a fence makes it difficult to handle warped materials.

The fence needs two half holes. One on the under side for chip clearance and one on the face side to allow space for pilot bearings to be isolated. See figure III-B-a-1.

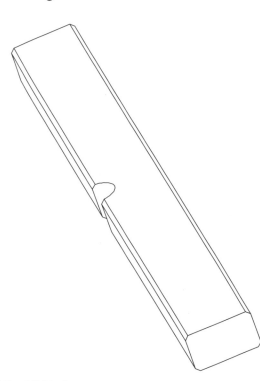

Figure III-B-a-1 Table fence.

The best way to secure a table fence is with two C clamps. It is not necessary for the fence to line up with the table because the bit is round. Whatever the angle at which the fence is attached it will always be lined up.

Any time a fence is installed on the router table, you should hand turn the chuck to be sure the bit is NOT touching the fence. Make sure the router is unplugged. It is possible to damage the carbide on the bit from a sudden contact before the bit is up to speed. Do not use damaged router bits.

b. Chip breaker

Decorative bits, like the roman ogee, tend to chip or tear out. This chipping can be reduced by taking a new fence, clamping one end to the table top and swinging the fence into the cutter while the router is running. The exact profile of the bit is cut in the leading edge of the fence and will act as a chip breaker when the work piece is being cut. JUST REMEMBER to clamp both ends of the fence before the work piece is cut. It is a good idea to keep a stock of table fences available to use for this chip breaker feature for different bit profiles.

Safety tip: Never trap the work piece between the fence and the bit. See figures III-B-b-1 the right way and III-B-b-2 the wrong way. Trapped material will be pulled in the direction of the router bit rotation. The router will take the piece away from you.

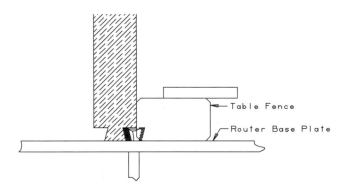

Figure III-B-b-1 Right way to cut.

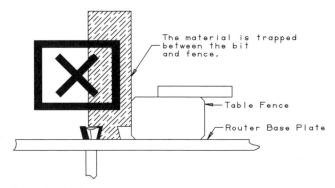

Figure III-B-b-2 Wrong way.

c. Isolating the bearing with the fence

It is a good practise never to depend on the pilot bearing to interfere with a fence cut. The bearing follows the irregularities in the wood and transfers them into the cut. Because the bearing is smaller than the bit these irregularities are exaggerated. When using a table fence you should always isolate the bearing.

Chuck up the bit in the table mounted router. Attach the fence on the out feed side of the table. Using a small, straight piece of wood tight to the fence, adjust the fence until the wood just touches the pilot bearing. Secure the infeed clamp on the table fence. Run the wood back and forth along the fence to see if you can feel the bearing. With your fine adjusting tool (hammer) tap the fence in or out until you can no longer feel the bearing. Do not loosen the clamps on the fence as you will lose your location. The above set up is done with the router unplugged.

d. Making stopped cuts

The router should be unplugged during set up. Put a piece of masking tape over top the bit hole on the fence and mark the centre of the bit. See figure III-B-d-1.

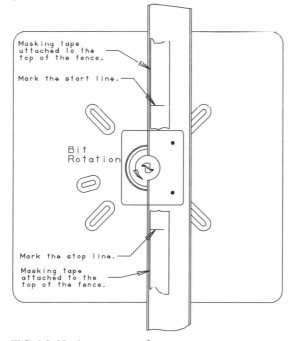

Figure III-B-d-1 Masking tape on fence.

To determine where to start and stop the cut, mark a line on the tape on either side of the centre line marked on the tape. The start line in-

dicates the point where the stock end will be on the outfeed side of the bit when the cut is begun. The finish line shows where the other end of the stock will be when the cut is complete. The diagram above shows these reference points on the tape to guide you in starting and stopping the cut.

Making the stopped cut

To make the stopped cut, start by resting the back end of the stock against the fence, move the front end into the bit so that the end of the piece lines up with the start mark on the tape. Feed the piece along the fence until the other end of the board reaches the stop mark. Keep the head end of the stock against the fence while you carefully rotate the back end out of the way of the bit.

Following this method puts you in control of the stock. The rotation of the cutter keeps the stock tight against the fence while the lines on the fence allow you to start and stop the cut precisely without seeing the bit itself. Use this method when you are making stopped cuts on either an edge or end of a work piece.

Stopped dados

Stopped dados differ from stopped edge or mold cuts. They require the use of stop blocks on the fence. These stop blocks serve the same purpose as the stop lines on the tape but they allow you control of the work piece when the cut is in from the edge.

Clamp the infeed block in place first then determine the location for the outfeed block. See figure III-B-d-2.

Figure III-B-d-2 Stop blocks on the table fence.

To cut the stopped dado

Put the heel of the stock against the infeed block and lower the stock onto the running bit. Feed the piece along the fence until the end of the stock contacts the out feed block. At this point STOP THE ROUTER. When the bit has come to a full stop lift the work piece away from the bit. This operation can not be done with a bit that has a pilot bearing. You must use a plunge bit.

Tip: Complete all stopped dado cuts of the same length at one time. This eliminates setting up the same cut more than once. It also assures uniform cuts for the project.

e. Rounding or cove corners

The corners of any piece of stock can be rounded easily and effectively by using the table fence and a round over or cove bit. Create a chip breaker in the fence with the chosen bit. This assures that the contour will make a smooth curve. Stand the piece to be rounded or coved on edge against the fence. Use a back block to prevent tear out and pass the corner by the bit. Do all four corners of the block for evenly rounded or coved corners. See figure III-B-e-1 and III-B-e-2.

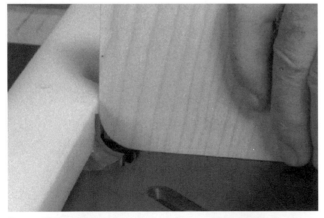

Figure III-B-e-1 Round corners with a round over bit.

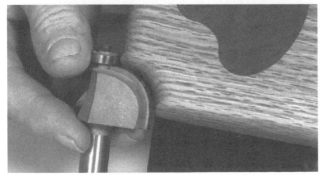

Figure III-B-e-2 Use a cove bit to cove the corners.

III-C. Jointer Fence

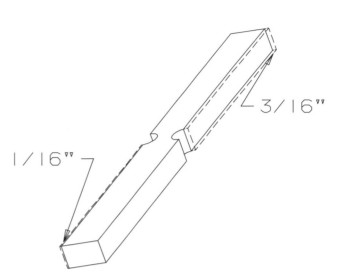

Figure III-C-1 Jointer fence with different infeed off sets.

Using your router as a jointer

Before we start to talk about using the router as jointer lets talk about the important parts which make the jointer work. The principle of the jointer is simple, the cutter is in line with the out feed table and the infeed table is lower by the amount which has to be removed. The infeed table is used to start the piece on the cutter and the outfeed table is used to receive the piece after it has been cut. These three parts, the outfeed, the infeed and the cutter must be set up correctly for the jointer to work.

The outfeed

This is the most important part to the jointer because the table or fence in this case has to be even with the outer cutting edge of the cutter in order to have the jointer work properly. See figure III-C-1. If the cutter is ahead of the outfeed fence the result is the project piece will have a snip or notch in the end of the board once the piece has left the infeed fence. See figure III-C-2

rough position with the router bit in the profile groove. Then the router bit is put behind the fence and a straight piece of material is placed even with the outfeed of the fence. The cutter is now rotated until the cutter is positioned with the outer most cutting edge in line with the piece of material. Caution: this is only done with the router unplugged. Once the outer most part of the cutting edge is touching the material the clamp is placed on the infeed side of the fence. After clamping the pieces check the cutter once again. Use your fine adjusting tool for additional minor adjustments.

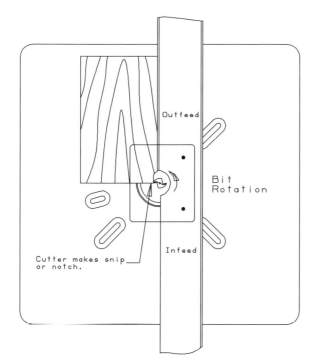

Figure III-C-2 Results of the cutter ahead of the out feed fence.

If the cutter is behind the fence then the results are a taper cut on the project piece. See figure III-C-3

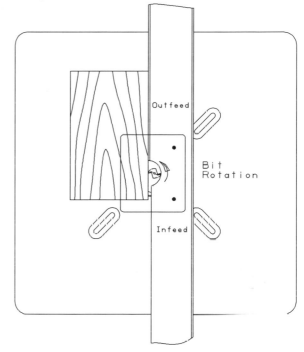

Figure III-C-4 Set up for the jointer fence.

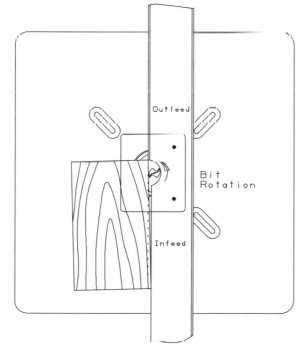

Figure III-C-3 Results of the cutter behind the outfeed fence is a taper.

It is important to have the outfeed fence even with the outer most cutting edge of the cutter. The easiest way to do this is shown in figure III-C-4. The outfeed fence is clamped in a

III-D. Measuring

Don't measure too much. If you can avoid using a tape measure or ruler, do so. If you need to step off equal lengths, cut a stick and use it. More mistakes are made in measuring than in any other part of woodworking. Measuring can be made easier by using some of these hints.

a. Half the thickness of the material

Any time you are required to make a rabbet or dado it is best to make these cuts at half the thickness of the material for several reasons. First it maintains the strength in the material. Second it is easier to compute the sizing of materials. Also if it becomes a habit, you never have to remember what you did for the last cut because it is a standard that you stick to.

How can you set half the thickness without measuring? Well first of all just guess at it. Lay the piece beside the cutter and raise the bit to what you think is half the thickness. You will be close but you want to be right on. So check it.

Any time you mill material for a project you should mill several extra pieces to use for test pieces. Set up the table fence on the router table and run a test piece into the cutter just on the corner. Turn the test piece over and run the same corner into the cutter again. Three things can happen. You can be right on and the two cuts meet exactly. You can be too high and there will be a notch between the two cuts. Lower the bit half the size of the notch. Or you can have a feather piece between the two cuts because you are too low. Raise the cutter half the size of the feather piece. Test the height again with another corner of the test piece.

As you use this method of depth adjustment you will get good at it and eventually have the setting right most of the time without any changes.

b. Set the full thickness of the material

To set the depth of cut to the full thickness of the material DO NOT measure. Set the work piece beside the cutter. Lay a small piece of wood over the work piece so it extends over the bit. Raise the bit to the underside of the wood piece and lock it in place. You have set the depth of cut to the material thickness without measuring. See figure III-D-b-1.

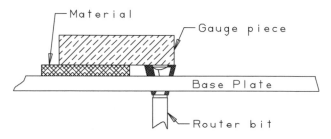

Figure III-D-b-1. Set full thickness of material.

c. Finding the circumference of a circle

To determine the circumference of a circle just lay a steel square on the circle as shown in figure III-D-c-1. The circumference is three times the diameter plus the distance between the points D and E.

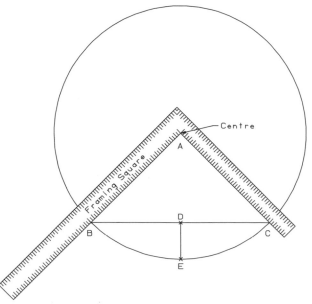

Figure III-D-c-1 The easy way to find circumference with a square.

d. Parallel lines

Drawing a long line parallel to the edge of a board, when you don't have a long enough straight edge, is not difficult. Just use a stick, a clamp and a pencil as shown in figure III-D-d-1.

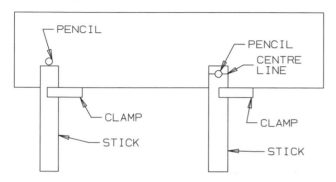

Figure III-D-d-1 Parellel lines with a shop made scribe.

e. Octagon lay out

If the square to be used is less than 6" on each side, place a ruler over the square so that the zero mark and the 6" mark are at the edges. Then scribe a line at the 1 3/4" mark as shown in figure III-D-e-1. Repeat for all four sides of the square.

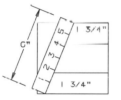

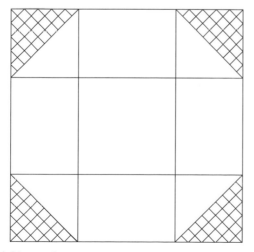

Figure III-D-e-1 How to layout a octagon.

The point at which these lines meet the ends of the square indicates the location of the corners of the octagon.

For different size squares do this. If the piece is exactly 6" square, use the 1 3/4" method. If the square is larger than 6", use a 12" ruler and scribe lines 3 1/2" from the ends. If the square is over 12" use a 24" ruler and scribe lines 7" from the ends.

You can use the same method to change linear square stock to linear octagonal stock.

f. Equal parts

There is an easy way to divide odd width stock into equal parts, a way that does away with clumsy fractions. Simply put your ruler at an angle across the stock until you have a total length that is readily divisible into the number of pieces you require. Then mark as shown in figure III-D-f-1.

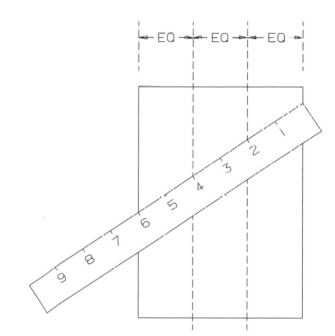

Figure III-D-f-1 Dividing the piece into equal parts.

g. Shop compass

A shop-made compass can be produced to draw large or small circles. All you need is a thin piece of wood longer than the radius of the largest circle you intend to draw. Fix a radius by locating a centre pin hole the distance you want from the end of the stick. Drill this hole with a drill press to insure that it is perpendicular. In fact, using a finishing nail as a drill, the same nail that you will use in the compass, works best.

Use your compass by locating the centre pin hole over the centre of the circle you wish to draw and, holding a pencil against the end (which can be notched to make things easier) draw away. See figure III-D-g-1.

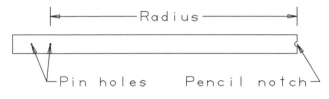

Figure III-D-g-1 Shop made compass.

h. Check your framing square

Framing squares, as you will discover, are not created equal nor are they all square. Check yours from time to time to see if it is still square. Dropping it accidentally may cause unwanted adjustments.

To check all you need is a straight board. As shown in the diagram position the square against the board and draw a line. Flip the square and draw another. If they do not coincide, your square is not square.

If the square you are checking is brand new, return it to where you got it and demand a square that lives up to its name.

If it is an old favorite, you can adjust it with a hammer and a centre punch. Just imagine a 45-degree line running from the point of the square to the inside angle. If the square is more than 90 degrees as shown by your check, use the centre punch near the inside corner to bring it back. If less than 90 degrees, use the punch near the outside corner.

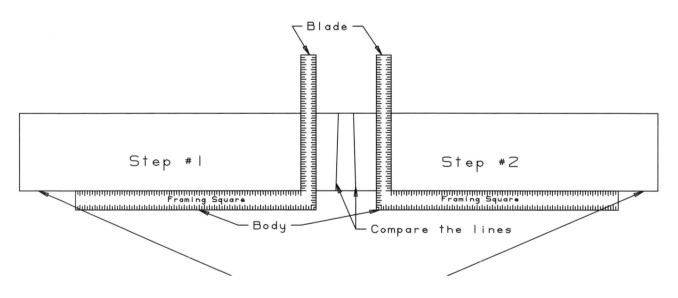

Figure III-D-h-1 Checking your square to see if it is square.

III-E. Bit Tips

❑When unpackaging a new router bit check to see that the bearing rolls freely.

❑Check to see that this bearing is tight. It is not uncommon to find the screw that holds the bearing in place is just finger tight. Tighten it with a key.

❑Check to see that there are no fractures in the carbide.

❑Check to see that the shank is smooth with no burrs or rough spots.

❑When installing a bit, bottom the bit shank out in the chuck, then lift it out about 1/16" to ensure it does not contact the bottom. The router bit generates a lot of heat. If the bit is bottomed out in the chuck the heat is transferred directly from the cutter to the router motor. This causes over heating and early burn out of the router motor.

❑NEVER use a dull or chipped router bit.

❑REPLACE all damaged bearings.

❑The shank material in a good router bit will always bend before it will break. If you notice a slight wobble in a router bit, do NOT use it.

NOTE: SOLID CARBIDE ROUTER BITS are very brittle and require special care by the operator. The slightest jambing in the work piece may cause the bit to break. When chucking up a solid carbide bit be careful not to hit it with a wrench. When installing a solid carbide bit into the chuck be sure there is a smooth surface of shank against the router collet. The bit's cutting edge should not be in the collet.

❑All router bits need good storage. Drill holes to hold the router bit shanks and space them to keep the bits from touching one another. (Brittle carbide is easily chipped).

❑Store router bits in a clean dry place.

❑Keep all bits and cutters clean and do not allow resin to build up as this will cause burning.

❑When purchasing cutters check to see that there is good clearance between the carbide cutting edge and the bit body.

❑When a bit becomes dull sharpen it. You may wish to send it out to a professional sharpener.

❑When a router bit becomes stuck in a chuck a stiff tap on the bit will jar it loose. Do not use a metal tool for this. A piece of wood works well. Be careful not to tap the carbide.

❑If a router bit is constantly coming loose, try a different bit. It may be that the shank of that bit is not round or is slightly undersized. This problem is most often present when you use a reducing sleeve in a 1/2" chuck.

❑When using a split sleeve in a 1/2" chuck, be sure that the split in the sleeve aligns with the split in the collet.

❑Some bits only come in 1/4" size shank so you must use a sleeve to bring it up to 1/2" shank if you have a 1/2" collet router.

❑Whenever possible choose router bits with shank size to fit the collet. Proper shank size bits last longer and stay sharp longer than under size bits that require a sleeve. WHY? Heat and vibration.

❑When routing abrasive materials use dust masks for the top and bottom of the router. Cut a hole to go over the chuck in one mask and pull it over the chuck end of the router. The other mask goes over the top of the router over the fan grill. Put another mask on your face. When the face mask requires changing, change all three masks. Your router will last longer and your lungs will thank you.

❑Be very careful what kind of spray you use to clean bits. Some sprays react chemically with the solder used to fasten on the carbide. Always remove the bearing before you spray the bit.

❑In a plunge router protect the columns on the router by setting up your wrenches to squeeze together to loosen the chuck. Avoid pulling wrenches apart to loosen the chuck because the wrench may slip and nick the columns. This will interfere with the smooth up and down plunge of the router.

❑Pull the wrenches to tighten the bit into the chuck. To be sure the bit will not come loose during the cutting operation, tighten the collet as tight as you can with the wrenches provided.

III-F. Remove Springs

For the ease of table mounting your plunge router, remove the springs! A five minute job for most routers.

When table mounting your router, making the height adjustments require you not only to lift the weight of the router but also to compress the springs. The purpose of the springs is to compensate for the weight of the router when using for portable routing. We do not need the springs with the router in a stationary position. So here's how we remove springs from most common plunge routers.

1) On most routers the base is held to the router with a threaded rod and double nut. When the router is to it's highest height the nut is stopping the base from being removed from the router motor. We want to locate the router in it's highest position and lock the base.

2) The next operation will be to remove the double nut. CAUTION: The springs in the columns are still under about 25% compression and we must not unlock the router base until we have the base facing in a safe direction.

3) Unlock the base and separate the base from the router. **About the lock.** The lock is a threaded pin and behind the pin is a brass cylinder which protects the columns from scaring with the bolt. NOTE: This cylinder is loose on some models and if lost you will not be able to lock the base to the router.

4) What's inside the columns? Inside the columns you will find 2 springs and 2 short metal rods inside the springs. We want to remove these springs and rods. Put the springs and rods in a place that you can find them for the next time you want to reassemble the router for portable operations. CAUTION: You cannot use the router for portable operations without the springs, so do not lose them. Do not forget about the brass cylinder as you need this to make the lock work.

Note: This is a good time to clean the grease that is around the springs and columns. Remember grease attracts dust, which will clog up the columns. After you have cleaned the columns, coat with a lubricant that will not attract dust like "Kity speed."

5) Reassemble the router and put the double lock nuts back on the threaded rod. The only spare parts that you should have after the operation should be the 2 springs and 2 rods. Don't put these parts in your special hiding place as you might misplace them. Note: Your plunge router should be set at it's lowest height for storage. This will protect the columns from the atmosphere and moisture.

Notes:

Appendix IV
Spacer Joinery

IV A Using Spacer Fences

How to make a good box joint

A good joint depends on three things being equal. These are the size of the bit, the space between the bit and the fence and the fence itself. As an example, if you are using a 3/8" fence then you should have a 3/8" straight bit and the space between the bit and the fence should be 3/8".

Only two things can go wrong with a box joint. It can be either too tight or too loose. A joint will be too tight if the space between the bit and the fence is larger than the bit. To correct, simply tap the fence in towards the bit slightly. If the joint is too loose, then the space between the bit and the fence is smaller than the bit. Tap the fence away from the bit slightly to correct. Use your fine adjustment tool to make the corrections. If your local hardware does not know what a fine adjustment tool is, ask for a hammer. The spacer bolts are designed with enough give in them to allow for these fine adjustments. Tighten the bolts after you are satisfied with the fit.

What makes a good joint

The answer is simple. What makes a good joint is the right fit. The larger the box the looser the fit should be, to give you enough time to get it together between the time you put the glue on and you finish the assembly. Always remember that glue, even a thin film of glue, occupies space. Use scrap to reach the desired fit before cutting into your project wood.

Joining even and uneven thicknesses

Remember, it is the height of the bit that determines both the depth of the box slots and the length of the box fingers. It is better to have the fingers protrude slightly, so they can be sanded off than to have them too short. However, the more the fingers protrude, the more work you will have sanding. The best rule for the length fingers should stick out is simple. Just enough to require a bit, but not a lot of sanding.

Same thickness

If the pieces you are joining are the same thickness, you will have to set the height of the bit only once. If one piece is thicker than the other, remember to have the fingers on the thin piece long enough to cover the thick edge of the other piece.

Keeping the sides even with an offset jig

If you cut box joints in two pieces of wood and try to fit them together, you will discover that the pieces do not line up. To make them line up you need a simple, home-made offset jig. See figure IV-A-1.

Figure IV-A-1 The offset jig for the second cut.

After you have determined what makes a good fit, take a longer piece of wood and run a lengthwise dado by holding the piece against the fence. Then, with the router switched off, turn this piece so that the dado you have cut fits over the fence. The edge should be flush against the inside of the router bit. Make this piece long enough so that you can clamp it on the in-feed side of the table, and so that the piece itself extends beyond the bit. Be sure to clamp it securely.

Keep the piece and mark it. It will come in handy the next time you want to make similar box joints. It allows you to make the initial cuts in two of the four pieces you will use to make a box. The other two sides will be cut against the spacer fence without an offset.

How box joints affect dimensions

If the bit is set to the exact thickness of each material, a box joint will leave the project the same size as the pieces that have been cut. Deeper cuts will reduce the dimensions slightly. If the specifications you are using are inside measurements, be sure to include the thickness of the material on each side before cutting the pieces you want to join.

If you are working with really close tolerances, allow for the finish to be applied.

IV B Building A Box

First, let's build a box using the same thickness material all around.

Sort your sides and ends, selecting the face sides of each piece. Mark the edges that will be on the top.

After you are satisfied with the fit of the joints by using scrap, clamp the two sides of the box together and, using a backing block to keep them vertical, run a series of box-joint cuts across both ends. Start the cuts with the marked top edges toward the fence.

Take the two ends and clamp them together. Clamp your offset jig in place, and with the marked top edges toward the fence, make the first cut on each end. This may be a bit tricky since you have to remember to flip the pieces so that the marked edge is toward the fence for each cut. Turn off the router and let the bit come to a complete stop.

Remove the offset jig and proceed with the remainder of the cuts on both ends, again remembering to keep the marked top edges toward the fence.

You should have a box that fits well and has an even top and bottom.

If your ends are thicker than your sides

Proceed as above, cutting the joints on the sides first. Remember to adjust the height of the bit to accommodate the thicker material being used for the ends.

After both ends of both sides are cut, reposition the bit to the thickness of the sides. Clamp your offset jig into position and clamp the

two end pieces together and, keeping the marked top toward the offset, make the initial cuts in both ends of the end pieces. Turn off the router and let the bit come to a complete stop before you remove the offset fence. Complete the cuts in the ends over the spacer fence.

A few tips

If your material has a tendency to chip, you may wish to wrap each side and end piece with masking tape before cutting the box joints. Just peel off the tape after you have made the cuts.

IV C Angle Box Joint

Set up the fence

Chuck up a 3/8" spiral bit in the table- mounted router. Attach the 3/8" spacer fence over the table leaving a 3/8" space between the bit and the fence. See figure IV-C-1. Check the box joint as done when making the standard box joints. Check the fit.

Figure IV-C-1 3/8" spacer fence over the spiral bit, fasten to the table with two bolts and wingnuts. Now the fence can be mounted in the same place every time.

Make the support block

To keep the pieces at the correct angle, a holding block is needed. The angle in this case is going to be 30 degrees. See figure IV-C-2-a and figure IV-C-2-b.

Figure IV-C-2-a Holding blocks with the 30 degree angle.

Figure IV-C-2-b Make the support blocks with the two angles.

Use a piece of 4 7/8" X 12" X 1 1/2" material and mark on one end of the block the letter A. On the other end mark the letter B and put a mark along one edge of the piece. Now drill two 1/2" holes 3/4" deep in the blocks as shown. Next cut the 30 degree angle in the center of the 12" block. See figure IV-C-3.

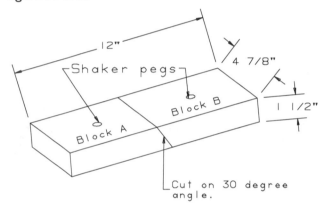

Figure IV-C-3 Drawing of the angled holding blocks A and B.

The holes are used to put in a shaker peg to hold the block. Using the spacer fence, cut the grooves into the holding blocks. Block A is cut with the marked side tight to the fence and block B is started with marked side tight to the offset block and then cut as block A. The grooves are cut with the grain and are made through the entire block.

Preparing the project material

Do not change your setup on the saw. To prepare the project material, one end of the pieces need to be cut at the same angle as the holding block. The setup for the block makes this a good time to cut the project pieces.

Making the angle box joint

With the angles cut on the one end of each piece, now mark the fence edge of each piece.

The marked edge is the edge that is to be put up against the fence. See figure IV-C-4.

Figure IV-C-4 Marking the fence side of the pieces.

The first piece

The angle box joints are the same as making regular box joints but the pieces are cut on an angle. Stand one of the project pieces on the angled end with the holding block A on the spacer fence and cut the box joint. See figure IV-C-5.

Figure IV-C-5 The first piece cut with block A.

Be sure to have the piece tight to the table and fence. Always keep your fingers away from the router bit. Make the same cut throughout the entire width of the project piece.

First cut on the second piece

The second piece needs to fit with the first piece. The first piece has a finger, then a groove and to match the second piece it has to start with a groove then a finger. An offset is needed to start with a groove. See figure IV-C-6.

Clamp this offset in place on the spacer fence and make the first cut. To make the joint match the angle cut, use block B. Remove the offset block and make the rest of the cuts. Make sure that the marked side is against the offset block.

Figure IV-C-6 Offset block for the first cut on the second piece with block B.

Dry fit the pieces. if satisfied with the fit, cut the angle box joints in the project pieces. See figure IV-C-7.

Figure IV-C-7 Pieces dry fit for the angle box joint.

IV D Rabbet Dado Joint

The easiest way to produce this joint is to use a spacer fence one half the thickness of the material. For example, if your material is 1/2" thick, use a 1/4" spacer fence.

Chuck up a spiral bit of the same size as the fence in the table mounted router. Position the spacer fence over the router and set the depth of cut to one half of the material thickness. This need not be a precise measurement since it will not affect the fit of the joint.

Use cut off pieces of scrap to check the set up. Rout a dado cut in the back face of one of the pieces to be joined. See figure IV-D-1. Then clamp an offset block on to the fence, stand the second piece to be joined on edge and make the rabbet cut with the front face of the piece against the offset block. See figure IV-D-2. Check the fit, as shown in figure IV-D-3.

Figure IV-D-1 The first cut is the dado joint.

Figure IV-D-2 The rabbet joint is cut with the offset block in place.

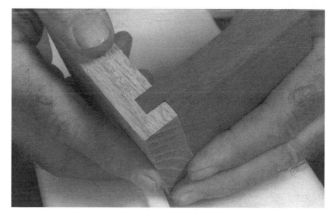

Figure IV-D-3 The rabbet dado joint.

Most problems in rabbet dado joints occur because the material thickness is wrong. Remember, the material should be twice as thick as the fence. The joint is sometimes spoiled because the rabbet cut was made when the material was not tight against the offset block. Whenever a rabbet joint is cut, the material left over fits in the dado groove.

IV E Dovetail Splice

Chuck up a 1/2" dovetail bit in the table-mounted router. Position the 3/8" spacer fence over the table with a 1/2" space between the fence and the router bit. Set the height of the bit to cut a 3/8" slot. If using a 14 degree dovetail adjust the height to 5/16". This slot will fit over the spacer fence. Since the height of the bit determines the shape of the slots, use two cut off pieces as a test and see how close the fit will be. See figure IV-E-1.

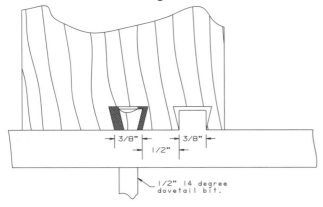

Figure IV-E-1 Dovetail setup on 3/8" spacer fence.

Setting up the pieces

Contrasting woods make interesting dovetail splices. Four pieces of contrasting material are needed to make two spliced sides. When you have determined where the splices will be made, mark the edges that will go against the fence when being cut. To get an even splice, the second piece will have to be offset by 1/2" (the size of the bit). Setup bars are an easy way to determine the offset, and remember to keep the ends flush on the bottom.

Making the cut

Keeping the marked edges against the fence, run the dovetail groove in the ends. Put the groove over the fence and repeat the cuts until the dovetail slots appear along the entire end.

HINT - By carefully clamping the pieces together, allowing for the offset, you can cut more than one piece at once.

The rule for getting a tighter or looser fit with dovetail splices is the same as it is for box joints. If the test piece is too tight, tap the fence toward the bit. If it is too loose, tap the fence away from the bit.

IV F Sliding Dovetails On A 45 Degree Angle

Building the jig

This particular joint, used in constructing the coffee mug tree, is much easier if you take the time to build yourself a simple jig first. To do this you will need two pieces of wood 2 5/8" x 1" x 6" and two 2 5/8" x 3/4" x 3". Deal with the thicker blocks first. In one end of each of these blocks make a 90 degree angle V cut centred on the 2 5/8" width. See figure IV-F-1. Just behind the centre of this cut, rout a 3/4" wide by 1/2" deep dado across the piece to receive a clamping support. Insert and glue these supports.

Figure IV-F-1 Jig used to hold the pieces to be cut on a 45 degree angle.

What you have is a pair of holders that will support the 1 7/8" square by 3" blocks that make up your coffee mug tree. Use a piece of scrap this size to finish the jig. Just insert this piece between the V cuts and clamp accross the supports.

Setting up the fence

Chuck up the 1/2" 14 degree dovetail bit in the table-mounted router and position the 3/8" spacer fence just as if you were making the dovetail splices described in appendix IV-E. When making these sliding dovetails, be careful not to make them too tight. Check the fit using scrap. See figure IV-F-1.

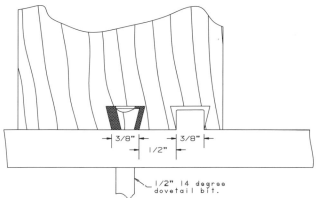

Figure IV-F-1 The measurements for the sliding dovetail.

Make the first dovetail cut through the jig blocks and the scrap representing the project block while holding the jig tight against the fence. Place the groove produced over the fence and continue routing to produce dovetails across the entire holding block. Discard the scrap blocks and install the coffee mug tree blocks. Cut 45 degree dovetail slides in all blocks according to the mug tree plans.

To make a different sized tree you will need another jig. To maintain the spacing you must increase the size of the square by 1/2" or multiples of 1/2". This is necessary because the bit you are using makes a 1/2" wide cut. The holding block must be made to fit the project blocks.

Notes:

Appendix V
Guide Work Basics

V-A Guides

Why guides and not pilot bearings

The guide has many advantages over the bearing bit. The first advantage of the guide and router bit is the router bit is running independent from the guide. The guide flange follows the pattern without rotating at the same speed as the router bit. The pilot bearing is rotating at the same speed as the bit, but it skids to a stop whenever the pattern is contacted. This pratice will change the shape of the pattern. If the bearing is on the top of the cutter we cannot plunge into the internal pattern. We need a pre-drilled pilot hole and must have the pattern on the bottom of the pieces. If the bearing is on the shank of the bit, we have to plunge into the pattern cavity freehand without any support from the router bearing until it is fully plunged into the pattern. The guide can rest on the pattern before the router bit enters the wood. This gives support and prevents the cutter from moving into the pattern. With the bearing on the shank you also have only one depth of cut that can be used, the full depth. With the guide independent from the bit we can make cuts at the required depths. We do not have to cut at full depth only. The guide gives better control and is safer to use. Because guides are used with the router where vibration is always present, we use brass. The brass ringnut on a brass guide will not vibrate loose like steel. If the router bit does come in contact with the guide it will most likely damage the brass and not the bit.

V-B Inlay work

Producing inlay work is really quite straight-forward. To make an inlay simply rout a cavity and cut a plug to fit it. See figure V-B-1

Cutting the cavity

Select the pattern to be used. It must be securely fastened to the material to be cut. This can be done by using a pattern jig, double-stick tape, nails, clamps or screws. Just remember that once positioned, the pattern CAN NOT BE MOVED until the cavity is completely routed.

V-B-1 A 1/8" inlayed piece of walnut into a piece of cherry.

Inlay work has to have a guide and an inlay bushing that are designed specifically for the task. Because it is critical, Oak Park recommends the portable 7" base plate which will automatically centre the brass guide. Brass guides and bushings are suited for pattern work because brass naturally clings to itself, and needs only to be finger-tight to work.

Use a 7/16" guide with a 1/4" router bit and a 1/4" inlay bushing. See figure V-5-2

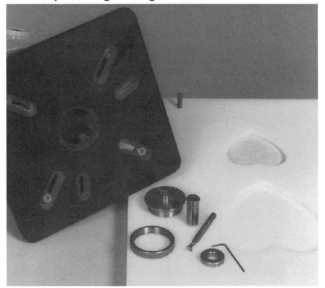

Figure V-B-2 Parts required to make inlays.

Set the depth of cut on your plunge router. You can use the plug material to set this depth. Start the router, plunge to the preselected depth and begin cutting from left to right in a clockwise direction.

Figure V-B-3 The inlay cavity made with the router, 1/4" bushing, 7/16" guide and the 1/4" router bit.

You should remove the chips and sawdust generated by the cut several times during the routing operation. Chips particularly have a habit of working between the guide and the pattern, altering the shape. Continue to clean out the material until you have a smooth bottom on the cavity.

Cutting the inlay plug

Remove the 1/4" bushing from the 7/16" guide. See figure V-B-4. Position the pattern over the inlay material and fasten the material securely. Use double-stick tape and your pattern jig or other fastening devices. The pattern must remain fixed during the cutting operation.

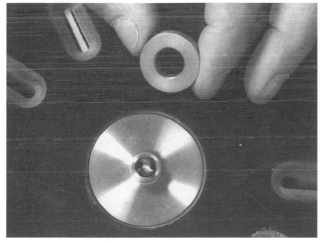

Figure V-B-4 Remove the 1/4" bushing before cutting the plug for the inlay cavity.

Set the depth of cut with the plug material. The depth should be a little deeper than the plug material, this will make sure that the cut is made completly through the piece. See figure V-B-5

Figure V-B-5 Setting depth of cut with plug material.

Begin your cut with the guide snug against the pattern. Move from left to right, working slowly to ensure that the guide stays tight against the pattern. It is important that no shavings or cuttings get between the guide and pattern as the cut is being made. See figure V-B-6

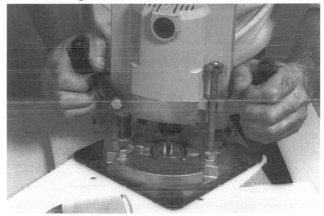

Figure V-B-6 Moving the router from left to right.

If you are careful, the plug and cavity should fit perfectly. If it does not, recheck your router bit. The guides and bushings are designed for bits that are exactly on size. See figure V-B-7 Position the inlay in the recess.

Figure V-B-7 Plug ready to be put into the cavity.

V-C Wheel jigs

Wheels have been used since people discovered the mechanical advantage to rolling something as opposed to carrying a heavy load. Most wheels are round and consist of a network of spokes radiating from a centre point called a hub. The hub becomes the centre for attaching an axel around which the wheel revolves. See figure V-C-1

Figure V-C-1 Various wheel designs.

Wooden wheels can be used for wheeled projects or for decoration on stationary projects. The problem is to get wheels of uniform size, thickness, and design. The wheel jigs explained here allow you to cut unlimited wheels all exactly the same using an incremental internal cut.

You will require the following:

Backing board - a piece of 3/4" plywood large enough to be fastened solidly to a bench or work top. Use the sub top. See Appendix VIII-F.

Project stock - a square at least 1 1/4" larger than the wheel size you wish to make.
Plunge Router, 1/2" straight router bit.
Guide - 1" (outside diameter). and ringnut.
Wheel jig - comes in 3 patterns and 3 sizes for each pattern giving you a choice of 9 variations.

Making wheels

Drill a 1/4" axle hole in the center of the project material. See figure V-C-2 The 1/4" axle hole must go through the project material and into the backing board. The project stock must be fastened securely to the backing board or sub top.

Mounting the blank

You may use 4 screws up from the back of the backing board extending into the hub (1" diameter around the pivot pin) or you can use double-stick tape to secure the stock to the backing board.

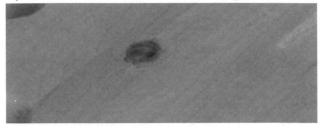

Figure V-C-2 The axle hole is put in the center of the wheel material.

The center point

Insert the pivot pin into the axle hole of the project material, setting the bottom of the pin into the backing board hole. Place the wheel jig on top of the project material. Make sure the pivot pin is flush with the top of the wheel jig.

Making the first cut

Install a 1/2" straight bit and a 1" guide in the router. Position the wheel jig for the first spoke hole. You may wish to expose certain wood grain or cut out a knot in the project material. This is the time to determine this aspect and position the jig accordingly. See figure V-C-3.

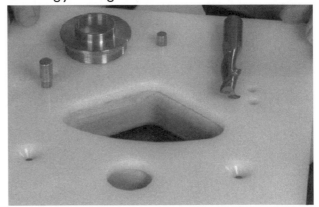

Figure V-C-3 Parts required to make perfect wooden wheels.

Run a screw into one of the counter-sunk screw holes to hold the jig in place for the first spoke hole. Cut the first spoke hole either right through the material, or partially through for a patterned wheel effect.

The next cut

Remove the screw and rotate the wheel jig to position it for the second spoke hole. You can rotate either right or left. Insert the aligning pin in hole. Index the wheel jig by bringing the pin up against the previous spoke hole edge. While indexing do not force against the pin as it could cause you to distort the alignment. If using the left pin rotate to the right or use the right-hand pin and rotate to the left. This is a personal preferance. Run the screw into the counter-sunk screw hole to hold the jig in position. Remove the aligning pin and cut the second spoke hole. Repeat the above operation for the next two spoke holes.

The last hole

For the last spoke hole use two aligning pins in holes. This allows you to adust the remaining space to center the last spoke. Insert the screw in the counter sunk screw hole. Remove the aligning pins and cut the last spoke hole. Remove the screw.

Figure V-C-4 Place 1" guide in the hole to make a circle cut.

Cutting the outside

Insert the 1" guide in the 1" hole. See figure V-C-4. Plunge the router bit into the project stock, rotating counter clockwise to cut the circular outside diameter of the wheel project.

The blank size

Be sure the project material is large enough so the bit is cutting in material on both sides of the router bit. For example: An 8-inch wheel requires a 9 1/4" square of project material.

Wheel jigs are available in the following variations: Standard wheel spokes in 8" or 10" or 12" wheel sizes. Tea Wagon spokes in 8" or 10" or 12" wheel sizes. Star spokes in 8" or 10" or 12" wheel sizes.

Wheels with inlays

Inlays instead of spoke holes are accomplished with ease using the same wheel jig. The jig is designed to use the 1/4" inlay bushing with 1/4" bit. You would follow the same procedure but use aligning holes for inlays instead of the aligning holes for the spokes.

Then use the Wheel Jig as the pattern for the inlays by double-stick taping it to the inlay material.

Use this same wheel jig to make a dish. Leave a bottom in each spoke cavity and mold the outside edges.

Notes:

V-D Pattern Fixture

The pattern fixture is a simple fixture designed to hold any size work piece to a maximum size of 8" x 12". It may be furniture blocked to accomodate smaller sizes. See figure V-D-1.

Figure V-D-1 Work piece blocked in the pattern cavity.

The bottom of the pattern fixture has cleats which fit exactly into the plate hole in the router table. Simply remove your table mounted router and the pattern fixture fits in the same hole.

The patterns are easily interchanged. The fixture has dovetail slots milled on the outside edges. The patterns are all dovetailed to match. Simply slide the chosen pattern into the fixture. See figure V-D-2. Blank pattern pieces are available if you wish to design your own patterns.

Figure V-D-2 Slide the pattern over the work piece.

Making it work

Remove the base plate and router from the table. Slip the pattern fixture (cleat side down) into the table hole. Center and secure the work piece in the fixture hole. Center the chosen pattern over the work piece and drill the pin hole from the bottom of the fixture up through the pattern on the top. Insert the pin in the hole to keep the pattern from moving. See figure V-D-3.

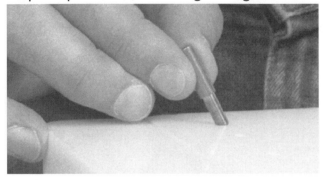

Figure V-D-3 Pin keeps the pattern from moving.

Choose a plunging bit (no pilot bearing) with any profile. Select a brass guide sized to allow the plunging bit to center and run free inside the guide. Attach the guide securely to the portable base plate (7" base plate) with the brass ring nut. Do not use pliers on these brass pieces. Finger tighten only. Attach the base plate to your plunge router. The guide flange will extend 1/4" below the base plate. The bit should be exactly centered in the guide without touching the flange of the guide. See figure V-D-4.

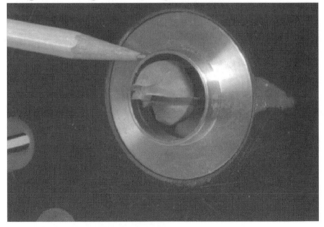

Figure V-D-4 The bit must center in the guide.

Setting the depth of cut

Place the router on the pattern jig with the bit in the cavity. Plunge the bit until it comes in contact with the work piece. Lock it in this position. Set the depth of cut by putting the required brass set up bars between the pole stop and base. See figure V-D-5. Lock the pole stop in place. The depth of cut is set.

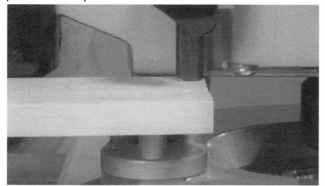

Figure V-D-5 Set the depth of cut.

V-D-6 Dish project in the shape of a club.

The cut

Direction of feed is important. When inside a cavity always move the router from left to right. With the guide snug against the pattern edge, start the router and plunge the bit into the cut. Move the router from left to right around the pattern. Ensure that debris does not get between the guide and the pattern. You may have to stop periodically and clean the cut or use a vacuum. Continue routing until the cut is complete. See figure V-D-6.

This could be a dish or frame project. This fixture also works well for inlaying contrasting shapes in a work piece. The pattern fixture is ideal for reproducing many small items quickly and precisely.

Notes:

Appendix VI
Furniture Construction

VI-A. Panel Construction

Molding panels with the router is a very easy process, there are three operations 1) the cope 2) the bead 3) the panel. The cuts are made in that order.

Marking the pieces

The best way to keep track of the pieces and where they fit is to use a system which identifies the parts immediately.

Marks are made on the best face or the front of each piece. Cut all of the parts face side down. When the parts are assembled we use the marks to tell us where we have sanded and where we have not sanded.

Tip: When just starting to make raised panels, before you make any cuts, you should sort the pieces to make sure that the right cuts are on the pieces. Lay all the pieces on the table for each panel. Sort for colour, grain, general look and best face. Mark the specific parts and their location. Then mark what cut is made where.

You do not have to mark the cuts on the panels because you cut all around the edges. The stiles, rails and mullions have a choice of cuts, cope or bead. While the parts are laid out on the bench, mark the bead and the cope. Now you know where and what cut to use. This is a simple way to avoid mistakes and frustration. See figure VI-A-1.

Good safety tip: Do all of your thinking and marking before you make the cuts.

Here are some suggested markings for the panel. Top rail (TR), Bottom Rail (BR), Stile (S), Mullion (M), and Panel (P).

The cope on the ends

The first cut made on the router is the cope cut on the ends of the rails and mullions. All of the pieces that need to have a cope cut should be in this group. Do not worry about mixing up the parts because you have all the parts marked right.

Router set up

Next is to set up the router. Keep the set up simple and divide the process into small segments. Set up the table mounted router. Mount the router bit, stile (bead) and rail bit (cope). The bit height will come after we have mounted the fence. See figures VI-A-2-a and VI-A-2-b.

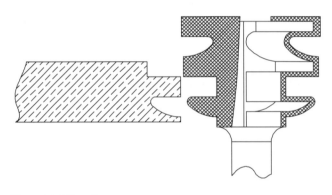

Figure VI-A-2-a Cope set up.

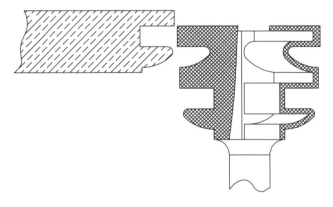

Figure VI-A-2-b Bead set up.

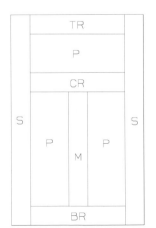

Figure VI-A-1 Mark the cope and bead cuts.

Mount the fence

When setting up your router there are only two things to be concerned about, is the fence the correct distance away from the router bit and is the router bit set at the correct height. What is the distance away from the fence? This is determined by the cutter and whether it is standard or not. Standard inside diameter of a cope and bead cutter is 7/8" and the standard inside diameter for a panel cutter is 1/2". The fence has to be mounted at these diameters, exposing the cutter on the 7/8" and 1/2" measurement.

The best way to do this is to use a jig which gives these distances automatically. Mount the stile and rail fence and clamp it to the table. See figure VI-A-3. This fence has steel pins that protrude below and fit into the pre drilled holes in the base plate. This is how the distance is set automatically.

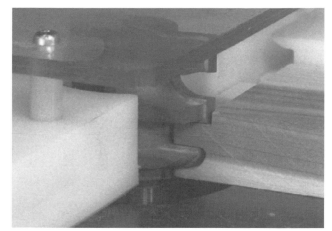

Figure VI-A-4 Cope cutter set up.

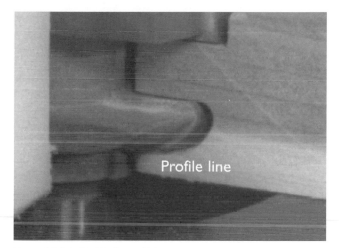

Figure VI-A-5 Profile line of the cutter.

From the end of the profile shape you want to have a 1/16" to 1/8" space between the table set up and the start of the profile. Remember, the cutter that you see cuts the opposite.

What is set up now?

The panel fence is locked in place at the proper distance from the cutter. The router bit should be mounted and the height set. The parts are sorted and marked where each piece needs to be cut and what kind of cut needs to be made.

The only safe way to cut these pieces on the end is to use a mitre block. The mitre block is designed to hold the pieces tight to the table and square to the fence during the cutting of the

Figure VI-A-3 Raised panel fence.

The router bit (cope)

The bit pictured below is a single cutter with both profiles on it. The cope cut is on the bottom part of the profile and the bead cut is on the top part of the profile. Start by putting in a router bit designed to make the cope cut. See figure VI-A-4.

The router bit looks like it might be difficult to set up but let's look at the most important part of the cutter, the profile line. The profile line of the cope is where you base the set up of the cutter. See figure VI-A-5.

cope. A toggle clamp holds the pieces in the mitre block and has a fixed position. If you hold it properly your hands will be away from the cutters. Test the set up with a scrap piece first. When satisfied, cut all of the cope cuts. See figure VI-A-6.

Figure VI-A-6 Mitre cutting the cope cuts.

How to check the cut

Here is how we check to see that the cut has been made successfully right after the cut. On the profile line we need to have two parallel surfaces see figure VI-A-7.

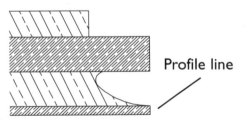

Profile line

Figure VI-A-7 The parallel profile line.

The second check point is on the back of the cut. This cut must be made straight and parallel with the end. See figure VI-A-8.

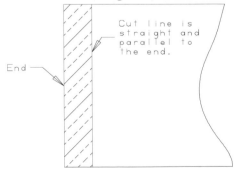

Cut line is straight and parallel to the end.

End

Figure VI-A-8 The cope cut made straight from the back.

Remember to check these cuts while you have them in your hand because if you check later two things have happened. The set up is no longer set up and you have to check and handle the pieces again unnecessarily.

Setting the bead

Where is the bead cut set? Do we have to set it or is it already figured out? Look for the answer on the pieces that we have already cut. The cope cut has to fit into the bead cut so we have to match the cope with the bead. The best way to match cutters is to use a point on the cutter that is the most important part and easiest to set from. To set up the bead cutter we need to drop the cutter until the top slot cutter of the bead matches the tenon part of the cope. See figure VI-A-9.

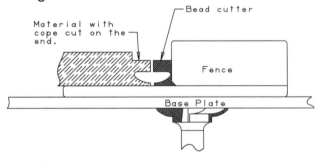

Bead cutter

Material with cope cut on the end.

Fence

Base Plate

Figure VI-A-9 Matching cutter with material.

Test the cut

The material is matched but the cut is not proven yet so make a small cut on the end of the cope. See figure VI-A-10.

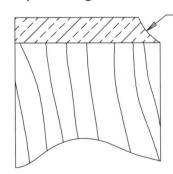

Test cut the bead on the coped end.

Figure VI-A-10 The test cut to match the cope and bead cut.

The perfect cut will have no lumber on the tenon where the cope joint meets the bead joint. If the cutter is high the lumber will be left under the cutter or on the side of the tenon closest to the front face. If the cutter is low the material from the tenon will be on the top of the cutter. Now is the time to change the position of the cutter because we know for sure that if the cutter is set up wrong it does not get better as we cut more pieces.

Thinking time before the bead cut

Before you jump right in and start cutting, sort the pieces and group them into single sided bead cuts and double sided bead cuts. The single sided cuts are the first to be made and the double sided cuts are the second to be made. They are easy to sort because the pieces that are on the outside of the panel, the stiles and rails, are singles. The pieces that are to be cut on both sides are the centre rail and mullion. Sort the pieces and make the cuts. Always use the push stick and keep your fingers clear of the cutter. See figure VI-A-11.

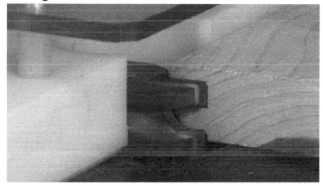

Figure VI-A-11 The bead cut.

Be sure to check the cuts

After each cut be sure to check if the pieces are going to fit together. You do not need to fit each piece now but just inspect the parts. See figure VI-A-12.

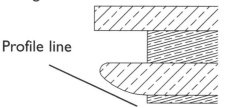

Profile line

Figure VI-A-12 Things to look for on the bead cut.

On the bead cut look to see how parallel the profile line is on the front and how well the shape is molded. The molded edge should be

clean and free of mill marks. If it is not to your satisfaction, recut the mold. Check right after you have cut the piece. This will make it easier to correct.

The added touch for the panels

Before cutting the panels you should radius the corners of the panels that are inserted into glue at the joint of the stile and rail. This prevents glue from the stile and rail joint coming in contact with the panel corners. Use a 1/8" radius. Check the radiusing techniques that have been talked about in the book PAGE 4-8. You *can not* have the panels glued into the panel door. The panels move and shrink so they have to float in the groove of the rails and stiles.

The panel cutter

The last operation to be cut is the panel. What is important when cutting the panels? The panel must fit into the cope and bead cut. The molded edges on the corners should meet on the 45 degree. First install the panel cutter. The cutter we are using is designed to make sure that the panel will fit into the cope and bead cut. See figure VI-A-13. It has a front and back cutter with the distance between the cutters designed to fit in the bead groove.

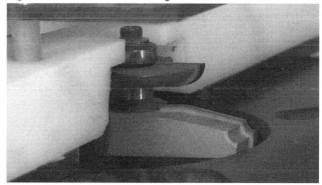

Figure VI-A-13 Panel bit.

Now set up the height of the router bit. The height is already determined by what was done with the cope and bead cut. Look at the profile line on the cope and bead and match the distance on the panel bit. Use the cope cut that was made on the end of the rail to assist in the height setup. See figure VI-A-14. This setting will make the panel flush with the front face of the door.

Setup the fence on the panel side and reposition the pins. The panel side is 180 degrees from the cope and bead side. Clamp the fence securely to the table.

Figure VI-A-14 Set up of the panel bit.

Molding the panels

Sort the pieces so you have all the parts facing the same way. When cutting the panels, cut across the grain, then with the grain, then across the grain and then with the grain. Use a pushstick at all times. Now we have finished molding the pieces and need to sort them back into their specific groups.

The dry assembly

What is a dry assembly? The best way to see if the pieces are going to fit or not is to first put them together without glue. Ask yourself these questions before gluing. How is the fit? Do they fit in my clamps and do I have enough clamps? Is the clamping pressure in the right place?

How is the fit

Now that you have dry assembled the milled pieces, look at a few things about gluing them together that might speed the process. In the dry fit process the assembly starts with one of the stiles and the rails. Keep a 90 degree corner in mind and be sure to keep an open end and side and the assembly will go smoothly. The last piece to be assembled should be the other stile. Make sure that all of the pieces have all router chips removed from the beads and copes and all of the joints are in good shape. If the assembly does not go just right, remember a bigger hammer doesn't help. Stop and look for the problem. Be careful not to drop the pieces on the floor as this is the best way to ruin the match.

Glue and clamp

Where do we need the glue and how much glue? What kind of clamping pressure and where to clamp? The gluing process requires that we put glue in the cope joint only. One caution when putting glue on the cope joint "more glue is not always better, but a little glue in the right place makes all the difference." The panels will float and move so you can not have glue attaching the panels to the stiles, rails and mullions. We have tried to take care of the glue in the corners by making the 1/8" radius on the panel corners.

The clamping pressure

Always clamp the panels together with the face side up.

With the wrong clamping pressure the door could be crooked, warped or twisted. The clamps must be parallel and level before you start to clamp. The clamping area should have enough room to set up the clamps. Because some woods react to the glue, it's a good idea to place a plastic sheet (plastic garbage bag) between the clamps and the wood. The bag will make the clean up easy and keep the glue stain marks off the finished pieces.

Put equal clamping pressure on the clamps by tightening one clamp about 1/2 the capacity and check the joint then move to the next clamp and give 1/2 the capacity and so on. Once all of the clamps have 1/2 the clamping capacity, finish tightening the clamps. Make adjustments and check to see that the door is square. This process will help prevent the parts from moving too much, and give you an opportunity to change the position of a moved part before you have the full clamping pressure on the panel.

VI-B. Mitre Gauge

a. Mitre Gauge Stopped Dovetails

When a drawer front is the overlapping type, we can use sliding dovetails to fasten the sides to the front. You can stop the dovetail from coming right through the top side of the drawer front by making a stopped dovetail. See figure VI-B-a-1. You can also use stopped dovetails in other projects. Case work is an example. The two drawer storage utilizes stopped dovetails in the case work.

Figure VI-B-a-1 Stopped dovetail for the drawer front.

Install a 1/2" dovetail bit in your table mounted router. Put a 1" brass guide and ring nut in position in the table plate. Place your mitre gauge slot over the guide.

When setting the bit depth, raise the dovetail bit to approximately 3/8" above the mitre base. Lock the head at 90 degrees. Now you can get a sample piece of 3/4" material, clamp it in the gauge, and cut a trial slot. See figure VI-B-a-2.

To cut a trial pin and check the fit, lock the mitre head at 90 degrees. Pull the mitre gauge as close to you as possible.

Position the 90 degree side of the pin fence in the indexing holes in the mitre base with the fence facing the mitre base slot. For 1/2" material you will use the left side and the outside left hand holes for the first cut.

Figure VI-B-a-2 Cut a dovetail slot.

The material should be tight to the pin fence and to the mitre head. Be sure to clamp the material in place. See figure VI-B-a-3. Holding the mitre gauge with one hand, turn the router on. With one hand on the mitre head and one hand holding the pin fence in position, push the mitre along the guide slot cutting one side of the dovetail pin. Cut until the bit has disappeared into the replaceable block of the mitre head. The bit should now be hidden from view. See figure VI-B-a-4. Turn the router off leaving the bit in this position. Never lift the mitre gauge while the bit is running.

Figure VI-B-a-3 Clamp the side to the pin fence.

Figure VI-B-a-4 Make sure the router bit is in the mitre block before changing the pin fence.

With the material still clamped to the pin fence move the pin fence to the next set of holes in the mitre base. See figure VI-B-a-5. With one hand holding the mitre head, turn the router on. With one hand on the mitre head and the other maintaining the pin fence in the proper location, cut the second side of the pin by pulling the mitre gauge toward you on the guide slot. Remember to keep your hands away from the cutting area.

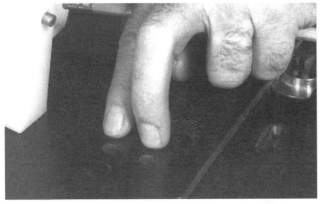

Figure VI-B-a-5 The movement is determined by the holes in the mitre gauge.

Unclamp and check the 1/2" dovetail pin by trying it in the slot made in the sample material. If the fit is too loose, raise the bit up slightly. If the fit is too snug, lower the bit slightly. Continue to use practice cuts until you get the type of fit you like. When the fit is right leave the bit set at this height until you have completed all the slot and pin cuts. When adjusting the bit height for fit remember that both the pin and the slot must be cut to the same depth.

A good shop tip is to cut a slot in a piece of stock once you have established the proper fit.

Save this block for a setup block for the next time you would like to set the depth of cut on your mitre gauge. If you change router bits you may have to adjust the height. Router bits vary slightly and this could change the necessary depth of cut you like. The higher the bit the tighter the fit. It is a good idea to use a test block each time you install the mitre gauge.

Once the proper bit depth is ready, set a stop block on your table to allow the mitre to slide only to the correct distance. Position the material so there is 3/4" between the bit and the edge of the stock. Clamp the material parallel to the mitre head and cut the stopped dovetail slots in the drawer front or case work. See figure VI-B-a-6.

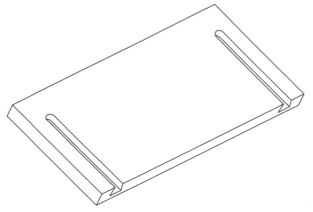

Figure VI-B-a-6 The stopped dovetail grooves for drawer fronts or case work.

Using the mitre pin fence on the left side, cut the dovetail pins on one end of each 1/2" drawer or case work side. See figure VI-B-a-7.

You will note that when sliding the dovetail pin into the slot it will not fit all the way up into the slot. Cut a notch in the top of dovetail pin to allow it to slide over and hide the rounded end of the slot. See figure VI-B-a-8. This completes the stopped dovetails in a drawer or casework.

Table leg brace

Make 45 degree pins on the cross braces for table/stool legs by laying the pin fence on the 45 degree angle. For 3/4" stock use the left side for the pin fence to center the pin. Be sure the pieces are positioned correctly and clamped to the pin fence. These pins will fit in the 1/2" dovetail slot.

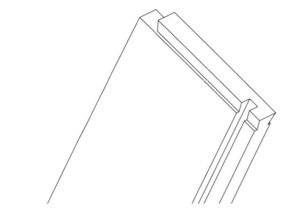

Figure VI-B-a-7 Drawer side with a dovetail pin on the front.

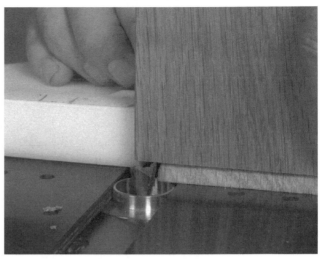

Figure VI-B-a-8 Cut the notch in the pin on the top.

VI-C Drawer Construction

When we are about to construct storage space, we tend to think of shelving. But probably the best type of storage for most items would be a drawer. The drawer has several advantages over the shelf. It allows easier access. It pulls out so we can see the items within. Organizes the contents simply and effectively. It is dust free compared to a shelf. It may be individually secured in the case of valuables or medicines.

If you are not a seasoned woodworker, you may mistakenly shy away from building drawers because of their complexity. Drawers do not have to be complex or difficult. The most common complaint that you may hear is that the drawer does not slide smoothly or that the front keeps coming off. Both problems are easily corrected.

The following is a simple, but successful method of constructing a drawer.

One of the first concerns would be the type of slide to be used. It is important if you are planning to use a manufactured drawer slide system, that you purchase all the slides before you build the drawers. Many times if you are short one set of slides, you may not be able to find that brand again and trying to match the same set of clearances may be impossible. Each manufacturer will have his own set of clearance specifications.

Some manufacturers require a 1/4" clearance all around between the opening and the drawer. Some call for a greater clearance at the top and bottom with a smaller clearance at the sides. Be sure to check these required clearances before proceeding with the construction of the drawers.

The next consideration is the type of drawer desired: flush mount, overlap, or inset. This simple drawer is an overlap style.

Simple Drawer

A drawer consists of five parts:

1. One Front - We would suggest that it be 3/4" thick wood which matches the rest of the cabinet.

2. Two Sides-Should be a minimum of 1/2" material. It may be solid stock or plywood. NOTE: We do not recommend particle board of any kind.

3. One Back-It should be a minimum of 1/2" thick and of the same material as the sides.

4. One Bottom-It should be 1/4" plywood.

Making the drawer

The first step is to establish the outside dimensions of the drawer after the allowance is made for hardware clearance. Example: The drawer pictured has a 3/4" thick overlapped

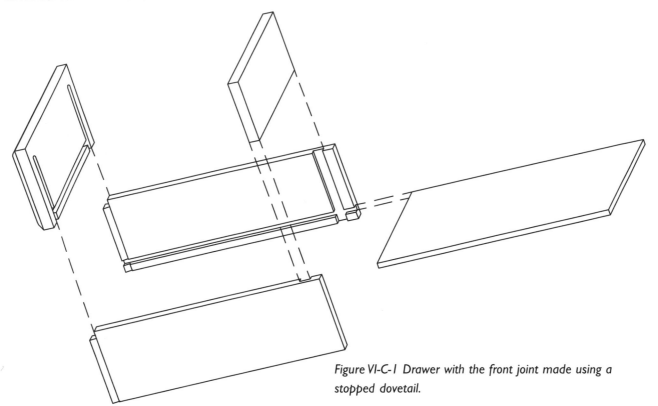

Figure VI-C-1 Drawer with the front joint made using a stopped dovetail.

front which uses a sliding dovetail to fasten the sides to the front. Figure VI-C-1.

When the front is of the overlapping type, we are able to use a sliding dovetail. Stop the cut from coming right through. This is called a stopped dovetail. See figure VI-C-2. The front is 4 5/8" wide and the sides are 3 1/2" wide.

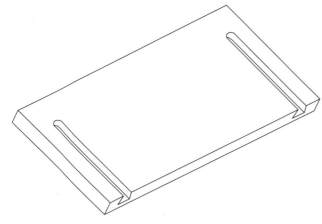

VI-C-2 Stopped dovetails for the drawer front.

Using a 1/2" dovetail cutter and the mitre gauge on your router table with a 1" guide installed, cut the two stopped dovetails in the front. Stop the cut 1/2" from the top of the

drawer front. For assistance with stopped dovetails, see Appendix VI, B. Mitre gauge.

Using the 90 degree pin fence on the mitre gauge, cut the dovetail pins on the two side pieces. Be sure you have a right and left side. Notch the dovetail pin at the top to allow it to cover the end of the dovetail slide in the drawer front. See figure VI-C-3.

Dadoing the Back

Install a 1/2" spiral (Straight) cutter in the table mounted router. Set the fence 1/2" away from the cutter. Use the 1/2" thick back to set this distance. Set the depth of the bit to half the thickness of the drawer sides (1/4"). Cut the dado in the back end of each drawer side. Use a push block to prevent tear-out.

Dadoing the Bottom

It is the drawer bottom that can indicate a good or bad drawer. It needs to have good support and be solid enough to keep the drawer square. Do not trap the drawer bottom between the front, back, and sides. Instead, from the back, slide the bottom into 1/4" dadoes in the sides and front.

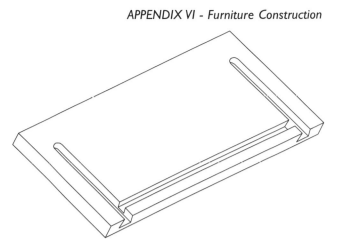

Figure VI-C-3 Notch the side dovetail pin.

Figure VI-C-4 Dado in the front for the bottom.

Making the dados

Install a 1/4" spiral (Straight) bit in the table mounted router. The bottom should be positioned 3/8" up on the sides and front of the drawer. This allowance will not only give strength but it also allows for most drawer slide hardware. Set the router table fence 3/8" from the bit (Use a 3/8" brass set-up bar). Set the bit depth to half the thickness of the drawer side.

IMPORTANT NOTE: This is the time when the two drawer sides become pairs. Pair them and mark the edges that must receive the dadoes. Cut the 1/4" dadoes in the sides.

The drawer front also needs to receive the bottom of the drawer. Be sure not to cut it from end to end. Cut the dado in the front from dovetail slot to dovetail slot. Clamp blocks to the fence to simplify this operation. See figure VI-C-4.

Molding

Mold the top edges of the drawer sides and the four edges of the front. For appearance sake the front of the drawer should have some kind of decorative edge. The top edge of the drawer sides should also be molded, to give a clean, smooth finish.

Rounding over the drawer

Install a 1/4" round over bit in the table mounted router. Set the table fence to isolate the pilot of the bit. Set the depth of cut to leave a clean round cut. (Practice on a scrap piece first). Round all the face edges of the drawer front. NOTE: Always do an end grain cut first, then a long grain, an end grain, and finish with a long grain side. This prevents chip out.

When putting a round over on the top edges of the sides be sure to start and stop short of the dovetail pin and the back dado.

Drawer Assembly

Flat sand all the drawer pieces. Apply glue to the dovetail pins on the drawer sides and slide them into place on the front. Fasten the drawer back into the dado in the drawer sides. Glue and nail it in place. With the drawer front face down on the bench, slide the 1/4" plywood bottom into place. It is not necessary to glue the bottom in place.

Lay the drawer face down and place a framing square with the tongue against the front and the body of the square along the side. Securely nail the bottom to the back once you are sure the side is square to the front. If you feel more support is needed, use screws rather than nails.

The drawer is now complete and ready for installation.

Appendix VII
Shop Made Fixtures

VII-A. Shop Made Jigs and Fixtures

The sole purpose of a jig or fixture is to make duplicates. Three things come into play: safety, setup ease, and speed. Our theory on this is when you need more than one identical part, make a jig. However, keep in mind the parts are only as good as the jig and the quality does not get better as you make more parts. Take time to construct quality jigs with safety in mind at all times. The jig should provide solid clamping ability while the piece is being fed into the machine. This is much safer than hand holding while cutting small parts.

Keep in mind what you have are jigs and fixtures for specific operations. If you look real close, they are all very simple and all employ the same method. Just the size and shape change. Use these ideas for many of your own designs and share your knowledge with a friend.

VII-B. Corner Pattern Fixture

Make the fixture

We wish to put small hearts in the corners on a project. It could be cut outs or inlays. It could be any pattern shape. It is best to make a corner fixture for this operation to be sure each design is positioned correctly in the corner and all four corners will match. We have shown this fixture using a back board of plywood but you may wish to fasten the stop blocks directly onto your sub top which is used over the router table. See figure VII-B-1

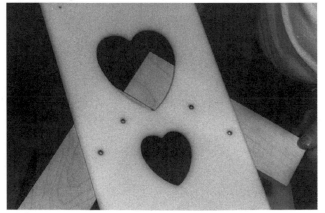

Figure VII-B-1 Fixture for corner inlays.

Material list:
    1 - polyethylene pattern (2 heart PA079)
    1 - 10" x 10" x 1/2" ply base/sub table top
    1 - 1 1/2" x 10" x 3/4" stop block
    1 - 1 1/2" x 8 1/2" x 3/4" stop block

Hardware:
    4 - #6 x 1" flat head wood screws
    10 - #6 x 5/8" round head wood screws
    2 - hold down clamps
    Double stick tape

How to build this project

Cut all parts to the exact size listed.

Locating the stop blocks

Double stick tape the stop blocks squarely on one corner of the back board. From the back side of the back board drill and screw the stop blocks in place with #6 x 1" flat head wood screws.

Centering the pattern

Use the framing square to center the small heart pattern across the corner at a 45 degree angle to the stop blocks. Drill and screw the heart pattern in place. Use #6 x 1" flat head wood screws. See figure VII-B-2

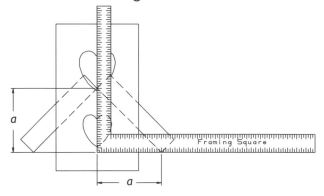

Figure VII-B-2 How to layout the pattern centre

The heart may be postioned any distance from the edges of the project piece. See figure VII-B-3. This fixture allows you to have four heart inlays in the corners in exactly the same location on each corner.

Figure VII-B-3 Uniform inlays without measuring.

VII-C. Shelf Bracket

Fixture

When making a shelf bracket two things are important

1) strength

2) appearance

Achieve both by cutting brackets out according to the following diagram. See figure VII-C-1.

Figure VII-C-1 Cut brackets for strength and appearance.

Cutting the brackets

Choose the thickness and width of the stock. Adjust the mitre gauge on the table saw to 45 degrees and make the first cut. Reset the mitre to 90 degrees. Place the first cut on the head of the mitre. This will make the second cut 90 degrees to the first cut. Cut the blank brackets as shown in the Figure VII-C-1. The long grain of the wood is now parallel to the long angle on the bracket.

Now when the bracket design is cut on the exposed edge it does not leave the end grain exposed. This gives you maximum strength and ap-

pearance because edge grain instead of end grain is exposed. See figure VII-C-2.

Right Way

Figure VII-C-2 Edge grain exposed after shaping.

In diagram figure VII-C-3 the end grain is exposed, this technique makes the bracket weak and detracts from the general appearance. Another point which makes the direction of grain important is that when mounting the screws in the bracket, end grain will be more likely to split than the edge grain.

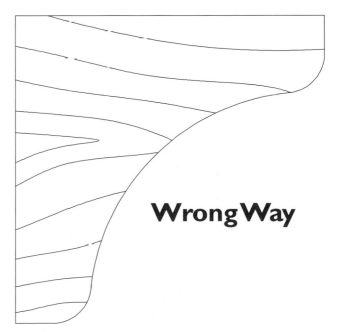

Wrong Way

Figure VII-C-3 End grain exposed after shaping.

Points to consider

When designing the pattern for the bracket:

1) Keep in mind the product is only as good as the pattern. Make a good pattern.

2) For safety be sure to incorporate a point or lengthen the pattern to use as a fulcrum point. This is an area where the operator can safely locate the guide to the pattern without touching the bracket stock. See figure VII-C-4.

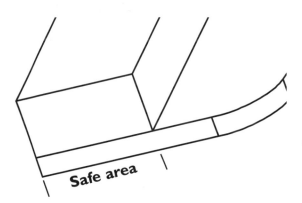

Figure VII-C-4 Pattern is lengthened for safety

3) When making the pattern you must take into consideration the distance between the edge of the cutter and the outside edge of the template guide. This calculation is important to determine the proper size of the bracket or finished part.

4) Make sure that the part is rough sized so that the router is not just trimming the part. To determine the size of the rough part add 1/8" to the distance between the router bit and the outside of the template guide. Make the part larger than the pattern by this amount plus material for the mold you desire.

5) The pattern needs a positive clamping system to hold the part in position during the routing process. Slide the rough cut stock against the positive locating blocks of the jig and clamp it with the hold downs. Mold and cut the pattern edge of the bracket by using a guide in your tablemount with a molding bit. See figure VII-C-5.

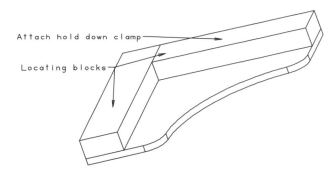

Attach hold down clamp

Locating blocks

Figure VII-C-5 Shelf bracket pattern jig.

6) Design the jig to account for the motion, direction of the router bit and wood grain direction. It is important to understand where to start and where to finish on each pattern.

This procedure is for making multiple parts which have to be the same. Examples are three or four legs to a pedestal table or six brackets on a shelf system.

Note:

VII-D. Pattern Fixture for larger size projects

Making the fixture

When the project is too large to fit inside the 8" x 12" pattern jig cavity, it is necessary to construct a suitable shop made fixture.

Shop made fixture

Choose a base piece of 3/4" plywood large enough to allow you to clamp or screw it to a work bench while the cuts are being made. Choose a piece of stock at least 2 1/2" wide and 3/4" thick (or the thickness of the project material you wish to use) and fasten it to the base along one edge. It should be long enough to fit all along the base piece on one side to hold the pattern and allow the mounting of two hold down clamps (one on each side of the pattern) in order to secure the stock in place during the cutting operation. See figure VII-D-1

Mounting the pattern

Fasten one edge of the pattern securely to the holder block allowing room below so the stock can be slid between the pattern and the base plywood.

When the stock is in the desired position use hold down clamps to ensure the stock does not move during the cutting operation.

The pattern can be fastened in this shop fixture on the end or the side depending on the project requirements. See figure VII-D-2.

Figure VII-D-2 Horizontal pattern fixture.

These fixtures can be used to hold the stock for the three heart frame (2-E) and the coat wallrack (3-C).

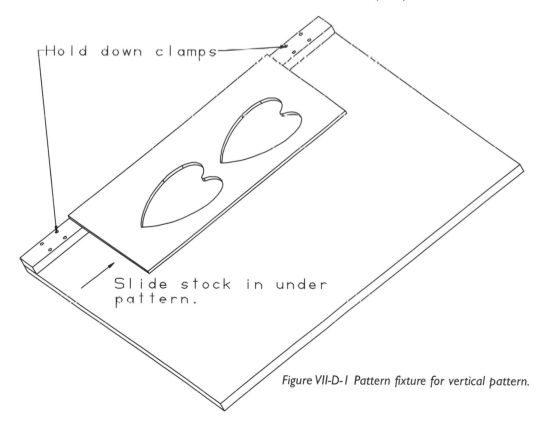

Hold down clamps

Slide stock in under pattern.

Figure VII-D-1 Pattern fixture for vertical pattern.

VII-E. External Guide Fixture (Monkey Finder)

Jigs and fixtures are designed and constructed to hold a work piece in a safe and efficient manner while a part is being cut. With a small part such as the monkey finder the part is so small that it is extremely important to make an efficient fixture and use it in a safe manner. See figure VII-E-1. Keep your fingers away from the cutters.

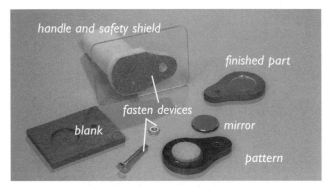

Figure VII-E-1 External routing fixture for small parts. handle and safety shield, fasten devices, blank, and pattern.

Material list:

    1 - 2" x 3" x 1/4" phenolic or masonite
    1 - 2 1/2" x 3" x 1/8" lexan guard
    1 - 2" x 5" x 1" polyethylene or hardwood handle
    1 - small scrap of pine for insert
    1 - 1" x 2 1/4" x 1" polyethylene or hardwood

Hardware:

    1 - 3/16" x 1 1/2" flat head bolt
    - flat washer and nut for above
    2 - #6 x 1" flat head wood screws
    - double stick tape

How to build this project

Cut all materials to size according to the material list and plans. Chuck up the 1/4" round over bit in the table mounted router and round all corners (four sides and top edges) of the handle. See figure VII-E-2.

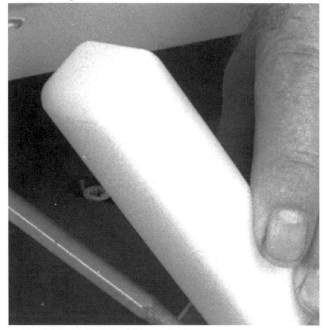

Figure VII-E-2 handle of small fixture.

In the 1/4" phenolic, cut the outside shape of the part according to the full size plan. You may use a scroll saw. Drill and counter sink a 3/16" bolt hole in the smaller end as per plan location.

Counter bore a 1" hole to a depth of 1/16" as per location and double stick tape a 1" mirror in the hole. The 1/8" thick mirror will protrude above the pattern surface by 1/16". You could use a 1/8" by 1" diameter wooden wafer instead of the mirror if you wish. See figure VII-E-3.

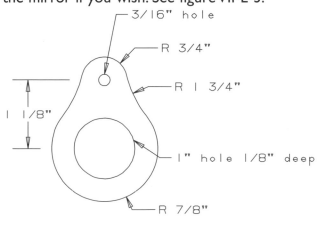

Figure VII-E-3 Pattern piece

Drill and counter sink a mounting screw hole in the small block and drill the 3/16" mounting bolt hole as per plan.

Double stick tape the lexan guard to the bottom end of the handle. Double stick tape the small drilled pine block to the bottom side of the lexan guard. Fasten all together by installing a #6 mounting screw through the small block, lexan guard and into the handle. See figure VII-E-4.

Figure VII-E-4 Handle, guard and block in place.

Sand and trim all sharp edges from the pieces. Install a rough blank and assemble the parts of the exterior guide pattern jig. See figure VII-E-5.

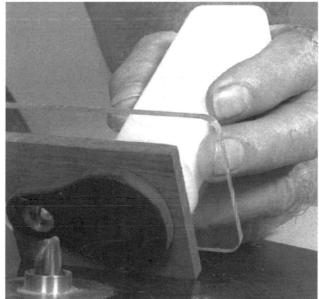

Figure VII-E-5 Monkey finder jig with blank installed.

This small jig allows you to cut and mold these small pieces safely by ensuring fingers are guarded from the cutter and the operator has positive control over the work piece. Exterior pattern work is done with the bit mounted in the table mounted router, a proper guide installed in the base plate and the proper use of the safety pin.

Remember to make safe efficient fixtures to hold and cut small parts. The shape can be anything as long as it allows you to hold it in two places to prevent the part from twisting as it is routed. The bolt hole and the mirror indentation prevent this little part from twisting in the fixture.

VII-F. The Sub Top

The sub top is simply a shop made accessory which you will find a valuable addition to your router tablemounting workstation. See figure VII-F-1.

The sub top will allow you to cut circles efficiently without worrying about damaging the workstation, and in addition, when your router is not in use, putting the sub top in place turns the workstation into an extra work bench.

A sub top is simplicity itself. All you need is a piece of plywood, any thickness from 1/2" to 3/4" cut to the size of your workstation top. Position the plywood on the top with a couple of clamps and from underneath, mark the opening where your router usually fits.

Unclamp the plywood, turn it upside down, and screw a couple of small square blocks cut from 3/4" plywood so that they will just fit in opposite corners of the opening. Round off the corners that will press against the opening of your workstation.

When you want to use the sub top, remove the router and mounting plate and simply position the sub top so that the blocks hold it in place. You can then cut into the sub top when you are cutting circles or following irregular patterns, without damaging the finished top of the workstation.

Other uses for the sub top include routing signs, free hand routing that requires nailing or taping the work piece in place and any cutting where the router bit needs to pass clear through the work piece. Cutting into the sub top will not damage the workstation surface. In addition, the sub top is handy when cutting splices and making cut outs. Use it with the wheel jig.

If you get to the point where you have made too many cuts in the sub top, you can ex-tend its life by simply flipping it over, transferring the blocks and using the other side.

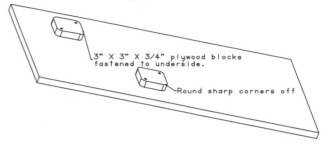

Figure VII-F-1 Sub top.

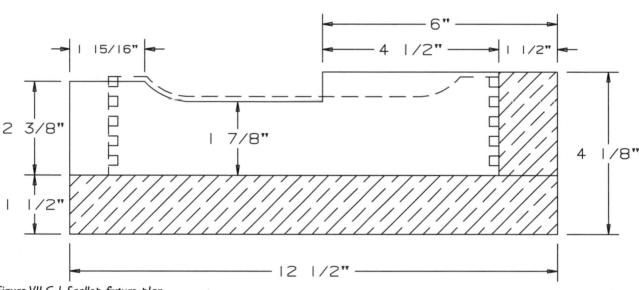

Figure VII-G-1 Scallop fixture plan.

VII-G. Scallop Fixture

This external routing fixture is very versatile for all kinds of scallop work. The size may be changed to suit the depth and width of scallop desired. This fixture allows you to cut the same design many times exactly identical without sanding. The design of the fixture makes a clean cut by always cutting down grain which eliminates tear out. Cut first one half of the scallop, then flip the work piece and cut the other half. This produces a clean chip free scallop and can be duplicated any number of times. See figure VII-G-1.

Material list:

1 - 3 1/4" x 8 1/2" x 1/4" phenolic or masonite

1 - 1 7/8" x 8 1/2" x 1/2" hardwood stop block

1 - 1/2" x 2 1/2" x 1/4" end stop block hardwood or polyethylene

Hardware:

1 - hold down clamp
4 - #6 x 5/8" round head wood screws
4 - #6 x 5/8" flat head wood screws
Double stick tape

Making the jig

Cut all parts to the sizes listed in the cut list. Use masking tape on the phenolic to provide a clean drawing surface to lay out the scallop design. Draw and cut out the 1/2" scallop according to the plan. Double stick tape the large stop block in place. From the back side drill and counter sink screw holes for #6 x 5/8" flat head screws and install the screws. Drill and screw the end stop block in place. Position the hold down clamp in the center of the scallop stop block and screw it in place. Sand any rough edges and test the jig using scrap material. See figure VII-G-2 and VII-G-3. You require a straight bit, guide, and safety pin.

Figure VII-G-3 Reverse the piece in the jig and make a second cut.

Figure VII-G-2 Cut halfway.

VII-H. Mortise Fixture

Making the jig

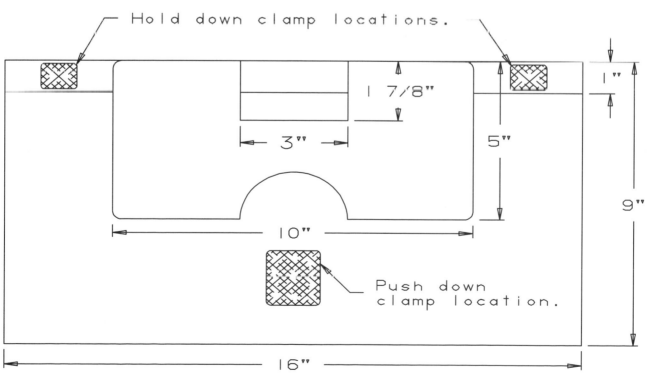

Figure VII-H-1 Plan for mortise fixture

Use 1/4" polyethylene or tempered mason ite. Use masking tape for marking.

Layout the size of mortise required. It may be used to make the mortises in the back of the full length mirror or to set butt hinges for a door. See figure VII-H-1.

Allowance for pattern

Make allowance in the pattern size for the guide and bit. We will use a 3/8" spiral bit and a 5/8" guide. There is a difference of 1/8" all around the pattern. Screw blocks in place on the pattern marks. See figure VII-H-2.

Figure VII-H-2 Wooden blocks along pattern lines

Making the pattern

Chuck up a 1/2" flush trim router bit in the table mounted router and trim the material along the wood blocks. See figure VII-H-3 and VII-H-4.

Figure VII-H-3 Cut mortise pattern

Assembly of the fixture

Remove the pattern from the trim blocks. Construct a hold down fixture as shown in the photograph. See figure VII-H-4. Mount the hold downs and the pattern to the mortise fixture.

Figure VII-H-4 Mortise fixture

Testing the fixture

Slide the cut mirror stiles into the mortise fixture. Locate, secure and cut the mortises using a 5/8" guide and a 3/8" spiral bit. Set the depth of cut to 1/2" using the set up bars.

Moving from left to right mortise out the gain for the rail to fasten to the mirror stiles.

This fixture can be used for other projects.

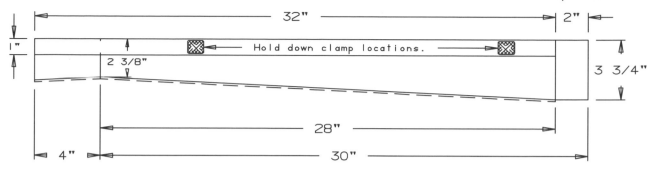

Figure VII-I-1 Plan for mirror stile fixture.

VII-I. Mirror Fixture

This fixture is designed to cut the long taper on a full length mirror using a brass guide and a spiral router bit. Direction of the grain is important when doing any cutting. This fixture allows you to cut inside tapers always routing down grain. Cut half the piece then reverse the project piece in the fixture and do the other half. Duplication is always perfect with a fixture like this because we are using the same pattern for each side and end cut. See figure VII-I-1.

Material list:

1 - 3 1/2" x 30" x 1/4" phenolic or masonite
1 - 3 1/2" x 4" x 1/4" phenolic or masonite
1 - 1" x 32" x 3/4" hardwood stop block
1 - 2" x 3 1/2" x 3/4" hardwood stop block

Hardware:

7 - #6 x 3/4" flat head wood screws
8 - #6 x 5/8" round head wood screws
2 - Hold down clamps
Double stick tape

Making the jig

Cut all stock to size according to the material list. Note: The base phenolic piece is in two parts. We have done this so the taper was easy to cut. It prevents getting trapped to a stop and then having to cut up taper on the next part. It also provides a halfway point to stop the taper cut and turn your project piece around and cut the same taper on the other end.

Suggestion: Use an angle fixture on your table saw to cut the pattern taper. See Appendix VII-J.

Double stick tape the stop blocks on the base of the fixture as shown in the plan. Turn the fixture over and drill and screw the stop blocks in place. Locate, drill, and screw the hold down clamps in place. Sand and trim any rough corners or edges on the pattern surface. The project piece will only be as smooth as the pattern. See figures VII-I-2 and VII-I-3.

Figure VII-I-2 Taper fixture.

Figure VII-I-3 The guide follows the taper pattern to the half way point.

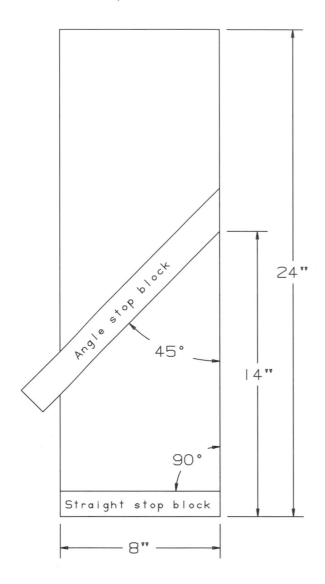

Figure VII-J-1 Angle fixture plan

VII-J. Angle Fixture - Table Saw Chute Board

Making the jig

We are often required to cut material at an angle. It could be a 45 degree angle as in the roll up box or a taper angle as in the plant stand. This fixture also works well to make a straight 90 degree cut. This chute board for the table saw is useful for many angle cuts. Because of the hold downs and design it makes it safe to cut smaller pieces. See figure VII-J-1.

Material list:

1 - 8" x 24" x 1/2" baltic birch plywood
1 - 1/4" thick polyethylene strip to match the slot in your table saw or use tempered masonite
1 - 1 1/4" x 8" x 3/4" hardwood stop block
1 - 1 1/2" x 10" x 3/4" hardwood stop block
1 - 3/4" x 1" x 1/4" polyethylene or masonite extended stop block

Hardware:

2 - hold downs clamps
4 - #6 x 5/8" round head wood screws
4 - #6 x 5/8" flat head wood screws
4 - #6 x 1" flat head wood screws
Double stick tape

Prepare strip

Cut the poly strip to fit the table saw slot. Drill and counter sink screw holes in the poly to fit the #6 x 5/8" flat head screws.

Figure VII-J-2 Mount the strip on the underside of the shute board.

Put a strip of double stick tape on the opposite side from the counter sunk screw holes in the poly strip. Lay the poly strip in the table saw slot with the tape side up. Position the plywood shute board over the strip extending it about 1/4" past the saw blade slot. Press down to stick the poly strip in place on the shute board. Turn the board over and put screws in place along the strip in the predrilled holes.

Raise the saw blade to cut 1/4" higher than the 1/2" plywood thickness. Place the poly strip in the table saw slot and pass the plywood shute board through the table saw. The strip and board edge will now be parallel.

Position the stop blocks

Mount the 8" hardwood stop block square with the infeed end of the shute board. Use 2 #6 x 1" flat head screws. Attach one hold down clamp near the center of this stop block.

45 Degree stop block

Prepare the 10" stop block by cutting a 45 degree angle on the end and make a 1/4" slot in the side to receive the 1/4" poly extend stop (used for 45 degree ends on the roll up box). See figure VII-J-3. See plan for position of the slot. Mount the 45 degree stop block on the shute board as shown in the drawing. Mount a hold down on the center of the angle stop block. Fasten the poly extend stop into the 1/4" slot. Glue will not work on poly but use double stick tape.

Figure VII-J-4 *Square cuts at 90 degrees.*

Figure VII-J-5 Angle cuts at 45 degrees .

Cut long tapers

To adjust the angle fixture for taper cutting, remove the 45 degree stop block. Position the long taper stop block up the length of the fixture. See figure VII-J-6.

Figure VII-J-3 Stop block for 45 and 90 degree angles.

Use a framing square to be sure the stop blocks are 90 degrees and 45 degrees respectively. Make sure your square is 90 degrees or square. To check see Appendix III-D-h.

This Angle fixture for your table saw can be used with many projects where 90 degree and 45 degree cuts are important. It is particularly useful with small pieces. See figures VII-J-4 and VII-J-5.

Figure VII-J-6 Taper stop installed.

Material list:

    1 - 1 1/2" x 24" x 3/4" straight hardwood for stop block

    4 - #6 x 1" flat head wood screws

    1 or 2 - hold down clamps

Procedure

Remove the 45 degree angle block from the shute board above. Leave the 90 degree end block in place. Put the proper angle on one end of the taper stop block and screw it in place on the shute board to make the desired taper. Position and attach the hold downs. Be sure to use the hold downs to fasten the work piece when you cut the tapers. This fixture can be used for the plant stand to cut the column tapers. See figure VII-J-6. It can also be used to cut the desired taper for the mirror fixture in Appendix VII-I. Make sure to adjust the angle to suit the project.

Figure VII-J-6 Cut long tapers.

VII-K. Drilling Fixture

The purpose of this fixture is to enable you to precisely drill 1/4" holes equally spaced from each end and centred on the 1/2" sides of the stacking trays. See figure VII-K-1. This same fixture or

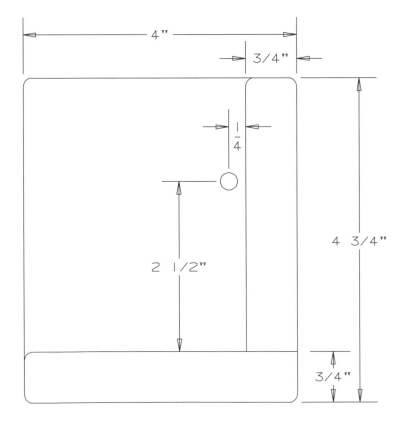

Figure VII-K-1 Plan for drill fixture.

design variation may be used for numerous other drill applications. Use it to drill screw locations for drawer and cabinet pulls or for hinge locations.

Material list:
4 - 3/4" x 3/4" x 4" hardwood stop blocks
1 - 4" x 4 3/4" x 1/4" phenolic or masonite

Hardware:
4 - #6 x 3/4" flat head wood screws
Double stick tape

Making the jig

Cut all material to the exact size according to the material list. Use double stick tape to stick the four stop blocks in place as shown in the plan. Be sure they form a square corner. Locate, drill, and counter sink holes for the mounting screws. Fasten the screws in place. Use masking tape to mark the location for the 1/4" drilling hole. It will be 3" from the end of the block and 1/4" from the side block and centred. Drill the 1/4" hole. Sand all the sharp edges and curves. See figure VII-K-2.

Figure VII-K-2 Drill precise holes every time.

If this same fixture is to be used for other drilling operations just drill more holes where needed but be sure to mask off with tape all holes except the ones you will be using. This saves having holes in the wrong location.

Notes:

Projects in Colour

BOXES

Another Small Box

Basic Box

Tissue Cover

Jewel Box

Box Drawers

Folding Box

FRAMES & DISHES

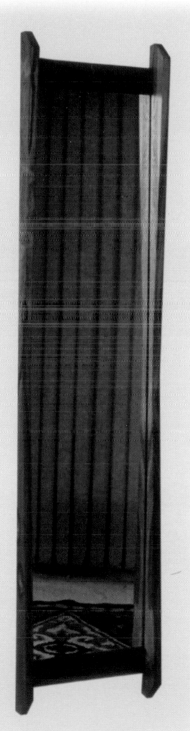

Full Length Mirror

Oval Picture

Wheel Nut Dish

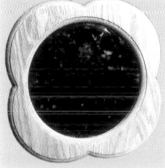

Circle Frame

Candy Dish

Mirror Frame

Three Heart Frame

HOUSE GIFTS

Coat Wall Rack

Small Chest

Two Drawer Chest

Basic Cabinet

Plant Stand

Walnut Chest

THIS & THAT

Wall Shelf

Pot Mat

Napkin Holder

Book Stand and Wooden Books

Mug Tree

Inlaid Heart Tray

OFFICE & HOME

Pen Gift Case

Clock

Pencil Box

Pen Storage

Desk Set

Pen Stands

In Out Tray

KIDS CORNER

Monkey Finder

Table and Chairs

Wagon

Wheel Barrow